James Bronterre O'Brien

The Rise, Progress, And Phases of Human Slavery

James Bronterre O'Brien

The Rise, Progress, And Phases of Human Slavery

ISBN/EAN: 9783744724012

Printed in Europe, USA, Canada, Australia, Japan

Cover: Foto ©ninafisch / pixelio.de

More available books at **www.hansebooks.com**

THE

RISE, PROGRESS, AND PHASES

OF

HUMAN SLAVERY:

HOW IT CAME INTO THE WORLD,
AND HOW IT SHALL BE MADE TO GO OUT.

BY

JAMES BRONTERRE O'BRIEN.

LONDON:

WILLIAM REEVES, 185, FLEET STREET, E.C.
G. STANDRING, 8 AND 9, FINSBURY STREET;
MARTIN BOON, 170, FARRINGDON ROAD, W.C.
SOUTH AFRICA: HAY BROS., WHOLESALE AGENTS, KING WILLIAM'S TOWN.

1885

TO THE PEOPLE!

THIS little Work, by an eloquent denunciator of the manifold evils of Profitmongering and Landlordism, whose entire life was devoted to the advocacy of Social Rights, as distinguished from Socialistic theories, is now given to the world for the first time in a complete form.

The Author, in his lifetime, was frustrated in his design of finishing his History through the ceaseless machinations of working-class exploiters and landlords. This has been at length achieved by the aid of his various writings preserved in print. The object steadily kept in view has been to give the *ipsissima verba* of the Author, so that no foreign pen may garble or mislead.

In order to provide room for so much additional matter as was essential to the elucidation of the great reforms needed in the subjects of Land Nationalisation, Credit, Currency, and Exchange, it has been found expedient to omit from this edition some disquisitions on subjects of ephemeral and passing interest, not closely connected with the scope of the Work. Ample compensation, however, has been given in the additions which have been made for the elucidation and enforcement of the saving truths herein contained.

" SPARTACUS."

CONTENTS.

CHAPTER I.

PROLETARIANISM SPRUNG FROM CHATTEL SLAVERY.

CHAPTER II.

ORIGIN OF SLAVERY IN PATERNAL AUTHORITY.

CHAPTER III.

CAUSES OF PARENTAL DESPOTISM.

CHAPTER IV.

INCREASE AND CONSOLIDATION OF SLAVERY.

CHAPTER V.

OPINION OF THE ANCIENT WORLD ON SLAVERY.

CHAPTER VI.

UNIVERSALITY OF PUBLIC OPINION AS TO MASTER AND SLAVES.

CHAPTER VII.

COMPARISON OF ANCIENT AND MODERN SLAVERY.

CHAPTER VIII.

EXPLOITATION-VALUE OF SLAVE AND FREE LABOUR.

CHAPTER IX.

HISTORY OF EARLY SOCIAL REFORMERS.

CHAPTER X.

PROGRESS OF EARLY CHRISTIAN PROPAGANDA.

CHAPTER XI.

THE FOUR GREAT PERSECUTIONS.

CHAPTER XII.

PROGRESS OF PROPAGANDA TO THE TENTH PERSECUTION.

CHAPTER XIII.

DEBASEMENT OF THE NEW POWER WHEN SEIZED BY RULERS.

CHAPTER XIV.

SERVICE OF CHRISTIANITY IN BREAKING CASTE-BONDS.

CHAPTER XV.

FORM OF SLAVERY UNDER MODERN CIVILIZATION.

CHAPTER XVI.

REFORMS AS MUCH NEEDED IN AMERICA AND IN COLONIES AS IN EUROPE.

CHAPTER XVII.

RELIEF TO UNEMPLOYED OR DESTITUTE A RIGHT—NOT A CHARITY.

CHAPTER XVIII.

GRADUAL RESUMPTION OF PUBLIC LANDS BY THE STATE.

CHAPTER XIX.

NATIONAL DEBT A MORTGAGE ON REALISED PROPERTY.

CHAPTER XX.

NATIONAL LANDS AND CREDIT FOR THE USE OF THE PEOPLE.

CHAPTER XXI.

NATIONAL SYSTEM OF CURRENCY AND EXCHANGE REQUIRED.

CHAPTER XXII.

EVIL OF MONOPOLIES AND EXPLOITATION OF INDUSTRIES.

THE

RISE, PROGRESS, AND PHASES

OF

HUMAN SLAVERY.

CHAPTER I.

PROLETARIANISM SPRUNG FROM CHATTEL SLAVERY.

Importance of Social Reform—Universality of Covert or Open Slavery—Partial
Prevalence of Working Class—Origin in Proletarianism—Advent of
Christianity—Its Effects on Slavery—Middle and Working Classes the
Produce of Emancipations—Classification of the *Proletariat.*

AT this critical period of the world's history, when either the whole
of society must undergo a peaceful Social Reformation that shall
strike at the root of abuses, or else be incessantly menaced with
revolutionary violence and anarchy, it becomes a subject of grave
interest to ascertain how Human Slavery came into the world; how
it has been propagated; wherefore it has been endured so long; the
varied phases it has assumed in modern times; and, finally, how it
may be successfully grappled with and extinguished, so that hence-
forth it may exist only in the history of the past.

Glancing over the world's map, we find nearly all the inhabited
parts parcelled out into various nations and races—some called civilized, some savage, and the rest, forming the greater part, in some
intermediate state of semi-barbarism. One sad feature, however, is
found, with hardly an exception, to belong to all. It is Slavery, in
one form or another;—it is the subjection of man to his fellow-man
by force or fraud. Yes, disguise it as we may, human slavery is
everywhere to be found—as rife in countries called Christian and
civilized as in those called barbarous and pagan—as rife in the western as in the eastern hemisphere—as rife in the middle of the nineteenth century as in the pagan days of the Ptolomies and the Pharaohs.

The only difference is, it is in the one case slavery direct and avowed ; in the other, slavery hypocritically masked under legal forms.   The latter is the phase slavery has assumed in countries calling them- selves Christian and civilized ; but it is a slavery not the less galling and unbearable because it is indirect and disguised.

What are called the "Working Classes" are the slave populations of civilized countries. These classes constitute the basis of European society in particular and of all civilized societies in general.   We make this restriction, because there are societies in which there is found nothing to correspond with what in England and France are called the working classes.   For example, they are unknown in Arabia, amongst the Nomad tribes of Africa, the Red-Indians of America, and the hunter tribes of Tartary ; and, although in process of development, they are comparatively " few and far between " in Russia, Turkey, Greece and, indeed, throughout the nations of the East in general.

Amongst those who write books and deliver speeches about the working classes, few concern themselves to note this peculiarity in their history, namely, the fact that they exist in some countries and not in others ; and the no less startling fact, that it is only at par- ticular epochs of history, and only under certain peculiar circum- stances of society, that they have been known to spring into social existence as a distinctive class.   Books, journals, pamphlets, essays, speeches, sermons, Acts of Parliament, all are alike silent upon this notable fact.   Nobody dreams of inquiring whether the working classes do, or do not, constitute a separate and distinct race in the countries they are found in ; or of asking themselves what cause or causes produced them at particular epochs and in certain climes, while they continue to be unknown at other epochs and in other climes ; and why we find them, as it were, sown broadcast in one country, while they appear but emerging into doubtful existence in other countries.   In truth, the history of the middle and working classes has still to be written ; and though it is far from our present purpose to undertake any such task, we shall, nevertheless, of neces- sity have to draw largely upon history for the elucidation of the facts and arguments by which we shall support our views upon the subject of slavery.

Not to encumber the question with details which, however inter- esting to antiquarians and scholars, would be out of place here, let us briefly observe at once, that the working classes, however general and extensive an element they constitute in modern society, are, nevertheless, but an emanation from another element, much more extensive and general, bequeathed to us by the ancient world under the name of Proletarians.   By the term Proletarians is to be under- stood, not merely that class of citizens to which the electoral census of the Romans gave the name, but every description of persons of both sexes who, having no masters to own them as slaves, and consequently to be chargeable with their maintenance, and who, being without fortune or friends, were obliged to procure their subsistence as they best could—by labour, by mendicity, by theft, or by prostitution.

The Romans used the term to denote the lowest, or lowest but one, class of voters—those who, being without property, had only their offspring (*proles*) to offer as hostages to the State for their good behaviour, or rather as guarantees for not abusing their rights of citizenship. We use the term in the more enlarged sense of its modern acceptation, to denote every description of persons who are dependent upon others for the means of earning their daily bread, without being actual slaves.

In the early periods of history, and, indeed, until some time after the introduction of Christianity, the Proletarians constituted a very small fraction of society. The reason is obvious. Actual slaves and their owners formed the bulk of every community. The few Proletarians of the old Pagan world were either decayed families who had lost the patrimonies of their fathers, or else the descendants of manumitted slaves, who, in succeeding to the condition of freemen (acquired for them by their enfranchised forefathers), succeeded also to their poverty and precarious tenure of life, by inheriting the disadvantage of having no patrons bound to protect them, no masters answerable for their maintenance, no market for their labour. But as such manumissions were, before the establishment of Christianity, comparatively of rare occurrence, and as the offspring of them were as likely to be absorbed in time by the slave-owning class as to sink into and swell the Proletarian, the result was, that until the times of Augustus Cæsar, and indeed for a considerable period after, the Proletarians were by no means a numerous class. In other words, there were comparatively few upon whom the necessity was imposed of obtaining a precarious subsistence by hired labour, mendicity, theft, or prostitution. Almost all kinds of labour, agricultural and mechanical, were performed by slaves ; masters had, therefore, little or no occasion to hire "free labourers." Prostitution was followed as a profession only by courtesans who were freed-women or the offspring of freed-women. The slave class who were devoted to that degradation were either the property of masters (of whose households they formed part) or else of mangones, or slave-merchants, who openly sold them or let them out on hire for that purpose. Of beggars and thieves there could have been comparatively few, for the same reasons that kept down the numbers of hired labourers and professional prostitutes : the conditions of society, as then constituted, did not make place for them. As already observed, almost every one was either an actual slave or an owner of slaves. If a slave-owner, he lived upon the revenues of his estates—upon his possessions, of which his slaves constituted a part, often the greater part. If a slave, his wants were supplied, and his necessities provided for, by those to whom he belonged. If a predial slave, he was kept out of the produce of his master's farms, just as the herds and flocks were kept, both being regarded alike in the light of chattel property. If a domestic slave, his keep was a necessary part of his master's household expenses. If let out for hire (an ordinary condition of ancient slavery), a portion of his gains was of necessity applied to his own maintenance. In any case—in all cases—he was exempt from want, and from the fear of want, as well as from all care and anxiety about providing for his subsistence. He could not, it is true, earn wages or acquire property for himself without his master's leave; but neither, on the other hand, was he liable to starvation or privation because there might happen to be no work for him to do.   Work or no work, he was always sure to be well fed, well housed, well clothed, and well cared for, as long as his master had enough and was satisfied with him. If he was incapable of acquiring property, so was he also exempt from its cares, and sure to participate in the use of his master's, at least to the extent requisite for keeping him in bodily health and in good condition.   Nor were slaves always debarred from the acquisition of property.   There are instances recorded of slaves having been permitted to amass considerable fortunes, though this was rarely the case till after their masters manumitted them.   Some also became celebrated as grammarians, poets, and teachers of *belles lettres* and philosophy.   Indeed, when they happened to have good, kind masters their lot was by no means a hard one;—it was an enviable one in comparison with that of a modern " free-born Briton," rejoicing in the status of an "independent labourer."   Of this we shall adduce proofs enough by-and-by.   Suffice it, for the present, to observe, that so well must slaves have been used to fare under the old pagan system, that terms corresponding with our " wanton," "saucy," " pampered," are of frequent occurrence in the old Greek and Roman classics as applied to slaves, particularly domestic or menial.   At all events, destitution, in the modern sense, was unknown to them; and, with it, were also unknown its inevitable consequences—mendicity, robbery, theft, prostitution, and crime—*as characteristic of a class or of a system*.   Individual or isolated cases there might be, and these chiefly amongst the manumitted; but there was no large class of persons subsisting by such means—no outlawed class compelled, as it were, by the very first law of nature—self-preservation—to erect such means into a system in order to preserve life.

Social evils there were—frightful evils—under the old pagan system. Slavery itself was an evil—an appalling evil—under even its most favourable conditions.   But fearful as those evils were—hateful as direct slavery must ever be while man is man—the ancient pagan world has exhibited nothing so revolting and truly abominable as the development and progress of Proletarianism, which was consequent upon the breaking up of the old system of slavery, and which has ever since gained more and more strength in every age, till, in our times, it has made Proletarians of three-fourths of the people of every civilized country, and threatens society itself with actual dissolution.

Strange that what God designed to be man's greatest blessing should be made man's greatest curse by man's own perversity! Yet so it is with almost every good thing designed or invented to perfect man in wisdom and civilization.   It is so with science and machinery, it is so with money; it is so with public credit; it is so with mercantile enterprise; it is so with the institution of private property; and so, also, it has hitherto been with the divine institution of Christianity itself.

Christianity was introduced into the world at a period when the cup of human wickedness was full to overflowing. The inequalities of human condition were then greater than at any antecedent epoch. Wars the most bloody and brutal, and on the most extensive scale, had just ravaged the whole civilized world, ending with the destruction of the Roman Republic and with the erection of a military empire which threatened all nations and all future generations with irredeemable bondage. The long internecine struggles of Marius and Sylla, of Julius Cæsar and Pompey, and afterwards of Anthony and Augustus, had crimsoned three parts of the globe with human blood, and let loose such a universal torrent of rapine, lust, proscriptions, conspiracy, and crime of every sort throughout Europe, Asia, and Africa, that hardly any nation or people escaped the general demoralization. Direct human slavery—the personal subjection of man to man as property—was at its height as a social institution. Thousands and hundreds of thousands who had been free citizens were taken prisoners and sold as slaves during those horrid wars. To escape similar disasters, whole nations and races without number placed themselves under the protectorate of Rome, paid tribute to the imperial exchequer, and basely bartered their independence and the rights and liberties of their subjects to win the smiles or to court the pleasure of Augustus and his successors. Rome herself was a mass of incarnadined corruption. To reconcile the Romans to their newly forged fetters it became the policy of their government to brutalize their minds with gladiatorial shows, or with the familiar sight of human beings torn to pieces by wild beasts, or by shedding each other's blood with a ferocity unknown to wild beasts, and to corrupt their hearts and manners with importations of all that was most debasing in the systematized lewdness and debaucheries of the Grecian stage.

It was at this peculiar crisis of human affairs that Christianity made its appearance in the world. Need we say the divine mission of its Author was to rescue humanity from the scourges we have been describing, to bind up its bleeding wounds, and to infuse into it a spirit the opposite of what had produced the appalling vices and evils so rife at the time of His advent? Need we expatiate upon the marvellous successes which attended the labours of Himself and his apostles in the early propagation of the Gospel, or upon the amazing revolution which His followers wrought in the minds of men during the three first centuries? It is quite unnecessary to do so: history has made the world familiar with the prodigies of those days. Suffice it to say that anything like so extraordinary and so universal a revolution in the opinions and manners of men had never before been conceived, much less operated. Upon this point, at least, all historians of credit and all true philosophers are agreed.

Amongst the greatest of these marvels was the gradual but rapid extinction of direct human slavery, which took place throughout the greater part of the Roman empire during the three first ages. Antecedently to the preaching of the Gospel, the emancipation of slaves was but of rare and casual occurrence: it happened only on those unusual occasions when a slave could purchase his freedom, or get somebody to purchase it for him; or when a benevolent owner conferred it upon him as the reward of long and faithful services; or when he broke loose from his owner, to become a pirate or bandit; or when some ambitious chieftain or conspirator conferred it illegally, by draughting him into his insurgent battalions. But how few the aggregate of these emancipations were, even in the early days of the empire, we may infer from a passage in Seneca, where he tells us that, upon the occasion of a discussion in the senate upon sumptuary laws, a certain senator, having proposed that all slaves should be forced to wear a certain uniform, was immediately reminded of the danger there would be in furnishing the slaves with so ready a means of contrasting their own numbers with the paucity of their masters. Indeed, Tacitus also informs us, that when the quæstor, Curtius Lupus, was dispersing a revolt of slaves which took place in Italy about the twenty-fourth year of the vulgar era, "Rome trembled at the frightful number of the slaves," as compared with the small number of free citizens—a number which, Tacitus further states, was diminishing every day. It would be easy to multiply proofs of this kind, but it is unnecessary, seeing that all historians admit that no emancipation of slaves upon a large scale—no systematic emancipations upon principle—took place antecedently to the introduction of Christianity; but that from the moment when the Gospel began to take root in Rome and in its tributary provinces—from that moment the manumissions of slaves began to take place frequently and systematically, till at last, upon the complete establishment of Christianity, direct personal slavery was entirely abolished.

Here, however, the perversity of man stepped in, to undo all that Christianity had done. The very emancipations it operated, and which it intended for the happiness of the emancipated, and to serve as the foundation of a new social edifice, in which all should enjoy equal rights and equal laws—these very emancipations were made a curse instead of a blessing to the emancipated, and to serve for the foundation of a worse system of slavery than any that was known under the Cæsars or the Pharaohs, or than any that existed in the Southern States of America or under any Oriental despotism.

Yes, the perverse ingenuity of man has turned the systematic and benevolent emancipations operated by Christianity into an evil greater than the evil it sought to redress—into an indirect and masked system of slavery more hideous and unbearable than the direct and undisguised slavery it warred against. For what did these Christian emancipations operate; and what have been their consequences to humanity? They turned well-fed, well-housed, comfortable slaves into ragged, starving paupers; and their consequences have been to fill Europe with a race of Proletarians by far more numerous and miserable than the human chattels of the ancients, whose place they occupy in modern civilization. Out of the systematic emancipations (the progressive and ultimately universal manumission of slaves) operated by Christianity have sprung what are now called the middle and working classes. The more fortunate of the manumitted and of their posterity have become our modern Bourgeois ; the less fortunate and more numerous have become our modern Proletarians. These latter are what the French call *le Prolétariat de l'Europe;* and this *Prolétariat* their Guizots and doctrinaires now divide into the four following classes,which we pray all true democrats to mark, learn, and inwardly digest:—1, les Ouvriers ; 2, les Mendians ; 3, les Voleurs ; and 4, les Filles Publiques : that is to say, 1, Workmen; 2, Beggars ; 3, Robbers; and 4, Prostitutes !—a classification which must be highly flattering to the operative class, and enamour them vastly of royal and doctrinaire governments.

These several divisions of the *Prolétariat* are thus defined by the doctrinaires :—

"A workman is a Proletarian who works for wages in order to live.

"A beggar is a Proletarian who will not or cannot work, and who begs in order to live.

"A robber is a Proletarian who will neither work nor beg, but who robs or steals in order to live.

"A public woman is a Proletarian who will neither work nor beg nor steal, but who prostitutes herself in order to live."

Such is the classification by which the vast majority of civilized society is nowadays distinguished by writers of the first eminence ! Such is the classification they justify and would uphold ! Nay, as we shall show, they offer it to us as the legitimate development of civilization, and as a just and righteous inheritance purchased for us by the blood of our Redeemer, and bequeathed to us through eighteen centuries of Gospel propagandism ! ! !

CHAPTER II.

ORIGIN OF SLAVERY IN PATERNAL AUTHORITY.

Antiquity of Slavery—Anterior to Legal Institution—Examples cited from Ancient History—Arose from Patriarchal Government—Despotic Power of Head of Family—Marriage Custom of Purchase—Aristocratic Governments favourable to Development—Decadence under Republics.

In the preceding chapter we have shown how the modern working classes sprang from the ancient Proletarians ; how the Proletarians arose out of the downfall of the ancient system of *direct* slavery; and how Christianity was mainly instrumental in bringing about the manumission of slaves in the Roman empire, and thence throughout western Europe. The Proletarians, past and present, are but the descendants and successors of the manumitted slaves, and of decayed families of the ancient master-class; and, as observed in our last chapter, the modern classification of them by writers of the Guizot school is—WORKPEOPLE, ROBBERS, BEGGARS, and PROSTITUTES. All who have escaped this classification are such descendants or successors of the ancient freedmen as have found their way into the class of burgesses, consisting of merchants, manufacturers, professionals, and money-dealers of all sorts. Of the remainder, by far the greater number fall within the description of work-people : these are the wages-slaves of modern civilization. Direct slavery was, then, the parent of Proletarianism; and Proletarianism the parent of wages-slavery. But how did direct slavery itself originate—the personal slavery of man to man? Was it instituted? Was it the creature of law, or of conventional compact? Upon this point the concurrent testimony of history and of philosophy is unanimous : it goes to show that slavery was not a public institution originally framed by human laws, but that it was what the Americans call a *domestic* institution originating in the despotic authority of parents over their offspring in the very infancy of society. This origin necessarily supposes slavery to have been amongst the earliest, if not the very earliest, of human institutions—to have been coeval with the institution of society itself. In point of fact, it appears to have been so. Tracing history back to its fountain-heads, before systems came to disturb them, we discover a countless variety of unmistakable signs to show that two distinct classes, not to say races, made up the aggregate of souls in every ancient community of which history makes mention. One is the master-class ; the other, the slave-class. The first possesses ; the second is possessed. This aboriginal condition of humanity appears, as an historical fact, universal. There is no ancient tradition, there is no authentic record purporting to be history, that does not make mention of masters and slaves.

There were masters and slaves amongst the ancient Hebrews, the proofs of which are abundantly scattered throughout the Old Testament and in Josephus's "History of the Antiquities of the Jews." There were masters and slaves amongst the Greeks in the remotest periods of their annals. This is shown by numerous passages in Homer's "Iliad" and "Odyssey;"—as, for instance, in book xxi. of the "Iliad," where Achilles boasts to Lycaon of the captives he had taken, and sold into slavery; and in book xxii. of the "Odyssey," where Euryclea, the governess of Ulysses' household, says to him, "You have in your house fifty female slaves, whom I have taught to work in wool-spinning, and to support their servitude." That masters and slaves existed at every epoch of the Roman republic and empire is evident from the testimony of every ancient classic whose writings or recorded sayings are extant. The Institutes of Justinian make slavery expressly a subject of legislation. That the relation of master and slave obtained in ancient Gaul and in ancient Germany we have abundant evidences in Cæsar's Commentaries and in several passages to be found in Tacitus's treatise "De Moribus Germanorum." Indeed, masters and slaves are known to have existed in France as late as the twelfth century, and in Prussia as late as one hundred years ago, as may be seen by the General Code of the Prussian States, published in 1794. Masters and slaves are still to be found in all Mahomedan countries, throughout the kingdoms of the East generally, and (tell it not in Gath!), until lately, in several of the republics of the United States of America.

But it is superfluous to insist upon the existence of a fact, the proofs of which are to be found in all ages and countries—in the oldest codes as well as in the oldest books, in the most ancient legends of poets as well as in the best accredited traditions of history. Indeed, the institution of direct or personal slavery is so ancient, that its origin is lost in the night of ages, and is nowhere accounted for. It appears to have been coeval with the origin of society itself. Wherever we find the beginning of civil institutions recorded, there we find slavery already established. Moses founded the institutions of the Jews ; and slavery is found in the books of Moses. Homer is prior, by many ages, to the historic times of Greece; and slavery is found in the books of Homer. The " Twelve Tables " are the basis of Roman institutions ; and Romulus, long anterior to the " Twelve Tables," opened an asylum at Rome to receive the runaway slaves of Laticum. At later epochs, the Salic law, the feudal and forest laws, the common or traditionary law of the Saxons, Thuringians, Germans, and Anglo-Saxons, are the starting points of the institutions of most modern nations ; and slavery is found in all the codes of the invaders—it is expressly mentioned or tacitly assumed in all. Let us note it here as an important consideration, that in all these monuments of legislation, whether poetic or historic, slavery is not treated as a thing instituted for the first time ; it is only made incidental mention of as a pre-existing thing, already acknowledged, accepted, established ; it was what the French call *un fait accompli*—a settled fact. Moses, Homer, the " Twelve Tables," the mediæval laws of invasion, do not institute or found slavery; they but bear testimony to its existence, either by incidental mention of it, or by imposing new conditions to regulate the relation of master and slaves; in short, they only go to show that slavery *was* before they *were*, or, in other words, that slavery was not (to use the language of jurists) the work of positive law, but a "great fact" anterior to all law, and as old as the origin of society itself.

The aboriginal character of slavery admitted, it remains to be shown, wherefore did society, in its infancy, establish slavery; or, rather, by what *modus operandi* was slavery made to develop itself in aboriginal society. History, reason, our very instincts, tell us there is but one satisfactory explanation of the phenomenon. It arose from the unbounded power which fathers, or the heads of families, exercised, in early days, over their households—wives, concubines, and children. All history is unanimous as to the fact that fathers exercised a supreme authority over their offspring in the early ages of the world. The same fact is found still to obtain amongst races retaining primitive customs. Evidences to this effect are to be abundantly met with in the Bible, in the Greek tragedians, in the legislation of the Romans, in Asiatic traditions. All go to prove that parental authority was bounded only by parental will,—that it extended even to the power of life and death over their offspring. The old pagans, in order to give the highest idea of the power of Jupiter, call him the "father of the gods." For no other reason have Jews and Christians, in like manner, named God the All-Powerful Father. Paternal authority was so absolute and extensive in primitive times, that it suffered no other, co-ordinate or paramount: it completely absorbed the rights and the very existence of wife and children. Out of this absolute paternal authority did personal slavery first arise. Sons daughters, and even wives were but slaves of the head of the family; they were amongst his chattels—a part of his estate. Aristotle calls children the "animated tools or instruments of their parents." In the days of the patriarchs, paternal authority over children was absolute amongst the Jews. Abraham's sacrifice of Isaac is one of many proofs that might be cited. It is evident God would not have ordered a thing contrary to the positive law—a law ordained by God himself. Moreover, divers passages in Josephus show in the clearest and most explicit terms that the absolute authority of fathers over their children continued undisputed, and to be held sacred, down to the time of Herod the Great, who was contemporary with the Emperor Augustus of Rome. The strongest evidence of this is the prosecution of his own two sons, Alexander and Aristobulus, before Augustus, wherein Herod took great credit to himself for his moderation in referring the matter to the emperor, "seeing that, in virtue of his rights as a father, he might put them to death without any other warrant or authority." The elder son, Alexander, in his reply, frankly admitted his father's right to give him death as he had given him life. Some years later, this same Herod exemplified the paternal power of the Jews in a still more impressive manner. In a speech which he delivered against these same rebellious sons before an assembly of the notables of his province, he reminded them that, independently of the law of nature, which gave him an absolute power of life and death over his offspring, there was an express law of his nation on the subject, which ordained that when a father and mother should accuse their children, and lay hands upon their heads, all parties present should be held bound to *stone* them; and that, accordingly, he might, without consulting them, have put his sons to death without any form of trial whatever, in virtue of his parental rights. These facts are decisive enough as respects the Jews. It is to be understood, however, that it was only aristocratic fathers—fathers amongst the higher orders—that ordinarily exercised this atrocious despotism over their own families.

The power of fathers over their children was quite as absolute amongst the early Greeks and Romans as amongst the Jews; and if it did not descend to so late a period of their annals, it is only because aristocratic forms gave place sooner to democratic, under their government, than amongst the Jews. That it existed in full force at the time of the Trojan war is forcibly demonstrated by the sacrifice of Iphigenia, which, as an historical fact, is a tradition corresponding exactly with the sacrifice by Abraham. In Sparta it prevailed as completely, in the days of Lycurgus, as it did in Judæa in the patriarchal times. Plutarch relates that, at that epoch, a sort of family council was usually held upon the birth of a child, to deliberate whether the newly born should be allowed to live or die. Even at Athens, where the democratic element prevailed more than at Sparta, and where humanity and refinement, the offspring of arts and letters, had made greater progress, the absolute power of parents was such that, even as late as the age of Solon, the Athenians were in the habit of selling their children for slaves—a practice which, Plutarch informs us, there was no law to prohibit. Let us here observe generally, that it was in the Homeric period that the absoluteness of parental authority displayed itself with the most vigour in Greece, and that this period corresponds exactly, in the history of their comparative legislation, with the patriarchal epoch of the Jews. For example, daughters were so completely identified with the chattels or property of their fathers, that their suitors had always to pay a certain price for marrying and taking them away. Thus, Jacob served Laban for seven years to obtain his daughter Rachel; and thus, among the Greeks, Othryon engaged to serve Priam during the siege of Troy, to obtain his daughter Cassandra without paying a dowry—that is, without buying her otherwise than by his services. Instances of this kind might be multiplied; but enough has been said to illustrate our position. Let us observe, however, as a general rule, that paternal authority was always greatest in the states most aristocratically constituted, and always least in those most democratically constituted; and that the period through which the absoluteness of paternal power prevailed was longer or shorter, in different countries, just according to the later or earlier development given to the democratic principle in their institutions. Such a barbarous power being utterly irreconcilable with liberty and justice, it could flourish only in times of ignorance and brute force. As democracy arose, and civilization spread, the parental despotism declined. It lasted longer in Judæa than in Sparta, and longer in Sparta than in Athens; because the barbarism of oligarchy prevailed longer in Judæa than in Sparta, and longer in Sparta than in Athens.

Amongst the Romans paternal despotism was carried to a fearful height. Roman legislation abounds in records of it; and her chronicles confirm all that is revealed to us by her legislatures. Dionysius of Halicarnassus tells us of an old law of the Papyrian Code which authorised fathers to kill and to sell their children. The Code of Justinian also makes mention of it. But the despotic authority of Roman fathers over their children is an historical fact, sufficiently familiar to most readers to dispense with the necessity of further proofs. It was one of the darkest traits of their legislation and national character, and it doubtless had no small share in imparting to their republic those harsh and overbearing qualities which involved them in perpetual broils amongst themselves and in endless wars of aggression against their neighbours.

To this barbarous and despotic power of parents over their offspring—a power extending over their whole lifetime—a power which applied to both sexes, and which appears to be coeval with the first existence of society itself—to this brutal, irrational, and inhuman power are we doubtless indebted for the origin of all human slavery. In what manner this despotic power manifested itself, and how the past and present order of things grew out of it, we shall endeavour to show in future chapters.

CHAPTER III.

CAUSES OF PARENTAL DESPOTISM.

Evidences from Egypt and Persia—Supreme Authority of Family Head—First Legal Limitation under Roman Empire—Necessity for gradual Growth of Slavery—Source of Paternal Riches—Importance of Chief of the Family.

We stated, in our last chapter, that human slavery, according to the concurrent testimony of history and philosophy, originated in the unbounded power which fathers or heads of families exercised, in the infancy of society, over their household—over wives, concubines, and children. Of the existence of this power amongst the ancient Jews, Greeks, and Romans we adduced some remarkable evidences. Similar evidences abound with respect to Egypt, Persia, Media, Asia Minor, and, indeed, of every other ancient people of which any traditions are preserved. The records of the various tribes and nations which inhabited Asia Minor go to show that the authority of fathers over their offspring continued to be supreme and absolute even down to a period not far removed from the Christian era. For example, Xenophon relates, in his "Anabasis," how a certain Thracian king, named Teutes, offered to give him his daughter, and to purchase one of his (Xenophon's), if he had any, "according to the law of Thrace." Plutarch, in his Life of Lucullus, furnishes similar evidences. He relates, that during the distress in which the proprietors of Asia Minor found themselves after the defeat of King Tigranes, those fathers of families who, upon the arrival of Lucullus, had not wherewith to satisfy the demands of the Roman tax-collectors, sold their little children and marriageable daughters. That such things should prevail under pure despotisms like those of ancient Asia Minor, Egypt, Persia, &c., or under the patriarchal *régime* of the Jews, when manners were primitive and the government a theocracy, is what we might expect in the natural order of things; but that they should occur under the more democratic and polished governments of Greece and Rome is what appears astonishing to our modern notions; yet so it was. The authority of paternity was no less supreme in the later than in the older countries. The early annals of Rome exhibit some glaring but curious instances of it, which, taken in connection with the revelations of later times, not only render the fact undoubted, but will account for many of the harsher qualities of the Romans, and, at the same time, strengthen our theory of human slavery. Going back to the very cradle of the Romans, we find that, when Rhea was delivered of Romulus and Remus, Amulius, her uncle, ordered the immediate exposure of the infants. This Roman fact corresponds with the exposure of Moses in Egypt, and with the Greek legend which describes Œdipus as having been similarly exposed and found suspended from a tree by the feet.

Dionysius of Halicarnassus, in relating the well-known story of the Horatii, tells us that the elder Horatius, assuming the defence of his son, the murderer of his sister, claimed the right of solely taking cognizance of the affair, inasmuch as his paternal quality constituted him a born judge of his own children. If we remember aright, Racine, in his tragedy of the Horatii and Curiatii, follows up the same idea. Plutarch, in the Life of Publicola, relating the conspiracy of the Aquilians in favour of the Tarquins, tells us that Junius Brutus in like manner arrogated the right of jurisdiction in the affair of his own son, and that he judged, condemned, and caused him to be executed in virtue of his paternal authority, without any of those judiciary observances which were adhered to in respect of the other conspirators. Titus Livius, an earlier and higher authority in such matters than Plutarch, gives a similar account of this affair.

Down to the times of Sylla, there does not appear to have been any considerable check or restraint imposed upon paternal power. The absolute authority of fathers was in some slight degree moderated by a law of that dictator, known to jurisconsults under the title of "Lex Cornelia de Sicariis"—a law aimed not so much at the domestic jurisdiction of fathers, as at the abuse of such jurisdiction for the purposes of private vengeance. But, that and similar laws notwithstanding, we find, even under the emperor, examples of domestic jurisdiction which go to prove that the sovereign authority of fathers was carried out through every epoch of the civil law. The philosopher, Seneca, reports the particulars of a process by a great personage, named Titus Arrius, instituted of his own authority, at his own domestic tribunal, against his own son. At this process or trial Augustus himself assisted as a simple witness. Seneca's account of this affair, which is brief and to the purpose, is worthy of notice. "Titus Arrius," he says, "wishing to judge his son, invited Augustus to his domestic council. The emperor repaired to this citizen's home, took his seat, and gave his presence simply as a witness of an affair in which he was not concerned. Augustus does not say: 'Let the accused be brought before me at my palace;' that would have been to arrogate to himself jurisdiction in the matter, and to deprive the father of his rights. After the cause had been heard—the accusation and defence—Titus Arrius demanded of each of the council to write down his judgment." Tacitus, in like manner, relates that a senator, named Plautius, sat in judgment upon his own wife, Pomponia Græcina, who was accused of addicting herself to superstitions. She was tried before the assembled household, and according to ancient usage. This happened in the reign of Nero. To these pagan we might add the Christian authority of Tertullian, who makes mention, at the opening of his "Apologetica," of domestic judgments which had just recently taken place at Rome, and which, like that of Plautius, would seem to have been directed against the Christians, whose religion, till the reign of Constantine, was looked upon (to use the language of Tacitus) as "a deplorable and destructive superstition." In short, the despotism of paternal authority appears to have prevailed in Rome at every epoch of her history, down to the period when paganism lost its hold upon the population. It is inferred from divers documents still extant, that the absolute authority of fathers did not disappear before the end of the third century; and the first law which positively prohibited fathers from giving, selling, or contracting away their children is said to be a law of Dioclesian and of Maximian. These laws are recited in the fourth book of the Justinian Code. Nevertheless, there is a law of Constantine, whereby the sale of children, in cases of great poverty or destitution, was made legally permissible. In truth, paternal despotism, like its offspring, direct slavery, perished little by little, or by slow degrees. Like direct slavery itself, it paled and sank before the rising light of the Gospel. The three first centuries witnessed one continuous struggle of Christianity against the establishments of paganism. Amongst the worst of these were parental despotism and personal slavery. As the Gospel gained ground upon paganism, parental despotism and slavery went down. Towards the close of the third century, the majority of the better classes of the Romans had embraced the new faith. Parental despotism and the servile subjection of man to man being imcompatible with that faith, these two relics of primeval barbarism began rapidly to disappear; and after the legal establishment of the Christian religion by Constantine, the relation of master and servant (though, as we shall see by-and-by, by no means improved) became altogether a new and different relation.

These preliminary remarks upon the history of fathers of families and of the ancient paternal authority must not be considered irrelevant, or otherwise than essential to our design. Without them, we could not account for the origin of human slavery; and, without knowing its origin, we could not well develop its progress and the various phases it has assumed up to the present time. No ancient record or tradition in existence goes to show that human slavery originated in positive laws or in coercive ordinances enforced by the sword. Reason and experience naturally coincide with history in this matter. That any portion of society, after living on terms of equality with the rest, should suddenly allow all its rights to be extinguished by brute force, or consent to have its liberties and independence voted away, when it had arms and instincts to defend them, is contrary to common sense and to all experience. Much less is it probable that the great majority would have everywhere suffered a contemptible minority to usurp the rights and powers of the whole. The ancient slave-class were everywhere a majority. Nothing but the force of early habit and traditional example could have made the majority the willing bondsmen of the minority. But as the relation must have commenced at some period before such habits and such traditional example could take effect, and as some sort of authority was absolutely necessary to establish the relation, it follows that, in the absence of all other competent authority, it must have been the natural authority of parents over their offspring that first established slavery. Such slavery must, of course, in the first instance have been direct; for, in a rude and primitive society, no other would be intelligible or possible.

If we be right in these antecedents, our conclusions from them must be, that the first fathers were the first masters, and the first children were the first slaves. To determine the history of the first masters is, therefore, virtually to suggest the history of the first slaves. Yes, the unbounded power of paternity in the first ages of the world was the origin of all human slavery; and therefore is slavery a thing anterior to all written constitutions, to all human laws, traditional or imposed.

Now come the questions, Why did our first parents make slaves of their children? and how came the domestic institution, established by parental despotism, to become a social institution diffused throughout the whole of society? Our natural instincts, undeveloped by reason and undisciplined by knowledge and experience, would, methinks, lead us to account satisfactorily for both facts. It was natural that the head of the family should govern the family. It was not unnatural that the parent, who had given life to the child, and who had preserved that life when the child was unable to take care of itself, should in some measure regard that life as his own; and as the maintenance of his offspring must have been a burden on the parent, and kept him comparatively poor in the days of early manhood, it is no more than what we should expect from the selfishness of old age—especially in a rude social state—that he should seek to indemnify himself, by the future labour of his children, for his cost and pains in bringing them up. Let us also bear in mind, that we are treating of those primitive times when man's animal instincts interpreted polygamy and the law of nature to be one and the same —times which Dryden describes as

> "Those ancient times, e'er priestcraft did begin—
> 'Twas e'er polygamy was deemed a sin."

In those days, the larger the family, the greater the wealth and power of the head of the household. In infancy, the offspring might be a charge and a source of poverty; but, as they grew up, they more than repaid the cost of maintenance,—they became, in fact, a source of wealth and power and aggrandisement to the parent. Now, according to all known traditions, the ancient fathers of families gloried in a numerous progeny. In the history of the Jews, families of fifty and upwards are frequently spoken of. Josephus informs us, that Gedeon had seventy sons; Jair, thirty; Apsan, thirty sons and thirty daughters; Abdon, forty sons—all of them living at the time of his death—besides thirty grandsons. Indeed, the Old Testament abounds in examples showing the multitudinous progeny ascribed to the old patriarchs—most of them, too, born of concubines, under what the modern world would call *disparaging* circumstances.

The traditions of early Greece harmonise, in this respect, with those of the Jews. Who has not read of the fifty daughters of Danaüs? In Homer, we find old Priam appealing to his numerous progeny, as the best means of exciting pity and respect in the vindictive breast of Achilles. We find him telling of his fifty children—

of nineteen born of the same mother, Hecuba; and all the rest, of concubines. Livy and Plutarch tell us of the three hundred Fabians —all of the same family—who perished in a great battle against the Tuscans, fought in the early wars of the Republic; and Plutarch also makes mention, in his Life of Theseus, of a certain personage, Pallas, who had fifty children.

From these and innumerable testimonies of a similar kind, we may readily conceive that these numerous wives and concubines kept by the heads of families in early times made fathers vastly more important personages than they are nowadays, and gave them progenies which, in comparison with modern ones, might be considered clans or tribes. What with wives, concubines, children, and grandchildren, every such father was veritably the head of a community; and inasmuch as his power was absolute over each and all, he had every motive that selfishness could dictate to make them, and keep them, slaves for his aggrandisement and pleasure. In fact, the more numerous his progeny and household, the greater was his source of wealth, the higher his status, and the better his security against personal violence in lawless times. That slavery should originate and grow up in this way appears to us perfectly natural. At all events, in no other way has it ever been, or can it ever be, satisfactorily accounted for.

What happened in the case of one father of a family would as naturally happen in respect of others. In the progress of time, some of the younger branches would naturally stray from the paternal home, and emigrate to other lands, where they would settle down and, in time, become the heads of families—the founders of new races of slaves. Indeed, we have but to imagine the case of one to apply to thousands similarly circumstanced, and we shall see the origin of human slavery at once satisfactorily explained. Those early fathers, or heads of families, would naturally love some of their children better than others; at least, they would have more confidence in some one than in the rest. To those so loved, or so favoured, would naturally devolve the headship of the family, or such portions of the patrimonial estate as might enable them to found new families elsewhere. These families, like the parent one, would as naturally resolve themselves into little communities of masters and slaves; so that in course of time, by the natural operation of one and the same first cause, the whole of society would find itself, what we find it to have been in all early history, an aggregation of souls divided everywhere into two great classes—a master-class possessing, and a slave-class possessed.

Let us not imagine, however, that a social order which appears to us so inhuman and so unnatural was viewed in this light, or inspired *our* feelings, in the ancient world; it would be a great mistake to suppose this. Nothing was further from the contemplation of the men of antiquity than our notions and theories about the equality of human rights. The idea of what man ought to be, or is capable of being made, was an idea unknown to the ancient world. The division of the human race into masters and slaves appeared to them a perfectly natural division: they saw no other; they never heard of any other; they appear never to have conceived the possibility of any other. Even the slaves themselves never complained of slavery *as an institution;* they never demanded liberty in the sense we demand it. When they did complain, it was not because they thought that one class ought not to be a master-class and the other a slave-class: that was an idea quite beyond them. When they complained—and they often *did* complain, and sometimes rebel too—it was either because they found their masters harsh and cruel, and wished to exchange them for new and better ones, or because they hoped, by breaking their fetters and becoming soldiers, pirates, or adventurers of some kind, to exchange their condition as slaves for the more enviable one of slave-owners. History records several insurrections of slaves that took place in ancient times; but in no one instance does it appear that the insurgents took up arms for the principle of equality, or for any cause common to other slaves as well as to themselves. Of this fact we shall adduce some notable evidences in the progress of this inquiry. For the present, we shall content ourselves with the assertion that, as a general rule, the religious doctrine of men's equality before God, and the political and social doctrine of man's equality before the law, or as a member of society, were doctrines utterly unknown to, or uncared for amongst, the old pagan world. In hazarding this assertion, we would be understood as applying it to all classes and callings of the ancients alike—to philosophers, poets, orators, and statesmen, as well as to mechanics, labourers, house-servants, even the very lowest description of menial slaves. That one or two philosophers and poets, here and there, may be found to have uttered sentiments prophetic of "the good time coming," or indicative of a tacit belief that man was made for a higher and brighter destiny than was his then lot, we pretend not to deny. But that any class or calling of men existed in the old pagan world who believed in, much less contended for, the political and social rights of man *as man* is what, we fearlessly assert, cannot be proved from any historical authority extant. With the exception of the Essenes of Judæa and the Therapeutæ of Egypt, we know of no attempt having been made in ancient times to realise the social views latterly so prevalent amongst the working classes in France, Germany, and, indeed, in most parts of Central and Western Europe, England included. The Essenes and Therapeutæ, however, can hardly be considered an exception to the general rule, seeing that the latter was a Christian sect, and that the Essenes, being Jews, believed in the same God that all Christians professed to worship. Besides, the Essenes were but a very small sect, hardly exceeding 4,000 souls in all; and though they held and practised the theory of human equality, and proscribed slavery from amongst them, yet, like the Shakers of America, they so mixed up absolute celibacy, and other ascetic doctrines and practices, with their community-system that, in the very nature of things, they could never be more than a small, isolated sect, utterly incapable of influencing, by creed or example, the destinies of the human race.

But how the cause of human liberty came to be hopeless under the old pagan systems, and how Christianity itself has hitherto failed in its divine mission, must be the subject of future chapters.

CHAPTER IV.

INCREASE AND CONSOLIDATION OF SLAVERY.

Sanction given by Law and Public Opinion—Various Causes of Enslavement— Practices of Ancient Germans—Analogy in Modern Commercial and Funding Systems, and Expatriation of Irish Peasantry—Slavery among the Jews.

HAVING shown how human slavery originated in parental despotism, let us now inquire how positive laws came to consolidate and regulate it, and public opinion to consecrate and perpetuate it, till it had become the normal condition of some three-fourths of the human race antecedently to the period of Christ's advent. Here we shall again find history our safest guide. If the oldest traditions show, on the one hand, that slavery did not originate in human laws, but was the spontaneous growth of the natural subjection of children to parents, there is equally ample authority, on the other hand, to show that, once introduced, all the forces of law and opinion known to the ancients were unsparingly applied to propagate and maintain slavery in every pagan country.

While families remained apart from each other, without intercourse, without social relationship, slavery knew no other law than the will or pleasure of the head of each household. But when, in the progress of early civilization, the families congregated in any particular locality or country came to find it necessary to constitute themselves into one great society for the purposes of exchange or commerce, intermarrying, mutual defence against aggression, &c., the despotic will of individuals gave place, of necessity, to a general law of the heads of families composing the society. It was then, and not till then, that slavery became a *legal* institution. The general law not only sanctioned and enforced it, but also greatly enlarged its bounds by creating new sources of slavery. For example, to be taken prisoner in war, to take refuge in the house of another, to be unable to pay one's debts, or, if a girl, being married out of her family or tribe,— these were so many new sources of slavery created by the general law. The rights of war were made to confer upon the vanquisher the same rights over the vanquished that belonged to their own fathers. Indeed, amongst the ancients the vanquished were considered as "men without gods," that is to say, men without ancestors of rank or dignity (for, in the language of the primitive poets, the gods and the ancestors of great families are one and the same thing); and they were treated as mere chattels, as appears from the very name given, viz., *mancipia*, which, though the ordinary term applied to slaves taken in battle, is, in its etymological sense, applicable only to things inanimate. Whether it was from a religious scruple, or for the purpose of divesting the vanquished of what prestige might attach to

them from the possession of their gods or ancestral images, we find
that the taking or keeping possession of these gods was always a vital
consideration in the sieges and battles of antiquity. Once taken by the
enemy, the capture and enslavement of their possessors was deemed
inevitable. Those left without gods, in this sense, were regarded as
outlaws by their fellow-citizens, and their future slavery was considered a *mere matter of course* by themselves, as well as by their
conquerors. We may readily imagine what a prolific source of slavery
this must have been in lawless times, when *might* alone conferred
right. We may also conceive how greatly it must have aggravated
and embittered the aboriginal relations between master and slave.

Asylums, or houses of refuge, were another means of extending
slavery under the positive law. The man who took sanctuary in one
of these places became the slave or chattel of the protector who had
given him safety. These asylums, of which we find mention made in
the primitive traditions of almost every old country, drew together
not only maltreated slaves from other quarters, but malefactors and
vagabonds of all sorts, and, in general, that restless and turbulent
class of people who love action for its own sake, and cannot live out
of broils and adventure. History testifies to the opening of such
asylums by rulers, and founders of cities, as an essential feature
of their policy. Thus, Moses determined six certain cities in which
manslayers might take refuge from the avenger. Theseus opened a
refuge at Athens, the remembrance of which was so fresh in Plutarch's
time, that that biographer thinks the phrase of the common criers in
his day, "All peoples, come hither!" were the identical words used by
Theseus himself. Romulus, as before observed, opened an asylum
at Rome for the fugitive slaves of Latium, which, it is said, remained
open for upwards of 750 years. Indeed, if we are to believe Suetonius,
it and similar places of refuge were to be found in Rome, and in the
provinces, till Tiberius formally abolished "the law and custom" of
them by an edict. It may be observed, generally, of these asylums
that, originally or primitively, the parties who fled for refuge to them
became the slaves, or subjects, or clients of their protectors, yielding
to the latter their personal liberty and service in exchange for their
preservation; but at later epochs the character both of asylums and
of those who fled to them changed altogether. When opened by free
cities within the boundaries of their liberties, or by priests in
their temples, they were sacred to freedom, and not to slavery. There
is no doubt, however, that in the early ages of the world both law
and custom turned them largely to account in extending the domain
of slavery.

Next to war, indebtedness, or the relation of debtor to creditor,
was probably the most odious and prolific source of slavery under the
positive law. Such appears to have been the case, at least, amongst
Greeks and Romans, with whose histories the moderns are better
acquainted than with those of other ancient countries. Plutarch tells
us, in his Life of Solon, that that legislator, on his arriving at power,
found a large proportion of the citizens in a state of actual slavery to
their creditors, and that one of his greatest difficulties and triumphs
was the adjustment of their conflicting claims.

Certain writers and commentators speak of an old Athenian law which gave money-lenders, as security for their money lent, the personal liberty of the borrowers—otherwise, a power to make them slaves. Others say the law in question extended the creditor's power to one of life or death—that he might expose or kill his defaulting debtor. The Roman laws of the Twelve Tables were, we know, borrowed from Greece ; and Aulus Gellius cites the express terms of the law of the Third Table to show that it armed Roman creditors with similar power over their unfortunate debtors. The rigour of this law was such, that in case there were several creditors, they had the option either to sell the debtor's person to strangers or to dissever his body and divide the pieces amongst them. Shocked and disgusted at the barbarity of this law, Aulus Gellius asks, "What can be conceived more savage, what more foreign to man's natural disposition, than that the members and limbs of a destitute debtor should be drawn asunder by a mangling process of ever so short duration ?" Tertullian, one of the early Christian fathers, bears testimony to the existence of that and similar laws under the pagan system. As he uses the plural word *leges* instead of the singular *lex*, it is clear there must have been more than one law of the kind. The murderous part of such laws was, however, too revolting to be carried into effect ; so the enslavement of the debtor's person was the course usually adopted by vindictive creditors. Indeed, Quintilian tells us expressly that public morals rejected the law of the Twelve Tables—at least, that portion of it which gave creditors the power to cut up the bodies of insolvent debtors. To imprison or enslave them was, therefore, their only practicable course ; and as the latter was the more profitable, it became the one usually resorted to. The sale of unfortunate debtors as slaves became, therefore, a part and parcel of the commerce of Greece and Rome. It was one of the ways by which hard-hearted creditors indemnified themselves for bad debts. And as neither law nor custom could reconcile any people to such a palpable outrage upon the rights of humanity, it never ceased to be a prolific source of disaffection and civil broils throughout every period of the Greek and Roman annals. Livy records some terrible outbreaks, arising solely from the laws of debtor and creditor. Indeed, next to agrarian monopoly, the workings of usury in pauperizing and enslaving free citizens was the principal cause of all the civil wars, and the ultimate cause of the downfall of the Greek and Roman republics.

But Greece and Rome are not the only ancient states in which debt multiplied slaves and slavery. Tacitus informs us that the ancient Germans were so addicted to gaming, that sometimes they staked even their bodies upon the last throw of the dice, and, when the game went against them, resigned themselves tranquilly to be bound and sold as slaves. 'Tis curious to observe the language made use of by Tacitus in describing this affair. It forcibly reminds one of the "national debts" of modern times, and of the cunning cant by which the toiling slaves, who pay the interest of them, are made to bear the burden with more than asinine resignation. Indeed, the whole passage, as given by Tacitus, might be strictly applied to the men and things we are living amongst, if we would but substitute a few of our modern commercial terms for the old dice-table terms employed by Tacitus. "They (the Germans)," he says, "practise gambling amongst their serious pursuits, and are quite sober over it. So desperate is their lust of gain or fear of losing, that when all other means fail, they stake their liberty and their very bodies upon the last throw of the dice ; nay, the beaten party (the loser) enters voluntarily and resignedly into slavery. Although younger and more robust than his antagonist, he quietly submits to be bound in fetters and sold. Such is their perverseness in depravity—*they, themselves*, call it FAITH, HONOUR ! The successful parties (winners) dispose of this class of slaves in the way of commerce, *that the infamy of their victory may be lost sight of by the removal of their victim.*" In this almost literal translation, we have paraphrased Tacitus no further than his elliptic style and the different genius of our language render necessary; yet we can hardly persuade ourselves that we have not been describing the process and the very terms by which commercial speculation and our system of public and private credit manufacture the slaves of our own day. The only substantial difference is, that our gambling and slave-making are upon an immeasurably larger scale, and that our enslaved Saxons, unlike their German progenitors, have not even a chance of saving themselves : for, though they are made to contribute all the stakes, they are allowed no further share in the game than to look on and pay the losses, whoever may be the winners. Tacitus's term, *fides (faith, honour)*, is the identical term made use of now-a-days to enforce the payment of national debts by those who never borrowed, and the payment of "debts of honour" by those who forget to pay their tailors' bills and their servants' wages. The old German gamester's trick, too, of getting his victim out of the way by disposing of him as merchandise, instead of keeping him to serve as a slave upon himself, is not without its analogies in our modern practice. Indeed, our whole system of commerce and of public credit is based upon a similar practice and similar motives. The slaves of our modern landlords, merchants, and manufacturers are always the *apparent* slaves of somebody else—of some wretched go-between underling, on whom the *odium*, though not the profits, of the system is made to fall. The landlord throws it upon the farmer or agent; the millowner, upon his overseer; the coal-king, upon his manager; the exporting merchant, upon the slop-shops and *sweaters;* and so on, throughout every ramification of trade and manufacture. The loanmonger retains not in his own hands his purchased privilege of rifling the pockets of all taxpayers twice a year for no value received. That would make his position as odious as that of Tacitus's successful old German gamester would have been, had he made the "plucked pigeon" his personal slave, who was whilom his boon-companion and equal. Business could not go on in that way. Our loanmonger knows it, and, therefore, no sooner does he get his bonds than he diffuses the "scrip" as widely and plentifully as the dews of heaven, till there is hardly a grade or calling in society that is not made directly interested and instrumental in enslaving the producer and defrauding him of his hire. At the moment we write, there are nearly a quarter of a million of families interested in what is called "public faith," "national honour," and all that sort of thing; and, amongst the whole lot, there is not one that was originally concerned in any of the hocus-pocusing transactions which have given us our "national debt," with its thirty millions of annual tax on the producing slaves of this country. The original loanmongers and their representatives have dexterously shifted the odium and the responsibility of their black job or jobs (for there were many of them) from their own shoulders to those of innocent parties; and, whatever may eventually become of these parties, they took good care to have more than their *quid pro quo* before they transferred their claims upon the public purse to the present recipients of the dividends payable half-yearly on account of the debt called "national." Another and, mayhap, a stronger analogy to the case of Tacitus's "plucked pigeons," sold into slavery, might be found in the expatriated tenantry and peasantry of Ireland. The landlords of that country do not *always* dispose of their human chattels by plague, pestilence, and famine; and there is no law of the Twelve Tables to authorise the cutting up of the bodies of their tenants in arrear. But there is a law—or, whether there is or not, they find one—which authorises them to eject tenants from their holdings, to raze their habitations to the ground, and to drive the said tenants, homeless and breadless, to find a shelter and a crust where they may. In such cases (and they are as plentiful as blackberries), it is not unusual for such landlords to smuggle their ousted victims out of the country, and even to pay their freight to Canada in some crazy old hull (provided their fare do not exceed the amount it would cost to bury them in case they died under a bush or ditch after the dilapidation of their homes). Once removed to Quebec or to the bottom of the Atlantic (it matters not which), there is an end of trouble to both landlord and tenant. In Canada the tenant cannot fare worse than in Ireland (for worse he could not), and he may fare better. At the bottom of the sea he is safe, and provided for, for all time to come. In either case he is out of the landlord's sight, and out of the sight of all to whom a knowledge of his treatment might suggest misgivings as to their own future. To the landlord who ousted him, his personal service as an actual slave would be as useless as that of Tacitus's ruined gamester would be to the successful one who had won him and sold him. He would be but an incumbrance—a lump of dead stock—an incubus upon the soil! His presence would be but a reproach to his landlord, and curse to himself! To get rid of him, then,—to dispose of him anyhow, or by any means, that will only get him out of the way,—is the one thing needful. Well, Tacitus has shown us how the lucky gamesters of his day got rid of their fleeced victims in Germany. Against his case we fear not to put the Irish "clearers" and the British farm-"consolidators" of our day, being perfectly assured that the Saxons of the present day will be found to excel those of Tacitus's day, or any other of the old German tribes, in the art of slave-making, as much as we excel the old Romans themselves in road-making, shipbuilding, money-grubbing, military manslaughtering, or any other art or science.

To return from this digression, the relation of debtor and creditor was unquestionably one of the direst and most fertile sources of slavery known to the ancient pagan world. Even God's chosen people, the Hebrews, were not altogether free from it. It is true, Moses's septennial release from debt, and the jubilee ordained at the end of every fifty years, were powerful checks upon the inroad of this form of slavery. But, nevertheless, indebtedness *did* furnish its contingent to slavery even under the Mosaic law; for do we not find Moses anticipating this curse in Leviticus, when he enjoins, "If thy brother that dwelleth by thee be waxen poor, and *be sold* unto thee, thou shalt not compel him to serve as a slave or bond-servant, but as an hired servant; and as a sojourner he shall be with thee, and shall serve thee until the day of the jubilee," &c. This shows clearly how inseparable was slavery from indebtedness under the ancient order of things, when Moses found it necessary to make provisions against its contingency, notwithstanding all the precautions he had ordained to prevent it. And Moses's foresight is fully proved by the subsequent history of the Jews. For we learn from Josephus, that at a later epoch, to wit, under King Joram, the son of Jehosaphat, the widow of Obadias (who had been governor of King Achab's palace) came to tell the prophet Elisha that, unable to reimburse the money that her husband had borrowed, to subsist the hundred prophets he had saved from the persecution by Jezebel, *his creditors laid claim to herself and her children as their slaves.* We might furnish other instances of a similar kind from sacred history; while from profane history we might cite proofs *ad infinitum* bearing upon the same point: but enough has been said for our purpose. The obligation of debtors to their creditors was undoubtedly one of the most grievous sources of slavery known to the positive law in ancient times. Next to war, it was probably the greatest.

The last remaining cause to be disposed of is the marriage of females—more especially of females married out of their own family or tribe. That much slavery was brought about in this way is provable in a variety of ways, and by the best traditional evidence. Homer's "Iliad" abounds in testimonies to this effect. We have already cited the example of Cassandra, whom Othryon purchased from Priam, even as Jacob bought Leah and Rachel from their father Laban. Other passages are still more conclusive on the point. We find in the 9th book, for instance, that Agamemnon, regretting his having occasioned the wrath of Achilles, offers him, by way of appeasing it, certain costly presents; amongst others, seven Lesbian female slaves, along with Briseis; and, when Troy should be taken, twenty captives, the most beautiful, after Helen; and as a climax, one of his own three daughters—Achilles to choose, and to have her without purchase. And again, in the 16th book, we find Homer making mention of a certain Polydora, the mother of Menestheus, whom he describes as having been purchased for a wife, by her husband, at a great expense. The poems of Virgil contain similar evidences,—as for instance, when Juno proposes to Venus to settle their quarrels, and to accept Dido as a spouse and servant to her son Æneas. The term *service* made use of by Virgil indicates clearly the servile relation to the husband which such marriages imposed upon women.

Having explained the *origin* of direct slavery, its legal establishment, and the principal known causes which multiplied it and consolidated it as a social institution, let us now inquire in what light it was regarded by the ancients themselves, wherefore it was able to maintain its footing all over the world, till the advent of Christianity; why it still obtains in so large a portion of the habitable globe; and why it has in nowise ceased, without giving birth to a masked or indirect slavery worse than itself.

In this inquiry, our task will resolve itself in establishing the three following propositions:—

1st. That direct or personal slavery was not regarded by the ancients in the light in which enlightened men of the present day regard it, that is to say, as an unnatural and inhuman institution, but, on the contrary, was considered to be a thing perfectly natural and reasonable in itself, and essential to the ends and purposes of society.

2nd. That the main cause of its permanence in the world was the universality of public opinion in its favour, rather than the force of law or custom; and that the slaves themselves fully participated in the general opinion.

3rd. That, all things considered, direct slavery, whether as practised by the ancients or by the moderns (wherever it is in use), was, with all its evils, less destructive of life, morals, and happiness to the majority than the present system of indirect or disguised slavery, as effected in most civilized countries by unjust agrarian, monetary, and fiscal laws.

CHAPTER V.

OPINION OF THE ANCIENT WORLD ON SLAVERY.

Permanence of Slavery under all Revolutions—Ignorance of Principle of Human Equality—Theory and Personal Experience of Plato—Contentment of Slaves with their Condition—Occasional Comfort and Happiness of Slaves —Absence of Revolts against Slavery—Social and Political Rights ignored by Greeks and Romans.

HAVING, in the preceding chapters, shown how human slavery came into the world, how it originated in the despotism of paternal power, before laws or governments were known, and how, coeval with society itself, it had grown up, flourished, and everywhere established itself, as a *domestic* institution, before any conventional act or delegated authority of society came to consolidate it as a *social* institution—having shown all this, and afterwards explained the subsequent modifications, enlargements, and aggravations of slavery made by positive legislation,—let us now ascertain why the diabolical institution endured so long in the world; why it still endures in very many countries; and, above all, why every attempt to get rid of it has hitherto only had the effect of aggravating the evils of society, and making the mass of mankind more miserable slaves, *without the name*, than any that ever bore the name in ancient or modern times. Having ascertained this, we shall then be prepared to comprehend the only just and practicable means whereby slavery of every sort, and in every form and degree, may be effectually and for ever banished from the world.

Had slavery, amongst the ancients, originated in, and been upheld by, their laws and governments, it may be fairly presumed that some of the revolutions which, at various epochs, swept away their laws and governments would have swept away the institution of slavery amongst the rest. Whatever is forced upon a decided majority of any people, by the will of a minority, can be upheld only by fraud and coercion. Had these been the conditions of slavery amongst the ancients, it is quite certain that the moment a successful revolution, from within or from without, came to break up the authority of rulers in any particular country, the slaves or bondsmen would, that very moment, seize their opportunity to emancipate themselves; and if it was the love of equality or of social justice that made them rise, they would not lay down their arms till they had established a just social order, based upon the recognition of *equal rights and equal laws for all*.

Now, there is hardly any ancient state or country we could name that has not had its revolutions, and that did not witness, at some period or other, a complete subversion of its government, laws, and institutes; yet do we find the institution of slavery survive in all.

In no one instance do we find the slaves of a revolutionalized state avail themselves of such a crisis to establish *the rights of man as man*. Intestine commotions, military insurrections, foreign invasions, popular triumphs over kings and senates—these and all other like incidents in the life of nations invariably passed away without abolishing the curse of slavery. Why was this? How happened it? Why did not the slaves of the old pagan world take advantage of some popular insurrection, or of the overthrow of their rulers by some invader, to vindicate the rights of humanity in their own persons, by at once establishing a free government for all, and by abolishing slavery altogether?

There is but one true and sufficient answer to these questions: it is this:—The doctrine of human equality, of equality in rights, duties, and responsibilities, was altogether unknown to the ancients: it was denied in theory; it was unheard of in practice. With the solitary exception before adverted to—that of the Essenes (of which more by-and-by), there is no historical record or monument extant to show that the slaves of antiquity, as a class, knew or cared anything about theories of government, much less that they comprehended what a Frenchman would understand by the words *république démocratique et sociale*, or what a member of the National Reform League understands by "the political and social rights of the people." Nor does there appear to have been a single writer, teacher, philosopher, legislator, orator, or poet, amongst the whole heathen world, to inspire the slave-class with any such notions. On the contrary, the idea that one class were born to be slaves, and the other to be masters, was an idea as sedulously inculcated by the educators of ancient society, as it was implicitly believed in by the slaves themselves. The poet and the two philosophers who, more than any others of their class, exercised a moral influence upon the ancient world—to wit, Homer, Plato, and Aristotle—agreed, to a hair, in considering mankind as naturally divided into two classes—those made to command and those made to obey, *alias* masters and slaves. Homer tell us, formally, in the "Odyssey," that Jove gave to slaves but the half of a soul. Plato, when citing this passage in his "Treatise on Laws," substitutes the word *mind* for the Homeric word *virtue*, and adds his authority to that of the poet, to inculcate that the Father of the Gods bestowed *mind* and *virtue* but by halves upon the children of slavery. Plato is still more expressive elsewhere. In his dialogue entitled "Alcibiades," he makes Socrates teach the same doctrine after his favourite fashion of question and answer. He makes him ask Alcibiades whether it is "in the class of nobles or in the class of plebeians that natural superiority is to be found;" to which the proficient pupil unhesitating makes answer, "Undoubtedly, in the class of nobles," or "in those nobly born." Aristotle is still more emphatic than Plato in laying down the theory of human inequality. In one place he goes so far as to call children "the animated tools of their parents," signifying by that, that children are by birth the natural slaves of their fathers. In his "Treatise on Politics," he tells us, roundly, that at the very moment of their birth all created beings are naturally fashioned, some to obey, and some to command—or, rather, some *to be commanded*, and the others to command; for it is the same verb he makes use of in both cases, using the *passive* mood for the slaves and the *active* for the slave-owners. In the same treatise he tells us, further on, that nature actually makes the bodies of freemen (genteel folk) different from those of slaves; that the latter are purposely made robust and hardy for the necessities of labour, whilst those of gentlemen are made so slight and upright as to be unfit for physical labour, but well qualified for the business of government. In citing this passage, we have given an almost literal translation of the Greek—a translation more expressive of the author's sense than a strictly verbal translation would be. The very terms made use of by Aristotle show clearly his belief that slaves were made to be slaves, and their masters to govern them. The words we have rendered by the free translation, "qualified for the business of government," mean, "*literally*, availably useful for political life," which, if not so intelligible, is stronger and of wider signification than our translation. At all events, there can be no doubt as to Aristotle's meaning. Like Homer and Plato, he was a firm believer in the *duality* of human nature—that is to say, that slaves were born with one nature, and their masters with another. Indeed, Plato carried this creed so far, that he made slavery to consist in the moral and mental man himself, and not in the servility of his condition as a slave. A wise man, he contended, could not be made a slave of: the natural superiority of such a man would rise superior to any, or all, conditions that might be imposed upon him. Plato lived to have his doctrine tried in his own person. Dionysius, the tyrant of Sicily, had him sold for a slave by one Pollio, a Lacedemonian chief; but history does not say whether Plato the slave held the same opinions on slavery as Plato the freeman and philosopher. It was one of his maxims that "a wise and just man could be as happy in a state of slavery as in a state of freedom." Dionysius took him at his word, and, tyrant though he was, we think he served Plato right. The sage who believed in two natures, one for slaves and another for freemen, and who taught that a wise and just man could be as happy in slavery as in freedom, deserved to have such doctrines tried and verified in his own person. Plato had them tried in his; but, great philosopher as he was, we suspect he must have found some little difference between slavery and freedom, when we find him seizing the first opportunity to recover his liberty, and preferring to live a freeman, in Athens, to living a slave at Ægina.

When such were the opinions of philosophers and poets (whose mission and function it was to live for other generations and other times than their own), what may we not expect from the vulgar herd who lived only for themselves? Their ideas were just what we might expect. High and low, gentle and simple, rich and poor, freemen and slaves—all, all believed in the duality of human nature—in the divine origin of kings, and in the no less divine origin of slavery. On these points the whole of pagan antiquity appears to have been unanimous. The treatment of their helots by the Spartans, who, in order to disgust their children with drunkenness, used to exhibit those unfortunates in a state of bestial intoxication, speaks volumes for the notions the ancients had of slaves and slavery. Their occasional decimation of the helots by wholesale and deliberate slaughter, for no other or better reason than to thin their ranks and reduce their numbers for their own convenience, is a still more glaring exemplification. It shows that a slave was a mere thing—a chattel —a nobody—even a nuisance, if his master only chose to think him so.

The Elder Cato, who was cried up for his goodness as a master to his slaves, thought it not unworthy of himself, nor unjust to them, to keep them always quarrelling with one another, by artfully fomenting jealousies amongst them. Plutarch tells us, too, that when they got old and broken down, Cato used to treat them as he (Plutarch) would not use the ox or the horse that had served him faithfully. He used to sell them, or dispose of them any way, when there was no more work to be got out of them. Yet Cato was a model for the gentlemen slave-owners of his day. He was the Benjamin Franklin of his republic ; the Adam Smith of the Roman political economy of his time. When *he* behaved so to his slaves, what must have been the opinions and behaviour of such masters as were brutes by nature, tyrants by instinct and culture? Seneca describes one of these worthies to us, under the name of Vedius Pollio, who, if we are to believe that philosopher, was in the habit of feeding the fish in his ponds with the flesh of his slaves! It is impossible to conceive that slaves must not have been considered of a different and inferior nature, when every description of masters, good and bad, are found (however differing in their mode of treatment) to deal with them as with beings having no rights of their own —no rights but what their masters might choose to confer.

The slaves, on their side, appear to have been perfectly reconciled to slavery as an institution. The writings of the ancients have left us nothing to countervail this opinion, but, on the contrary, much to confirm it. We can nowhere discover any evidence to show that the slaves of antiquity regarded slavery in any other light than as an institution natural in itself, and neither unjust nor unreasonable, provided they (the slaves) were well treated. It is true they often complained of their lot, and sometimes rebelled, too, in order to change it; but, in so doing, it is to be observed, they never complained of slavery *as an institution*, nor invoked the principle of Equality as the end and object of their complaints or rebellions. Their complaint was, not that slavery existed, but that they, themselves, and not others, were the slaves. And when they rebelled, it was not in order to put down slavery and establish liberty for all; it was to exchange conditions with their masters, or else to secure their own freedom at the price of taking away other people's. The idea of making common cause with other slaves, in order to emancipate *all* slaves, never entered their heads. Principle, or love of equality, had nothing whatever to do with their movements. The principle of *liberty for all* was too sublime an idea for them. Equality before God and the law was still further beyond them. Slavery, *as a principle*, they had no fault to find with; they complained only of the *accident* that made them slaves and others free. Even of this the vast majority never complained, because the vast majority (there is reason to believe) were content with their lot, and satisfied with their masters' treatment of them. Indeed, the whole tenour of what we read of in history respecting slaves leads to this conclusion. The vast majority were content with their condition. In general they were kindly treated; and as they knew no other state, and saw nothing unjust or unreasonable in slavery, they were attached to their masters as to benefactors (regarding them as the authors of their comfort), and might, mayhap, as a general rule, be pronounced happy.

The old classics are full of allusions and passages which go to show the high state of domestic comfort enjoyed by certain descriptions of slaves, and the free and familiar relations which subsisted between them and their masters. A kindly and homely sort of intercourse was the rule; harshness and ill-nature would appear to have been the exception. Indeed, slaves were regarded so much in the light of mere animals by masters, and masters so much as demi-gods, or superior beings, by slaves, that no possible rivalry, jealousy, or misgivings could subsist between them; but, on the contrary, that sort of mutual confidence, fidelity, and fondness with which favourite horses and dogs reciprocate the kindly treatment and caresses of their owners. Whenever we find slaves breaking out into insurrection, we may be sure it is either because they have harsh masters, or have been torn from distant homes, or are being seduced by insurgent chiefs who promise them rapine and freedom; or because they expect, through a successful insurrection, to become pirates or robbers, which was the highest occupation of honour and profit that a slave could aspire to in those days. In these insurrections, as already observed, equality was never invoked. The "rights of man" was a profound mystery in the womb of the future. The insurgents thought of no slavery but their own; and of no other or better advantages from liberty than the spoils of their masters, and exchanging conditions with them.

Limiting ourselves, for the moment, to Roman history, we find some six revolts of slaves recorded by Livy, and some three or four more made mention of by Aulus Gellius, Tacitus, and others. Livy does not go much into detail; but, from the little he says, he makes it manifest that real liberty or equality had nothing to do with any of the six revolts he treats of. The sixth revolt, which was headed by one Eunus, a Syrian, is related at greater length by Diodorus of Sicily. And what does Diodorus show? That Eunus was an impostor, who pretended a mission from the Syrian Venus, and, ejecting flames from his mouth by means of a hollow nut that he had filled with lighted sulphur, succeeded in fanaticising some 2,000 slaves, and inducing them to break loose from the work-houses. He had soon an army of some 60,000 men, gained several actions in the course of a long and bloody war, made himself master of the camps of four prætors; but at last, pressed by increasing numbers, and forced to shut himself up in the city of Enna with his followers, he and they, after defending themselves with courage and bravery amid indescribable difficulties, were at last overpowered, and perished all, by famine, pestilence, and the sword. This insurrection, which took place in Sicily, was no sooner quelled than another broke out, of a similar kind, and upon as large a scale, under the command of a slave named Athenio, who, after assassinating his master, and causing all the work-houses to rise in insurrection, had soon as large an army under his command as Eunus had. Like Eunus, Athenio had some incipient successes; he stormed and made himself master of two prætorian camps : like Eunus, however, he had soon to succumb to the united force of famine and the sword. He perished, with nearly all his followers. The immediate cause of these two servile wars—which, next to the famous one under Spartacus, appear to have been the most formidable of their kind—was the alleged violation of the work-house regulations by the masters. Indeed, Diodorus testifies, positively and clearly, that the revolt headed by Athenio arose solely from the inability of the prætor in Sicily to enforce the laws or regulations which had been made in favour of the slaves, and which, like our modern factory lords, the masters were continually seeking to evade. Plutarch lets it appear that a similar cause provoked the revolt of Spartacus.

Those three revolts, which took place during the last sixty years of the Republic—namely, the two under Eunus and Athenio, in Sicily, and the third under Spartacus, in Italy—were the most serious and destructive of the servile wars recorded of Rome. They had the ablest commanders, and met with the largest measure of success. In these, if in any wars of the kind, might we hope to find the dignity of human nature vindicated by the insurgent bondsmen. There was nothing of the sort. The harsh conduct of masters and the violation of work-house rules were the motive powers of each revolt : no higher motive seems, for a moment, to have actuated the revolters.

The conduct, too, of Eunus and Athenio, during their brief success, showed how thoroughly undemocratic, and even aristocratic, were their plans and objects. Instead of setting about the abolition of slavery and the establishment of equality, they began forthwith to ape the pomp and circumstance of their oppressors, and to deal with their followers as though they were little kings, and not fellow-slaves in rebellion. They wore purple robes and gold chains. Athenio carried a silver staff in his hand, and had his brow wreathed with a diadem, like a monarch. Indeed, Florus tells us that, while these adventurers assumed all the state and airs of royalty, they imitated royalty no less in the havoc, plunder, and devastations they spread around them. At first they contented themselves with plundering and pulling down the castles, villas, and mansions of the aristocrats and master-class ; but, this accomplished, they soon began to exact the same servility from their followers that they had themselves kicked against. Liberty and equality were out of the question. Had they succeeded, their wretched followers would soon have found that they had but exchanged masters.

The revolt under Spartacus is the most horrible of all, because it was a revolt of men who were gladiators as well as slaves. Liberty or the rights of man had no more to do with this revolt than with any of the others. It arose from brutal oppression on the part of one Lentulus Batiatus, to whom a portion of the insurgents belonged : he was training them, in fact, that they might combat one another to death in the arena for his recreation. Neither in its origin, conduct, nor results did this servile war differ from any of the others. Like all of them, it originated in private wrongs, was purely personal in its antecedents, and neither in its progress nor results did it exhibit a single indication of democratic, philanthropic, or any other virtues than the usual military ones common to all Romans at the time. In truth, what we moderns understand by political and social rights (and without which we know that real liberty cannot exist for any people) was an idea altogether foreign to every class of Greeks and Romans, and, indeed, to the whole of antiquity, with the solitary exception of the Essenes.

Thus, *public opinion* conspired with law and custom to uphold direct human slavery throughout the ancient world. This opinion must have been all but universal, since not even slaves in revolt ever dreamt of abolishing slavery as an institution. They warred against certain incidents and accidents of slavery ; never against the principle itself. This universality of public opinion in its favour, coupled with the fact that direct slavery is an evil of far lesser magnitude than the indirect slavery of modern civilization, we take to be the true explanation of the old pagan system having endured so long in the world.

CHAPTER VI.

UNIVERSALITY OF PUBLIC OPINION AS TO MASTER AND SLAVES.

System acquiesced in by Slave-Class—Insurrections and Rebellions from other Causes than Hatred of Slavery—Rising under Spartacus—Conditions wanting for Success—Contrast of Modern Aspirations after Freedom—Example from enslaved Roman Citizens—Preference of Slaves for their Condition.

ALTHOUGH the historical facts cited in the preceding chapter demonstrate satisfactorily enough that what, in our times, is called *public opinion* was amongst the ancients universally in favour of human slavery as a social institution, nevertheless we shall here adduce a few additional facts in confirmation of that proposition, before we pass on to our next, which will go to show that it was more owing to the prevalence of such opinion, than to the force of laws, that direct slavery endured so long; and that, viewing the question impartially and as a whole, that form of slavery was, with all its abominations, less galling and oppressive, and less destructive of life, liberty, morals, and happiness, than is the present system of indirect or disguised slavery, to which our modern civilization dooms the vast majority of Christendom,—at least, the vast majority of the proletarian and working classes.

The testimonies we have quoted from Homer, Plato, Aristotle, and Seneca were pretty decisive as to the light in which slavery was regarded by the teachers of antiquity. Cato's treatment of his slaves, the still more atrocious conduct attributed to such brutes as Vedius Pollio, and the habitual treatment of their helots by the citizens of Sparta, show clearly enough that the proprietory classes carried out, to the letter, the theory of their philosophers and poets; but the most decisive evidence of all is, unquestionably, that furnished by the various servile wars and insurrections to which we have made reference. The fact that in no one recorded instance did the slaves of antiquity rebel against slavery as an institution,—the fact, that in no one of the ten servile rebellions which, under the Romans, took place in Italy and Sicily did the insurgent slaves declare for liberty for all slaves, nor invoke the principle of Equality against the pretensions of the master-class,—the fact that, upon these and all similar occasions, the rebel-slaves never dreamt of emancipating any but themselves, uniformly betraying an utter disregard of other people's rights when they got the upper hand, and manifesting that no higher motive actuated them than to break their own chains, or transfer them to the persons of their masters,—these and the like facts banish all doubts on the subject, and render it matter of positive

D

certainty that no class or description of men, amongst the ancients, disavowed the principle of slavery, or dreamt of abolishing it as an institution of society.

We have seen how Eunus and Athenio, the two successful leaders of the two Sicilian insurrections, used their successes, not to proclaim equal rights and equal laws for all, but to rob and massacre, to ape the paraphernalia of royalty, and to impose upon others, as well as to rivet upon their own followers, the chains they had struck from off themselves.

If ever a slave-insurrection might have been expected to fly at nobler game, to strike at the very root of oppression, and to hoist the banner of universal freedom for all slaves, it was the insurrection of the gladiators under Spartacus, adverted to in our last, which was by far the most formidable of all the servile wars that occurred under the Republic. It was a war which must have succeeded in abolishing slavery, had it only been a war of principles—that is to say, a war against the institution itself; for it had every other essential element of success. It was provoked by a most atrocious abuse of power on the part of the master-class, by an outrage upon humanity so flagrantly indefensible that, but for the prevailing prejudices in favour of slavery as an institution, the conduct of the government in making common cause with the wrong-doers would be altogether inexplicable.

First, there was a good cause, to begin with—a cause to justify the very stones of Rome to rise in mutiny. Then, the bondsmen were in this instance regular fighting-men, trained for combat in the arena. They had first-rate captains at their head, in the persons of Spartacus, Crixus, and Œnomaus, of whom Spartacus was more than a match for the ablest generals sent against him. Moreover, these gladiators might be said to represent the entire brotherhood of slaves throughout the Roman empire; for they had amongst them Greeks, Thracians, Gauls, Spaniards, Germans, &c.—slaves from all parts.

If ever insurgent bondsmen might be expected to strike a blow for general liberty, to proclaim emancipation not for themselves only, but for the universal brotherhood of slaves, it was this formidable body. They had numbers, science, discipline, and commanders of consummate skill and courage. They represented not the slave-class of Italy alone, but the slaves of every country then subject to, or in alliance with, the Romans. To crown all, they had an unexampled run of military successes. Florus, Appian, and Plutarch give us copious and minute details of this famous war, which lasted about three years, and, from their accounts, we cannot help believing that the gladiators must have been successful, had they made their war a war of principle,—or, to speak more correctly, had the public opinion of their day allowed such a thing to be possible. From the moment Spartacus was raised to the post of commander-in-chief, the war might be said to be one continued series of brilliant victories for the gladiators. He defeated, in succession, not less than five Roman armies, led by prætors or consuls. At last the Senate, after charging Crassus with the responsibility of the war, found itself obliged to recall Lucullus from Thrace, and Pompey the Great from Spain, to unite their forces and their generalship with those of Crassus—so formidable was the foe, so imminent the danger. Not Hannibal himself struck more terror into Rome's proud rulers than did Spartacus the slave-gladiator.

But while history accords to Spartacus many noble qualities, and admits his consummate talents and bravery as a general, it tells us enough, on the other hand, to show that neither himself nor his companions in arms had any notion of fighting for general liberty, nor any other object in view than to accomplish their own escape from their merciless oppressors. In this respect Spartacus but shared in the universal opinion of his day. Possibly he had mind enough, himself, to comprehend the wisdom and the necessity of making this war a war of principle. A man of his superior parts was fully equal to that; but as such an idea could not have been appreciated, nor even comprehended, by his followers, he was too sensible to broach what would have, to them, appeared downright insanity. Like all men similarly circumstanced, he was forced to appeal merely to the lower order of motives. To promise them personal freedom and the spoils of war was his only means of keeping his followers together. Accordingly, we learn from Plutarch that the proposed end of all his victories was to pass the Alps, gain over the Gauls, and then, with their assistance, make their escape, each to his respective country and home.

At all events, the idea of abolishing the institution of slavery appears never to have entered their minds. Had the slaves of that age been capable of comprehending such an idea, it is almost certain Spartacus would not have been conquered. The prevalence of such an idea would have united the whole slave population, not only in Italy, but everywhere else, under his standard, and there would have been a simultaneous rising of the whole race. So exalted, so ennobling a motive would have made his officers proof against bribery, corruption, and jealousy, and would have effectually prevented that mutinous spirit amongst his followers to which, more than to the strength of his opponents, historians ascribe his downfall.

An ignorant people, actuated only by inferior motives, by considerations purely personal or selfish, cannot be emancipated from slavery. The narrow selfishness of such people will ever expose them to be cajoled or bribed into intestine divisions; and as the want of principle will preclude them from associating the rights and liberties of others with their own, in any struggles they may make, so will the aid of these others be wanting to them in their hour of need, and their ultimate discomfiture prove the inevitable consequence and just reward of their ignorant selfishness.

Indeed, it is to this narrow-minded disregard of principles on the part of the slave-class—a disregard founded wholly in a selfish ignorance of their true interests—we are to ascribe the continued prevalence of the slavery of our own times, as well as of that which vainly sought to disenthral itself by force under Spartacus. What happened to the insurgent slaves under Eunus and Athenio in Sicily, and to the gladiators under Spartacus in Italy, is just what will happen to the Red Republicans in France, and to the Chartists in England, should they ever attempt to recover their political and social rights otherwise than by a movement founded purely upon principle and wholly exempt from selfish or merely personal calculations on the part of men and leaders. Upon no other conditions is success possible, as we shall endeavour to demonstrate, with all but mathematical exactness, in the progress of this inquiry.

History has been defined, "philosophy teaching by example." It is in order to illume the future by the light of the past that we prosecute this inquiry. A vulgar belief prevails extensively, both in this country and upon the Continent, that human slavery is almost wholly the work of priests and religion, and that the genius of Christianity in particular is hostile to liberty and progress. Those who hold such opinions are apt to attach an undue importance to the words "monarchy" and "republicanism," and to fancy that there was more real liberty under the ancient republics of Greece and Rome, before Christianity was heard of, than it would be now possible to establish in any country concurrently with the kingly office, and with Christianity being a part and parcel of its fundamental law. Such persons are also apt to suppose that the slavery of ancient times was wholly the work of positive laws, operating by coercion to keep down an adverse public opinion, and to account in pretty much the same way for the abuses and oppressions of our own time, ascribing them almost wholly to individual rulers or governments, and scarcely at all to the ignorance and corruption of the public opinion around them. Believing such notions to be, in a great measure, erroneous and prejudicial to the cause of *real reform* (which must take possession of a people before it can of a government), we have been at some pains, and shall be at still greater, to make the true origin and character of slavery better understood than they appear to be. In so doing, we think we shall be able to show that an ignorant and unprincipled people cannot have a good or wise government, and that an intelligent, right-principled people would not tolerate, and therefore could not long have, a bad one. If we be right in this sentiment, a reform of public opinion must needs precede a reform of parliament; and as one great object of this treatise is to endeavour to operate such a reform, we shall avoid, as much as possible, mere assertions without proof; and therefore, even at the risk of being sometimes tedious, we shall continue to bring forward facts and details, as we proceed, in elucidation of our positions.

Now, without going into theological questions (which nothing shall induce us to do), let us request a certain class of French philosophers, who are at present labouring to solve the "social question," to ask themselves how it happened that, before Chistianity was heard of, the theory and practice of human slavery had got such a firm hold of the whole pagan world, that not even the slaves themselves ever. dreamt of calling the institution into question.

In the middle ages we have had Jacqueries, corresponding with the slave-insurrections under pagan Rome; but it is notorious that, in those Jacqueries, the principle of fraternity and equality was invoked by the disaffected. In the 16th century the Anabaptists of Munster rose against aristocracy and privilege, and, for a season, put down their lords and masters with as high a hand as Eunus and Athenio put down theirs in ancient Sicily. But mark the difference: the Anabaptists sought an order of things in which all should work, and none be drudges or slaves; the followers of Eunus and Parthenio sought quite a different thing,—they sought only to exchange places with their masters, and they had no objection at all to human slavery, provided they were not slaves themselves.

What is true of John of Leyden and his followers might be applied to our own Fifth-Monarchy men in Cromwell's time, and to the French revolutionists of 1793 and 1795 under Babœuf. If they sought to pull down those above them, it was upon the principle and the understanding that neither themselves nor anybody else should take the places of the dethroned oppressors. Something similar might be predicated of certain Socialist sects in modern France and Germany. If they are for making a clean sweep of the aristocracy, it is not that they may take their places. If they are against privilege, it is against the principle that they contend, and not against the mere accident that they themselves are not privileged parties.

This remarkable difference in the revolutionary movements of ancient and modern times cannot but strike every thinking man who will take the trouble to compare them. Nor let it be said that the difference arises solely from the disaffected having been slaves in the times of paganism and freemen in the times of Christianity. Cataline and his co-conspirators were not slaves, nor the friends of slaves: yet they acted precisely upon the same motives and principles as those ascribed to Eunus and Athenio. Cataline did not promise his brother-revolutionists a *régime* of liberty and equality for all orders of men; quite the contrary. In the first place, he indignantly repudated all co-operation with slaves; and instead of *equal rights and equal laws for all*, he promised one portion of his followers a cancelling of all their debts; another portion, *magistrates, sacerdotia, rapinas*—i.e. magisterial offices, the preferments and property of the Church, and general plunder; and to all he promised women, wine, horses, dogs, &c., according to their age and tastes. If we are to believe Sallust, he was to begin with setting fire to Rome, proceed with the massacre and spoliation of his enemies during the confusion, and end by putting his associates and friends in the place of the men they wished to get rid of. In other words, Cataline's doctrine was (to use an old Roman phrase), that every man must be either *prædo* or *præda*—either the *thief* or the *spoil*, or, as Voltaire expresses it, either *hammer* or *anvil;* and he was determined to be the thief, or the hammer. The doctrine of *equality*, at any rate, had no share in his system.

What history describes Cataline to have been is equally predicable of the whole of the revolutionary school in which he had had his political training. Sylla and his lieutenants, on the one hand, representing patrician revolutionists, and Marius, Sulpitius, Saturninus, &c.,

on the other, representing the plebeian revolutionists, had acted, every man of them, upon the principles ascribed to Cataline./ Not a chief or demagogue of them all, on either side, said a word or proposed a measure that savoured of justice or legality for all people. Principle was entirely out of the question. It is doubtful, indeed, whether either leaders or people understood anything at all of the matter. There is certainly nothing in history to evidence that they either knew or cared for any other rules or principles of government than those good old-fashioned ones, which the several agencies of gold, intrigue, and the sword resolve themselves into—the right of the strongest. To such republicans as Sylla, Marius, Clodius, Sulpicius, &c., our modern ideas of a *république démocratique et sociale* would be about as intelligible as a proposal to light old Rome with gas or to communicate *senatus consulta* by the electric telegraph.

Before despatching this branch of our inquiry, let us cite just one more fact from history, which we regard as perfectly decisive on the question—a fact sufficient of itself to convince any reasonable man that slavery, as an institution, had the public opinion of all classes in its favour in the times we are treating of; so much so, that not even Roman citizens and warriors, sold into slavery, thought of questioning its propriety.

In the second Punic war, some 1,200 Roman citizens were made prisoners by the Carthaginians, and by them disposed of to merchants, who, in the regular way of trade, sold them as slaves amongst the farmers of Peloponessus, by whom they were set to work in the fields. Now, if any class of slaves ought to be imbued with the sentiments of human equality, it is, undoubtedly, men like these, who had not been born in slavery, and who, from the very constitution of the Roman army, must have been men of family and station. Let us see. Plutarch tell us, in his Life of Flaminius, that some years after, when the Achæan cities demanded succour of the Romans against Philip of Macedon, Titus Quintus was sent to them with some legions, and made himself master of the disputed territories. While engaged in these operations, his soldiers fell in, one day, with the 1,200 Roman citizens who had been sold into slavery by the Carthaginians, and found them delving the ground, like any other slaves. As might be expected, the soldiers and the slaves embraced one another as fellow-countrymen and old friends; but mark the sequel: not a word is there in Plutarch or elsewhere to intimate that either soldiers or slaves regarded this bondage of Roman citizens as anything monstrous or degrading. On the contrary, after embracing, the soldiers went their way, and the citizen-slaves resumed their task-work. Flaminius, as being master of the country, might have set them at liberty at once, if he liked: he did no such thing. It would have been *to violate the rights of property*. It is true, those slaves afterwards obtained their liberty; but it was only through a voluntary subscription raised by the cities of the Achæan league, which, in gratitude for the services rendered by Flaminius, redeemed the bondsmen and made a present of them to their benefactor. And even when released by Flaminius they did not resume their former rank of citizens: that rank was irredeemably forfeited. They became *freedmen* only; which imposed upon them a sort of fealty to their patron, whose vassals they thenceforward were in the eye of the law. This one historical incident speaks volumes. It shows how completely the system of slavery was ingrained in the minds and habits of the people, as well as in their laws and institutes. Here was a victorious Roman general and soldiers so respecting the institution, that not even their own fellow-citizens, made prisoners by their most hated foes, were regarded as fit objects for freedom, until it pleased their masters or owners to give them up to the general for a sum of money; and had it not been for the subscription of the cities, the slaves would have reconciled themselves to their lot of slavery as to a thing quite natural and proper under the circumstances.

After this, let it not be said that it was the force of law or the strength of governments that maintained slavery in ancient times. No; it was the universality of the public opinion in its favour. Had it been otherwise, the slaves might have emancipated themselves in any of those revolutionary crises which were of such frequent occurrence, and when neither law nor government had any force adequately to cope with them. But, even in their own most successful insurrections against the tyranny of their masters, they never dreamt (as we have seen) of abolishing slavery. Nay, on one occasion, when Marius, unable to cope with Sylla's faction for want of sufficient troops, solicited the slaves to rise in behalf of the democratic party, and offered them their liberty if they would but join his ranks, only three individuals, we are told, out of the whole slave population gave in their names to be enrolled.

In the following chapter we shall endeavour to account for this, and show that, as a general rule, the slaves acted wisely, in preferring to remain slaves (when they knew so little of real liberty) to becoming "free and independent labourers," without arms, votes, lands, money, or credit, after British fashion.

CHAPTER VII.

COMPARISON OF ANCIENT WITH MODERN SLAVERY.

Forces which overthrew Chattel Slavery—Advantages of real Slaves over Freed-Men and Wages-Slaves—Natural Fecundity esteemed a Blessing, not a Curse—Condition of American Slaves under Slavery.

HAVING seen how firmly rooted was the institution of direct human slavery in the public opinion of the ancient world, let us now inquire what was the potent force or combination of forces which subverted that opinion, and which operated the mighty changes that afterwards took place in the social relation of man to man. By these changes, we mean the manumission of the slave-class, the consequent formation of proletarianism, and, in course of time, the universal substitution of indirect or disguised for direct or personal slavery—an order of things which has ever since prevailed, and which, at the moment we write, imposes upon the vast majority of every "civilized" country a bondage more galling and intolerable than was the personal servitude of man to man under the ancient system.

It will be readily comprehended what a potent agency was requisite, and what sacrifices must have been incurred, to subvert a social order so deeply implanted in the habits, prejudices, and even convictions of the whole world. To produce such effect, only the most potent causes, only the most powerful influences known to act upon human nature, could suffice. What are these? *Religion and self-interest.* For—not to encumber ourselves with subdivisions of causes—suffice it to say, that two overwhelming ones brought the change: one, the Christian dispensation, which gradually revolutionized public opinion amongst the slave-class, and among the pious and benevolent of the master-class; the other was of the gross and worldly kind, coming from quite the opposite direction, yet concurring to the same end—it was the force of selfishness. This force it was which, operating by calculations of profit and loss upon the mass of worldly-minded slave-owners, taught them, if not instinctively, at least by practical experience, that their bondmen might be made more servile and profitable slaves for them, *without the name*, than any that ever bore the name. The former or sublime Christian cause would, had it been allowed to operate freely and unalloyed with worldly selfishness, have extinguished human slavery of every form and degree from the face of the earth. The latter or more wordly cause, by turning the manumitted slaves into proletarians and mercenary drudges, only substituted a new and worse kind of slavery for the old.

But, before showing how the change was brought about, let us briefly compare the two kinds of slavery—the old and the new. Under the old system a slave was called by his right name—a slave.

He was, to all intents and purposes, the property of his master. He was liable to be bought and sold, or otherwise disposed of, the same as cattle, sheep, bales of goods, oil, wine, or any other kind of merchandise. If he had a harsh or cruel master, he was liable to all manner of ill-treatment, including corporal punishment and even death itself. Of liberty or rights of course he had none but what his master might choose to confer. Whatever wealth he might hoard or scrape together was at the mercy of his master; for as slaves were themselves but the property of their masters, whatever belonged to them belonged, by the same rule, to their owners. It is needless to argue in condemnation of such a system: it is self-condemned in the very fact that human nature recoils from such a state, and that it is only bearable by those who know no better, and only preferable to the sort of mockery of freedom to which it has given place. Let it not, however, be supposed that the evils of such a state were felt as we should now-a-days feel them, who have enjoyed the rights of liberty and conscience; it was quite otherwise. If the condition of direct slavery had its dark side, it had also its bright side—bright, at least, in comparison with what has followed. The slave of antiquity was not insulted with the name or mockery of freedom when he knew he had none. He had not the shadow hypocritically offered him for the substance. He had not to upbraid his masters with dissimulation and treachery, in addition to the burdens imposed upon him. He had not to complain that his master had robbed him or defrauded him of rights, and of a position which belonged to him by the same constitutional law by which the master claimed his own. Of these he could have known nothing, simply because they had never existed in or before his time. What men have never had, they can hardly be said to have ever lost; and what men have never lost, they can better bear the want of, than they can the loss of what was once theirs, and which they know and feel ought still to belong to them. In these respects the chattel-slaves of ancient and modern times have greatly the advantage over the starving proletarian drudges falsely called "free and independent labourers."

But the ancient bondsman had other and more substantial advantages unknown to his proletarian successors. He knew nothing of the actual wants and destitution, nothing of the manifold privations, in which the great mass of the labouring classes now-a-days live, move, and have their being. The very fact of his being his master's property caused him to be always well fed, well housed, well clothed, and well cared for, according to his condition and habits. If he had no property, nor the right to acquire any, independently of his master's control, neither had he any rent or taxes to pay, nor any other claims or demands upon him that were not all amply provided for at his master's expense. Food, clothing, shelter, firing, medicine, medical care—these and every other essential requisite for keeping him in health and good condition were abundantly supplied him by his master, for the master's own sake. Indeed, it was the master's interest to do so; for whether there was work for the slave to do, or not, it equally behoved the master to keep him always in good condition, that he might be the better workman when there was work for him to do, and that he might fetch a better price in the slave-market when his services were no longer wanted. Besides, it was the custom in those days for masters to take a pride in displaying the goodly state of their slaves—of both their prædial and domestic slaves—just as our modern gentry and graziers take a pride in displaying the stock upon their farms, the studs in their stables, and, above all, the plump and portly figures of their butlers, footmen, grooms, and all the other paraphernalia of modern flunkeyism. There was, in those days, none of that desperate competition, in vanity or in trade, which now-a-days makes starvelings of the millions in order to make millionaires of the thousands; which offers premiums for fat oxen, and the union workhouse to lean labourers; and which awards prizes for bulls and rams, and superior breeds of every description of brutes (not excluding even the stye and the kennel), while it degrades the human animal below the lowest description of savage man, and maintains its anti-christian pomp of circumstances for the few, at the expense of blistering the backs and pinching the bellies of those who, St. Paul said, should be "first partakers of the fruits." This kind of modern science was wholly unknown to the ancients. Not a line is there in the works of Homer, Hesiod, Plato, Aristotle, indeed of any of the old poets, philosophers, or historians, to show that they knew anything of our modern science of political economy. They believed in slaves and in slavery; but they had no idea of enriching a master-class by famishing the bodies of those to whom the masters owed everything, much less did they ever dream that the wealth and aggrandisement of the master-class were to be promoted by the expatriation, decimation, or diminution of the slave-class. If the ancient Spartans occasionally decimated their slaves, it was not because they looked upon them as a "surplus population," burdensome upon their estates, but because they feared their growing numbers, while their own ranks were being continually thinned by internecine wars with their neighbours. The idea of a slave being a useless incumbrance, a mere incubus upon the soil, was an idea utterly incompatible with their established custom of regarding slaves not only as property, but as that superior description of property which alone gave value to every other. Accordingly, though amongst the ancient philosophers we find many strange schools and sects, and very many eccentric and incomprehensible doctrines taught, yet nowhere do we meet with any sect or school corresponding with our modern political economists. There is no such philosopher as our Parson Malthus to be found in the whole circle of classic or Biblical lore. Had such a fellow as Malthus shown himself in the days of Alexander the Great, and gone about preaching that the gods had sent too many mouths for the meat and harvests they had provided, not even Diogenes would have associated with such a lunatic; and if the slaves had only got scent of the tendencies of his theory, not Alexander himself could, in all probability, have prevented them from flaying him alive. Fortunately for them, however, there were no Malthuses in the world at that time. In the absence of such philosophers, slaves were not only free to marry and to beget children, but their masters actually regarded every increase in their slaves' families as a direct gain—a direct increase of the most valuable portion of their property. The idea that at Nature's feast there was no cover for the new-comer was, at that epoch, an idea that would be as abhorrent to the master's notions of self-interest as it would have been to the slave's instincts of procreation and self-preservation.

It is true, the condition of slaves was a deplorable one when they had such brutes for masters as Seneca describes in the person of Vedius Pollio; but we are to regard such extreme cases as rare exceptions. All historic testimony goes to show that the general rule was in the other direction. Even Seneca's testimony proves this; for, in speaking of this very Vedius Pollio, he says, "Who does not detest this man, even more than did his own slaves, for fattening the fish in his ponds with human blood?" The treatment of his gladiators by Lentulus Batiatus is another indirect proof to the same effect. Had Lentulus trained his gladiators to appear in the arena in the usual way, to be matched against others on some great occasion of public games, &c., they would not have complained, much less rebelled. They would, in that case, but have been called upon to exercise a profession which was as familiar to the Romans, and as little distasteful to the combatants themselves, as that of prize-fighting in England or bull-fighting in Spain. But the brute, Batiatus, kept his gladiators locked up, and was professedly training them to *fight with one another* till they should die by each other's hands—a destination which, while it promised certain death, held out no prospect of honour, *éclat*, nor even safety to the greater number. It was this studied brutality, so much out of the ordinary course, which provoked the slaves to mutiny and revolt. And the fact of its being the only recorded instance of gladiators rising in rebellion against the laws is the best proof that such barbarity was unusual, and not sanctioned by the public opinion of the time. Indeed, so general appears to have been the contentment of ancient slaves with their lot, that only one or other of three causes is ever assigned by history for the servile outbreaks it records:—first, excessive cruelty on the part of masters; second, the non-execution of the laws regulating the labour and condition of slaves; and third, the chiefs of parties raising and embodying them with their insurgent bands in times of civil war. The fewness of the servile wars recorded as arising out of the two first causes sufficiently testifies that harshness on the part of masters, and the non-execution of the regulations in favour of the slaves, were but exceptions to the ordinary course of slave-life, and not the general rule. It proves also that it was not against slavery itself the slaves rose, seeing that it was only what they considered *an abuse of it*, and not the thing itself, they rose against, and that, even when victorious, they never set about abolishing the institution. And as to the third cause of slave-insurrections, it proves still more forcibly the general contentment of slaves with their lot; for, had it been otherwise, *three* slaves only out of the

whole population would not have responded to Marius's appeal for a
general rising of their order; still less would they have failed to profit
by the splendid victories of Spartacus, when, had they only felt the
sentiment of equality, or entertained any dissatisfaction with their
lot as slaves, they might have effectually exterminated the whole
master-class, and established whatever form of government and of
social order they thought fit. Indeed, they had frequent opportunities during the last sixty years of the Republic, and also during
the first century or two of the Empire, to make a successful rising
against the master-class, had they been inspired generally with a
hatred of their servile condition. But it was not so.

As a general rule, the slaves both of Greece and Rome were fully
reconciled to their condition, and had good reason to be so, considering how profoundly ignorant they were of the political conditions
upon which alone real liberty can exist for the many. With their
ideas and habits, any attempt to emancipate themselves would have
plunged them into deeper degradation and ruin. Even their masters,
much less themselves, knew little of the laws and institutions by
which liberty, with security and prosperity, can be established. The
proof of this is their interminable wars with one another, and with
their neighbours all around them. A still stronger proof is their
egregious folly in allowing agrarian monopoly and usury to make
such frightful progress amongst them, that "free citizens" became
actually greater slaves to money-lenders and land-monopolists than
the slaves so called; till at last the republics of Greece and Rome
were brought to such a state that a military despotism alone could
save them from tearing one another to pieces. When such universal
ignorance and barbarity prevailed amongst the master-class—an
ignorance and barbarity that virtually left civil liberty and equality
without any solid guarantees whatever—it would be madness to
expect that any revolution useful to humanity could have been effected
by a still more ignorant slave-class. They would but have made
confusion more confounded, and, by altogether suspending production,
annihilated society itself amid scenes of indescribable carnage and
cannibalism. At all events, the slaves knew better than to make
any such attempt. They preferred bearing the ills they had, to
flying to those they knew not of. Without land or capital, and freedom to use them in security, they were infinitely better off as slaves
than they would be by any revolution, however successful, that
did not give them these essential requisites. And seeing how the
poorer classes of free citizens fared (who had to make shift to live without the use of land or capital), it is no wonder they clung so tena-
ciously to their well-fed, well-housed servile condition. In plain
truth, the slaves of antiquity would have been mad to exchange
their slavery for what is, now-a-days, falsely called liberty, unless
in so doing they took good care that, along with liberty, *they had the
means of producing and distributing wealth on their own account.*
And as this supposes a species of politico-economical knowledge
infinitely beyond what might be expected from such a class in their
day,—as it supposes such a knowledge of agrarian, monetary, fiscal,

and other laws as are absolutely necessary to the preservation of even the semblance of liberty, and which knowledge was almost as dead a letter to their masters as to themselves,—we cannot but rejoice, for their own sakes, that the slaves of antiquity chose to remain as they were. When men have but a choice of two evils, it is desirable they should choose the lesser. The slaves of antiquity had but a choice between direct slavery and the miseries of proletarianism: in our opinion, they chose the lesser of the two. Had they been wise enough to understand their true political and social rights, they might have escaped both. Christianity came to teach them; but man's perversity stepped in between them and the light of the Gospel. Even to this day, after eighteen centuries of gospel-propagandism, not one in a thousand of the slave-class—whether they be chattel-slaves or wages-slaves—whether they be proletarians or the property of their masters—understands his political and social rights. The consequence is, the two kinds of slavery prevail still all over the world; and, of the two, direct or chattel-slavery is now, as formerly, the lesser evil of the two. In no part of the East, that we know of, would an Oriental slave of modern times exchange conditions with one of our Wigan handloom weavers, nor with a Dorsetshire labourer.

But, to bring this question to a test that will make the difference at once obvious to every one, let us just compare the condition of a modern American slave (so-called) with that of "a free and independent labourer" in England. We choose these two countries because they are inhabited by the same Anglo-Saxon race; because they are at the head of modern civilization; and because, from the commercial intercourse between them, we know more of their positive and relative condition than of any other two known countries.

First, what was the actual condition of a modern chattel-slave, as he was to be found in any of the Southern States of the great American Union? We shall give it from the lips of an eye-witness —from one who has visited that country and judged for himself, in the year 1849—above all, from one who is a rank abolitionist, and so thorough going a hater of slavery, and of everything pertaining to it, that in the paragraph immediately preceding the one we are about to extract, he buoyantly exclaims, "When we remember the ardour and perseverance of the American character, and the intelligence of their leaders, we must believe that the day approaches when the axe shall be laid to the root of this fell upas-tree." The author of this sentiment is a Mr. Edward Smith, who was deputed, along with another gentlemen, by an influential body of capitalists in London to make a survey and inspection of the north-western part of Texas, with a view to some extensive plan of colonization projected by the parties. This Mr. Edward Smith has furnished his employers with a printed report of his travels through several States of the Union; and in that report he utters not a few jeremiads upon the curse of slavery, and not a few withering invectives against its aiders and abettors. If, therefore, any testimony in favour of slaves and slavery can be pronounced wholly unexceptionable, it is that of Mr. Edward

Smith, the Abolitionist. Now, what says this gentleman? We quote pages 83 and 84 of his report:—

"From the slaves themselves and from other parties I have learned that, with few exceptions, they are kindly treated, are not overworked, and have abundance of food, clothing, and efficient medical attention. We saw them lodged in small cabins, sometimes rudely built, and in other places very neatly built, but always *partaking of the character of the planter's or overlooker's house* near to which they stand. A slave, his wife and family, occupy a cabin exclusively, unless the family be small, when two or more families live together. The planters find it to be their interest to use their negroes well. They always permit and, indeed, urge the slave to do overwork by planting a small plot of land, set apart for his use, with corn, tobacco, or other produce. This they do after the day's work is over, and also on Sundays, when the law does not allow the master to require them to work; and wherefore we saw them clean and well dressed, lying upon the banks of the rivers, as we passed by. When the produce is gathered, it is sold by the planters, and the proceeds given to the slaves. Some slaves prefer to cut wood, which is sold to the steam-boats; and all supply themselves with vegetables from their own garden. Many industrious slaves can thus obtain from fifty to two hundred and fifty dollars per year for themselves, which they expend in the purchase of tea, coffee, sugar, whisky, and other luxuries of the table, and in clothing fit for any European gentleman. In large cities, as New Orleans, they hire themselves from their masters at an agreed-upon sum, and work for others, as they prefer, and thus earn from twenty to twenty-five dollars per month for themselves. *Very many slaves own horses, kept for their own use; and others own lands;* and Captain Knight, of the ' New World,' stated that he knew a slave *who owned four drays and teams and seven slaves.* Indeed, when they are good servants, they are much valued, and obtain every enjoyment they desire."

This extract is, we think, pretty decisive of our position; yet there is another, just following, which is so strongly corroborative of what we have advanced in respect of the contentment with their condition which we have ascribed to the ancient slaves, that we cannot forego the temptation to quote it. "Free-born Britons!" "independent labourers!" mark this passage:—

"They" (the slaves) "do not usually care to save money wherewith to purchase their freedom, *feeling that the protection of their masters is an advantage to them;* but there are those, as the stewardess on board the boat on which we descended the Mississippi, who have paid from 1,000 to 1,500 dollars for their freedom!"

CHAPTER VIII.

EXPLOITATION-VALUE OF SLAVE AND FREE LABOUR.

Contrast of Plantation-Servants with British Workpeople—Affluence of former American Slaves — Misery of Free Labourers and Artisans—Value of Irish Peasants and English Workers—Free and Slave Children in America.

LOOK on the life of a modern negro-slave in America, and compare it with the life of a modern Irish or Scotch peasant, or even that of an English hand-loom weaver in the North or of an English labourer in the South and West. *Compare*, did we say? Alas! the two conditions will not bear a comparison. *Contrast* is the word we must use. To the damning disgrace of modern civilization be it said, we cannot *compare* the condition of our free workpeople in Europe with that of the negro-slaves of Louisiana,—we can only *contrast* them ; and the contrast is so truly appalling that, in contemplating it, one cannot help trembling at the prospective destination of humanity.

Mr. Edward Smith says: "Many industrious slaves can thus" (by overwork) "obtain from 50 to 250 dollars per year, which they expend in luxuries of the table and in clothing fit for any European gentleman." This, be it observed, is over and above an abundant supply of all their ordinary wants by their masters. It includes neither food, drink, ordinary apparel, medicine, firing, nor house-rents,—not even vegetables or poultry, for with these, it seems, the slaves are provided out of their own gardens and fowl-yards. It includes not one of those ordinary expenses which absorb the entire week's earnings of a modern "free-born Briton." The American slave's surplus earnings may be considered as so much pocket-money. He might save, or lay by at interest, the whole of his 250 dollars per annum towards the purchase of his liberty, if he liked to exchange his condition for that of an independent labourer. According to Mr. Smith, however, the negro knows better; for Mr. Smith tells us, "they" (the negroes) "do not usually care to save money wherewith to purchase their freedom, feeling that the protection of their masters is an advantage to them." If this protection be an advantage in America, where the wages of independent labour are still comparatively high, what would be the negro's feelings were it proposed to him to give up his master's protection in exchange for the independence of a Dorsetshire labourer or of a Yorkshire weaver? Ah! then, indeed, he would *feel* the difference between the two kinds of slavery; then he would know how to appreciate that condition of primitive slavery which Mr. Smith calls a upas-tree, and from which our saints of Exeter Hall so yearn to release him. "Very many slaves," again quoth Mr. Smith, "own horses kept for their own use ; and others own land." We should like to know how many operative cord-wainers or journeymen tailors in London keep horses for their own use, and how many of them own lands purchased with the proceeds of their overwork? We should like to know, too, how many of their masters can afford to keep horses for their own use? We apply this query to the tailors and shoemakers of London, because no other two trades are subject to less variation than these, and because the wages paid in them are higher in London than anywhere else in the United Kingdom. Is there a journeyman tailor or shoemaker in London that can afford to buy and keep a horse out of his wages? We believe not one. And if it cannot be done with London wages, certainly nowhere else can it be done in England, Ireland, or Scotland. As to an English field-labourer, or an artisan in one of our manufacturing towns, keeping a horse or owning land, the idea is absolutely ludicrous. Indeed, we are living in times when very few of their masters, much less themselves, can afford to indulge in such luxuries. For though we have many of that class who, having become millionaires and country squires, can keep carriages as well as horses, yet the majority, if the truth were known, are nearer the *Gazette* than they are to that easy condition in which men can afford to keep horses for their recreation and amusement. The case of the stewardess whom Mr. Smith met on board the boat in which he descended the Mississippi presents a startling contrast to the ordinary condition of industrious females in England. The stewardess had, it seems, with her own surplus earnings purchased her freedom at from 1,000 to 1,500 dollars; 1,500 dollars, at 4s. 2d. the dollar, is just £312 10s. of our money. Where is the woman engaged in any branch of industry in England that could show £312 10s., or a tithe of that sum, as the result of a few years' saving of wages? If there be such cases they are not one in ten thousand. According to the commissioner of the *Morning Chronicle*, to whose valuable revelations we referred in the preceding chapter, " there are now in London some 28,577 needlewomen whose earnings average but 4½d. per day. There are as many more whose earnings hardly exceed 3s. a week all the year round. Contrast (for we dare not say compare) the condition of these unfortunate beings with that of the black female slave who, besides living well, could save 1,500 dollars in a few years wherewith to purchase her independence! Yet there are hypocrites amongst us—hypocrites to be met with in shoals upon our platforms and in our pulpits—who would wring tears of pity from us for the poor negro slave, while not an atom of sensibility have they for their own white slaves whose condition is infinitely more to be commiserated.

But, after all, the real test is this :—What is a negro-slave's value in the eye of his master, and what is the British or Irish slave's value in the eye of *his* master or employer? A sorry, good-for-nothing slave indeed must he or she be whom an American planter could not find a market for! From 800 to 1,200 dollars was a common price for a good stout negro in New Orleans. In the case of the stewardess spoken of by Mr. Smith, we find that her master considered her worth from 1,000 to 1,500 dollars—*i.e.*, of that much value to himself. We know in the case of our own West India slaves, that our Parliament estimated their value to their owners at £20,000,000, the annual interest of which we taxpayers have still to provide. But how stands the British or Irish slave in respect of marketable value? In Ireland his value stands so high that, only a few years ago, the landlords of Kilkenny county, with the Marquis of Ormond at their head, actually memorialized the Government to relieve Ireland from the presence of 2,000,000 of the peasantry, offering to assist the Government even pecuniarily in any scheme of emigration or transportation, or expatriation or extermination, it might set on foot for that purpose! Indeed, hardly a Parliamentary session has passed over, for the last twenty years, without witnessing some kind of project, or proposal, or suggestion for getting rid of Ireland's "surplus population." Up to the winter of 1846-47 (the year of the famine) 2,000,000, at least, of the population were uniformly condemned as surplus! Instead of being considered worth so much per head, like the negroes, it was deemed worth making a pecuniary sacrifice to rid the land of them. At £10 per head, these 2,000,000 would fetch just the sum which the West India planters thought a very inadequate remuneration for the loss of their slaves. Instead of asking £10 per head for them, the Irish owners and occupiers of the land were disposed to give £10 per head to get rid of them. They would have jumped at the bargain, could they have found the money and the purchasers. Fortunately for those patriotic and Christian gentlemen, the famine of 1846-47 came to carry off about a million of the surplus. Emigration and starvation have since relieved them of another large batch. Starvation being a cheaper process than emigration, it is the favourite scheme of the Irish proprietary classes. But as there were then, and still are, many refractory Irish who hold the rich man's laws of *meum* and *tuum* in less respect than they do the great law of nature which forbids any man to starve in a land of abundance, the landowners and occupiers have found it necessary, and for their interest, to contribute largely to the emigration of the last few years. They have in this way expended some hundreds of thousands of pounds, besides sacrificing many times that amount in the voluntary cancelling of debts and in the remission of arrears of rent due. At all events, the proprietary classes of Ireland have furnished, and do still continue to furnish, proofs innumerable and irrefragable that they consider their white slaves as not only valueless, but to be worth considerably less than nothing, seeing that they will give something very considerable to get quit of them. There's the marketable value of an Irish white slave!

And how stands the case in England? Not very dissimilar from Ireland. Are not the ominous words, "surplus population," as familiar to us upon this side of St. George's Channel as they are to our Irish brethren upon the other side? Have we not all manner of emigration schemes afloat here, as well as there, to get rid of the surplus? How often has it been proposed to raise a gigantic loan of

millions wherewith to promote British emigration upon a gigantic
scale, and to mortgage the poor-rates as security for the repayment
of the loan ! We remember how, some twenty and odd years ago,
great numbers of the agricultural parishes in England had it gravely
in contemplation to get rid of their surplus in that way. We
remember some of the calculations made on that occasion. We
remember how certain wise men in certain places laid it down that
whole parishes might be cleared at the rate of £30 per family, on
the average, and how much better it was to sacrifice the interest of
this sum (£1 10s. for each) than to saddle a parish with the maintenance of a whole family of paupers. According to this estimate,
a whole family of English white slaves was worth just £30 less than
nothing ! In other words, their marketable value might be expressed algebraically thus :—

An English white slave and family = minus £30.

About the time this estimate was made of the value of live
Englishmen in this country, Burke and Hare, the murderers, were
selling dead men's bodies, in Scotland, at the rate of £10 per head
to the College of Surgeons in Edinburgh. Consequently, a dead
slave was at that time worth some £40 more than a whole family
of live ones, unless the latter could be made available for anatomical
purposes. Since that period the value both of live slaves and
dead ones has greatly fallen in the market. Subjects for the
dissecting-table can now be got almost for a song. And as to live
slaves, our "surplus population " has so vastly augmented since the
time referred to, that, notwithstanding the myriads already disposed
of by famine and the cholera, we feel assured our lords and masters
have still some 5,000,000 or 6,000,000 more they would gladly get
rid of upon any terms. There are full that number at present in
the United Kingdom for whom no regular kind of remunerative
employment can be had—who are, in consequence, regarded as not
only valueless, but as a positive incumbrance upon the soil—as a
dead loss to the country—and whose lives are thereby made a burden
to themselves as well as to others. To compare the condition of
these thoroughly oppressed and neglected beings with that of the
well-fed, well-clothed, well-housed, well-cared-for negro slaves described by Mr. Edward Smith would be to outrage common sense.
As already observed, we may *contrast;* we cannot, in decency, *compare.*
Why, according to that gentleman's testimony, any industrious
negro, with a kind master, could save more money in twelve months
(besides leading a life wholly exempt from care) than some of our
hand-loom weavers could earn in two years, or than an Irish white
slave could earn in four years at 6d. a day—which is more than
their average earnings throughout the year.

The writer of this happening to visit Leicester some twelve months
ago, he made diligent inquiry there touching the rate of wages and
the condition of the people generally, engaged in the staple trade of
the town. From the very best sources of information, he learned
that their average wages did not exceed 6s. a week throughout the

year, although at that period the hosiery trade was unusually brisk, and all hands full of work. Only twelve months before, nearly one-half the artisans were out of employ, and the streets literally swarmed, at all hours of the day, with men, women, and children roaming about in a state of utter destitution. To beg or steal was their only resource; for they were absolutely starving.

Talk of negro slavery, indeed! No chattel slaves of ancient or modern times ever knew the dire distress and torturing privations of these poor Leicester people. Indeed, except in the midst of a civil war, such sufferings as theirs could not have happened under the ancient system of chattel-slavery. In ordinary times of peace, it could not have been even conceived; for neither masters nor slaves could have possibly had any experience of such a state of things. It was only in desperate civil wars, or occasionally from plagues, pestilences, or famine, that such calamities arose in ancient times; and then all classes shared alike in the visitation. Indeed, upon such occasions the slaves were generally those that suffered least; for as they possessed nothing to invite spoliation, and as their productive uses made it the interest of all parties not to molest them, they necessarily escaped most of the evils which, in times of war and commotion, ravaged every other class. Hence their uninterrupted increase in numbers in Italy, Sparta, and elsewhere; whilst the free citizens, or master-class, were being continually thinned by the calamities referred to. And seeing that their owners could have valued them as property only on account of their labour, the idea of their roving about in famished gangs, like the poor Leicester weavers, without bread or work, and of then being forced, as a means of preserving life, to beg a brother-worm of the earth to give them leave to toil, is an idea that would be as novel and as difficult of explanation to them as (to borrow an illustration from Locke) the peculiar flavour of a pine-apple would be novel and indescribable to one who had never tasted that particular fruit.

But man lives not by bread alone; he has other wants besides those of food, clothing, and shelter: he has certain moral wants, and certain sympathies, the gratification of which is as essential to his well-being and happiness as the satisfaction of his mere animal wants. It is in respect of these, even more than in respect of his physical requirements, that the chattel-slave had, and still has, so immeasurably the advantage over the proletarian wages-slave. Waiving, for the present, the numerous proofs and evidences of this to be found in the ancient classics, let us prove it by less fallible evidence—by the actual condition of the chattel-slave in our own time. And here we shall again cite the testimony of an abhorrer of chattel-slavery, to show its superiority over the wages-slavery of proletarianism. What says Mr. Edward Smith, the Abolitionist, in treating of those moral relations between master and negro slave, upon which the well-being and happiness of the latter must depend, as much as upon his physical comforts? He says, " The planters find it their interest to use the negroes kindly." He says, the cottages built for them " usually partake of the

character of the planter's or overlooker's house,
stand." He says, "The young coloured childr
with the planter's children, and thus learn to rea
he admits " the planters forbid their learning to
" most of the planters encourage ministers i
instruction to their slaves ; for they have disc
Christian is not a bad servant." He says that, a
the sort of paternal care bestowed upon the co
the planters, and of their being brought up as co:
mates with the planter's own children, " the
attached to the place of their birth and to the
with whom they were raised, or whom they nurse
he adds, " this attachment is commonly returned
that he will not part with the slaves so long as he
them." These are pretty strong evidences. Ye
still. It relates to that event in every man's
his coming into the world and leaving it, is a
important of his life; at all events, his happine
in the humbler ranks, is said to depend more up
other event, or upon any other relation in wl
towards his species ; we mean, of course, m
intercourse. Now, how stands the negro-slave in
us see whether the planter scowls at him for m
whether he incurs the wrath of poor law g
missioners, and the withering anathemas of M
one of the ends of his being. Let us see, in s
menaced with starvation and death, like a "free-
proletarian order, for obeying a paramount l
enforced by scriptural injunction. Upon thi
point in the negro's condition Mr. Smith obser
planters) " uniformly encourage marriage amongs
not require a man and woman to marry unless
If the man fancy a woman on another plantatio
to the marriage, and one will sell the husband
one master may own them both." Compare
conditions of negro marriages with those
marriages amongst the poor of this country.
British or Irish landlord encouraging the " peas:
Where do we find an English or a Scotch cott(
ironmaster promoting early marriages amongsi
Whoever heard of any of these gentry taking
young woman into his service, in order to facili1
those they love ? On the contrary, early marriag
proscribed by these gentry, and, indeed, all mai
amongst the poor. Nothing is more common, i
for landlords to make it a condition, when lettin
that he (the tenant-farmer) shall not, on any
son-in-law or daughter-in-law beneath his roc
establishment ; whilst he (the landlord) take!
time, that there shall be no other habitations for

estate. What is this but interdicting marriage by taking the most stringent precautions against it? We know a certain *noble* lady, now living, who, not many years ago, when appointing a master and mistress to instruct the young people in a boys' and girls' school (established upon one of her estates), made it a positive condition of their appointment that, although they were man and wife, they should have no children while they held their situation! This titled Malthusian is by no means a rare specimen of her rank or sex; on the contrary, she is but a sample of the sack; and the sack is judged by the sample. In truth, from Lord John Russell and his Grace of Richmond down to "penny-a-line Chadwick," of poor-law notoriety, and the very lowest of his understrappers, there prevails but one sentiment on this subject, namely, an unmitigated dread and hatred of affording any encouragement to the labouring classes to marry. And, from the manner in which they have contrived to frame and administer our present system of poor-laws (throwing the weight of the burden where there is least strength to bear it), we may add, with truth, that they have succeeded in making the great body of our ratepayers as anti-matrimonial and as thoroughly Malthusian as themselves.

As the tree is known by its fruit, so may we judge of the relative merits of the system which facilitates and encourages marriages amongst chattel-slaves, and of that which prescribes Malthusianism to our free and independent proletarians. The result of the latter system in this metropolis alone is 100,000 women obliged to subsist themselves, wholly or in part, by prostitution! The result of the former system is prostitution reduced within very narrow limits amongst the slave-class, and what there is of it is directly chargeable to the masters' own account, and not to that of their male slaves.

But enough has been said to establish our position that chattel-slavery, with all its abominations, is less destructive of life, liberty, and happiness than the wages-slavery of modern proletarianism. Were other facts and arguments necessary, we could supply them to redundancy. We therefore dismiss the subject, and shall proceed to show how Christianity unconsciously caused the greater evil in attempting to rescue humanity from the lesser.

CHAPTER IX.

HISTORY OF EARLY SOCIAL REFORMERS.

Intention of foregoing Contrast—Difficulties of Christian Revolution, and comparative Facility of Coming Ones—Essenes as Early Reformers—Difficulties in
the way of Christian Innovations on Pagan Slavery.

BEFORE proceeding to show how Christianity, on the one hand, and
worldly selfishness on the other, concurred in superimposing the evil
of proletarianism upon that of chattel-slavery, and in gradually supplanting chattel-slavery itself, to make place for the wages-slavery of
modern civilization, let us guard ourselves by a word or two against
a misconception that might possibly arise in the minds of some from
the perusal of the two last chapters.

Let no one suppose that it was any part of our intention to exten-
uate the abomination of serfdom or chattel-slavery under any condition, or to mitigate that just abhorrence of it, in all its forms, which
we feel assured the reader, in common with ourselves, feels towards
it. Far be from us any such purpose. The object of this part of our
inquiry was simply to show that wages-slavery with proletarianism
may be the worse evil of the two, and is positively at this moment a
greater curse to the human race than any form of chattel-slavery or of
serfdom known in ancient, mediæval, or even in modern times. The
inference, therefore, that should be drawn from the last two chapters
is, not that we regret the social revolution which has taken place, but
that it did not take place in the right way, and that, in consequence,
another and greater revolution is still indispensable and inevitable
for the major part of the human race.

That such revolution or, as we prefer to call it, reformation is
ardently desired by the millions everywhere cannot be doubted. The
existing condition of every country in Europe—our own included—
affords unmistakable evidence of it. The revolutionary struggles of
1848, and the counter-revolutionary barbarities of 1849, resorted to
for their temporary suppression, are but forerunners of the great
social reconstruction we refer to. Whether this reconstruction shall
be effected peaceably in the way of social reformation, or emerge, like
order out of chaos, from the throes of a violent convulsion, is a secret
of the future, which time alone can disclose. It ought to be, it may be,
and, we trust, will be a peaceful reformation. The times are favourable for such a change. The amazing revolution which has lately
taken place in the arts and sciences, as applicable to the purposes of
human economy, ought naturally to give birth to another revolution
of a kindred quality in the political and social mechanism of society.
This latter change need have nothing in common with the innovations or revolutions of times past. We live at an era of the world's
history when science may be made to yield more treasure for all than

ever was won for the few, by war and commerce, in the past. We have agencies and powers at command for the production of wealth, and facilities for its rapid interchange, which the ancient world never dreamt of, and which to even our own grandfathers in the last century would have seemed as marvellous as a Barmecidal feast or any other brain-creation in an Arabian tale. By the agency of a single inanimate power, that consumes not and never tires, we can do more to change the face of terrestrial creation than could be done by the labour of all the men and horses in the known world. We have already in full play, though misapplied, a sufficiency of this power to equal the labour of 700 or 800 millions of hands, with a capability of enlarging its application and uses *ad libitum,* and with mechanical contrivances within reach whereby that gigantic power may be made available for the performance of every operation now performed by human hands, and for the production and distribution of every description of wealth and luxury desirable for man's use. We can raise more sustenance for man and beast from an acre of land than could the ancients from six. We can transport tons of merchandise in ten or twelve hours to distances which our ancestors could hardly have reached within as many days. We could, were it worth while, light up the whole of this vast metropolis at a single stroke of the clock. We have learned to ride by vapour, to sketch and paint with the sunbeam, and to transmit our messages by the lightning. In the subjugation of the elements to man's use, we have opened new fields for ambition, new roads to glory, whose trophies will, ere long, throw those of kings and conquerors into the shade, and render statecraft, priestcraft, lawyer-craft, and every other description of craft now in the service of landlordism and money-mongering, as odious and as obsolete as the occult sciences.

With these powers and appliances at command, no portion of the human race needs the subjugation of any other portion for the gratification of its utmost legitimate wants and desires. With such prodigious advantages in its favour, the age we live in ought to witness the extinction of every vestige of every description of slavery known to man. The transition from chattel-slavery to proletarianism and wages-slavery cost, as we shall see, rivers of human blood; and, nevertheless, man's ignorance and barbarity have, as we have seen, made the change rather a curse than a blessing to the majority of his fellows. The second social revolution—the transition from proletarianism and wages-slavery to real and universal emancipation —may be effected without the loss of a single life, or the sacrifice of a shilling's worth of his possessions to any man of any class. Such, at least, is the creed of us, National Reformers. To make that creed known and appreciated by submitting it to a full and impartial examination by the public, and thereby to enlist as many as we can of the good and wise of all classes in the cause of human · redemption, is, we hardly need say, the main object of this inquiry. In entering upon it, we found it necessary to begin at the beginning. The light of the past, though a lurid one, has appeared to us necessary to illumine the present; and, to see our way clearly into the future, both lights will, we think, be found serviceable. In other words, to render clearly intelligible *what ought to be*, we have deemed it an essential part of our inquiry to ascertain *what has been* and *what now is*. In the prosecution of this task, we now proceed to show how Christianity and selfishness concurred in changing the slavery *that was* into the slavery *that is*.

As already explained, the institution of slavery was never called in question by any class of the ancients before the advent of Christ, if we except that small obscure sect amongst the Jews known by the name of Essenes. Even these are supposed by some to have been a society of Christian monks originally formed by St. Mark, who is said to have founded the first Christian church at Alexandria. The accounts given us by Jesephus and Philo, however, make it much more probable that the Essenes were Jews, and not Christians, and that they existed before the birth of the Messiah. Those who ascribe their origin to St. Mark evidently confound them with another sect of later growth, established at Alexandria by Christian monks, and known by the name, Therapeutæ. The bulk of this latter sect are supposed to have been Greek Jews, converted to Christianity, and settled in Egypt. The Essenes lived chiefly in Palestine, and spoke the Aramean and not the Greek language. As far as certainty can be had in such matters, there is reason to believe that the Essenes existed before and in the time of Christ; and though no mention is made of them in the New Testament, they are supposed to be alluded to by St. Paul in his Epistles to the Ephesians and Colossians and in his First Epistle to Timothy. From Josephus's and Philo's account of them, we should suppose them to have been enthusiasts and ascetics, who occupied pretty much the same position amongst their contemporaries and co-religionists, the Jews, as the Shakers in America do amongst the modern Christian sects of that country. That they were not *necessarily* Christians might, we think, be fairly inferred from the very doctrines and practices ascribed to them; and that the existence of such a sect might well have preceded Christ's appearance will appear strange to no one who considers how very popular St. John the Baptist was, and what crowds of enthusiastic followers he attracted by his preachings and asceticism before the Saviour made known His mission. Assuredly the Essenes were not more ascetic than St. John the Baptist, whose raiment was camel's hair, and food locusts and wild honey ; and assuredly their mysticism and social equalitarianism bear less analogy to veritable Christianity than the doctrines and practices of John.

This argument alone, independently of historic authority, ought, we think, to suffice to set aside the ill-grounded belief of many that the Essenes were *necessarily* an early Christian sect. Their holding certain doctrines in common with Christians, such as the immortality of the soul and man's spiritual responsibility to and equality before God, is no more a proof that they were followers of Christ, than the holding of similar doctrines by Socrates and Plato would prove these philosophers to have been believers in a religion which was unknown till near four centuries after their death. Dr. Neander's account of the Essenes is, that they were a society of pious Jews, who, disgusted with the cant and hypocrisy of the Pharisees, and wearied with the trials of the outward and of the inward life, had withdrawn themselves out of the strife of theological and political parties, at first, apparently (according to Pliny the Elder), to the western side of the Dead Sea, where they lived together in intimate connection, partly after the fashion of the monks of later days, and partly like mystical orders in all periods have done. From this society other smaller ones afterwards proceeded, and spread themselves all over Palestine. They employed themselves in the arts of peace, such as agriculture, pasture, handicraft works, and especially in the art of healing according to the simple but unerring ways of Nature. Dr. Neander thinks it also probable that they imagined themselves supernatually illuminated in their search into Nature's secrets and use of her powers; and that their natural knowledge and art of healing assumed, moreover, a sort of religious or theosophic character, since they professed to have peculiar prophetic gifts. Comparing this account with what we know of similar sects in our own time—with the Mormons, for instance, or with the Shakers, or with the White Quakers of Dublin—it seems probable enough. It is the way of all such enthusiasts to run from one extreme to another. Despising the Pharisees for their hollowness and canting adherence to mere traditional and ceremonial law, in which the *letter* was everything and the *spirit* nothing, the Essenes went right into the opposite extreme, and almost sacrificed the outer to the inner man. They believed firmly in the immortality of the soul and in future rewards and punishments; they were absolute predestinarians; they observed the seventh day with peculiar strictness; they held the traditions of the Old Testament in great reverence, but only as mystic writings which they expounded allegorically; they sent gifts to the Temple, like other Jews, but offered no sacrifices; they admitted no one into their society till after a three years' probation; they lived in a state of perfect equality, except that they paid great respect to the aged and to their priests; they considered all secular employments ungodly and immoral, except agriculture and the trades and occupations connected with it. They were practical communists in the largest sense of the word, for they had no separate or individual interests, and held all things in common; they were industrious, quiet, orderly, and free from every kind of vice practised in ordinary society; they held solitude and celibacy in high esteem. Some say they allowed no marriages or sexual intercourse in their society; but this is doubted. They allowed no change of raiment till necessity required; they abstained from wine and other fermented liquors; they were not permitted to eat but with their own sect, and then a certain portion of food was served out to each person, of which they partook together after solemn ablutions.

It is, no doubt, the similarity of many of these practices to those of some of the early Christians, and of the Therapeutæ in particular, hat has led some Roman Catholic divines, and also some philo-

sophic writers, to speak of the Essenes as of a Christian sect.
Were the supposition of these writers correct, history would in that
case be without one single testimony to show that the theory or
practice of the equality of human rights was known to any ancient
people on earth, Jew or Gentile, before the propagation of the
Gospel. We believe, however, that the supposition is without
foundation. We believe the Essenes were a Jewish, not a Christian
sect. We believe their sect was anterior to Christ, and even to
John the Baptist. We believe it consisted of ardent Jews, who,
inflamed by the pious, fervid, and truly democratic outpourings of
Nehemiah and others of their prophets, and disgusted by the
manner in which they saw all Moses's laws in favour of the poor set
aside by the scribes and Pharisees of their day, to the profit of
usurers and land-monopolisers, resolved, in the language of their
own Scripture, to "come out from amongst them and be separate;"
and that, accordingly, in the words of Dr. Neander, they were
"distinguished from the mass of ordinary Jews in this—that they
knew and loved something higher than the outward ceremonial and
a dead faith—that they really did strive after holiness of heart and
inward communion with God." We believe moreover, that, instead
of owing their origin to Christianity, Christianity in a great measure
owed its early progress and successes to the Essenes; and that the
Therapeutæ, with whom they have been confounded, were but an
offshoot of their society, which subsequently engrafted itself upon a
Christian stock. With these considerations we hold it to be an
established fact that the Essenes do constitute a veritable exception,
but the only solitary one recorded in all history, of any people, before
Christ's advent, repudiating the doctrine and practice of human
slavery. This singular exception, if it be one, proves two things worthy
of every serious man's notice. One is, that if we are not indebted to
Christianity for the first or earliest repudiation of human slavery,
we are indebted for it to the purest fraction of that people, and to
the purest form of that religion, to whom and to which we owe
Christianity itself; in other words, it is to believers in the God of
the Jews and of the Christians, and not to the believers in any pagan
gods or in no God, we are indebted for the first authoritative inter-
ference with the pretended right of man to hold his fellow-man in
bondage. The other is, that the Essenes must have purposely
avoided propagandism and proselytism, kept themselves few and
select, and courted retirement and obscurity, in order to escape
persecution and perhaps death at the hands of their Jewish brethren.
Upon no other supposition would it be easy to account for their
fewness and impunity. For everything recorded of them goes to show
that they were as singular a people amongst the Jews, as the Jews
themselves were singular to the rest of the world; and those
who did not spare Christ and his Apostles were not likely to have
spared them, had they been equally bold and zealous in the propagation of their principles. It was, probably, from similar motives
that they mixed up celibacy and other asceticisms and eccentricities
with their system. What was singular and unpopular was not likely

to alarm rulers, or to excite a dread of innovation, because not likely to excite imitation and to attract followers; and what the authorities or the ruling classes saw no cause to dread, they would not be forward to prosecute or persecute. The apparent absurdities and vagaries of many other levelling sects might probably be accounted for in a similar way. Had the Mormons mixed up celibacy and other repulsive asceticisms and absurdities with their politico-religious system, like the Shakers and White Quakers, it is not improbable that they would be still under the patriarchal care of Joe Smith at Nauvoo. This fact alone speakes volumes for the dangers and difficulties Christianity had to encounter a few years later, when, for the first time in the history of the human race, a few fishermen and other obscure persons, headed by the supposed son of a carpenter, proclaimed open warfare against all that, up to that time, had been held sacred and indestructible in the constitution of human society.

And what pen, what tongue, can describe the zeal, the labour, the sacrifices, the dangers, the trials, the persecutions, of the early Christians in their first onslaught upon the powers of might and darkness? Never, never, can a tithe of a tithe of what they achieved and suffered in the cause of human redemption be known to their Christian successors of our day. It is only the profound politician, conversant with men and with the world, as well as versed in the history of his own and other times, who can even imagine what they must have suffered, or approximate to appreciating the miraculous virtues they must have displayed, and the herculean labours they must have performed.

Had the slaves of the ancient world been as conscious of their own degradation, or as discontented with their lot, as are their proletarian successors, the wages-slaves of our day, the case would have been vastly different. But it was not so; on the contrary, the slave-class of old was the very class that least of all was susceptible of the sentiment of equality, and least disposed by inclination or habit to countenance equalitarian innovators. What Mr. Edward Smith says of the negroes of America is still more applicable to the ancient slave-populations:—"They never tasted freedom, and do not feel the want of it; and to be as happy as a nigger is a common phrase in free and slave States alike." If the modern negro has never tasted freedom, he has at least heard of it, and heard that slavery is accounted a crime and a felony in most Christian countries. But the ancient slave never heard of, or imagined, any such a thing. Besides, except when he had a downright brute for his master, he was really comfortable and happy—"as happy as a nigger," and for the self-same reasons.

Here was the first great difficulty Christianity had to cope with— a difficulty almost impossible of conception in our times. To appreciate it properly, we must only try to conceive what a Chartist or Socialist lecturer's difficulty would be as a propagandist in London or in the provinces, provided all our labourers, artisans, and other workpeople were so fully employed at light work and ample wages, that "as happy as a hand-loom weaver," "as happy as a London

needlewoman," or "as happy as a Dorchester labourer" would be
as current proverbial phrases in England as the phrase, "as happy
as a nigger," is in America.   Add to this the difference between the
toleration allowed to opinions now-a-days and formerly, and the fact
that as slaves were the property of their masters, to tamper with
them was, in the eye of the law and of public opinion, to tamper
with the master's rights of property and with his personal security.
Just imagine these things, and we shall then have some faint idea of
what the early Christians had to contend with from this source alone,
in the first propagation of *liberty*, *equality*, *and fraternity*. But of this
and their other difficulties, dangers, and sufferings more in the next
chapter.

CHAPTER X.

PROGRESS OF EARLY CHRISTIAN PROPAGANDA.

Opposition from corrupt Slave-Caste—Detestation of Christian Doctrines by Slave-
owners—Incomprehensibility of new Doctrine of Equality—Absence of a
destitute Free People a Drawback on Reform — Spread of the New
Teachings—Alarm, and Persecution of the New Faith.

WE have seen, in the preceding chapter, what apparently insur-
mountable difficulties the early Christians had to struggle with in
the ignorance, contentment, traditional habits, and deep-rooted prejudices of the slave-class. To these hereditary bondsmen, who knew
no gods but their masters' gods, no law but their masters' will, the
sublime dogmas of the Gospel appeared altogether incomprehensible
and out of nature's course. Slavery they had ever regarded as decreed for them by fate ; and as they had no wants, spiritual or temporal, but such rude ones as were abundantly provided for by their
owners' care, they regarded with alarm and distrust the apostles of
a new faith, which was characterised as subversive of everything
human and divine. In a word, the slave-class was, of all classes
existing at the time, the least accessible to evangelical doctrine,—
the least susceptible of the new dispensation so freely and so bountifully offered, for the first time, to the whole of humanity in the name
of the Creator of all. Undoubtedly, this, if not the first, was the
greatest stumbling-block in the way of the new reformers.

That the master-class and the civil magistrate should encounter
such unheard-of innovations with the fiercest resistance was but
what might naturally be expected. To these the new religion was
at once sedition and rank blasphemy. A religion which treated
their gods and oracles as the offspring of fraud, begotten upon the
body of folly, was subversive of everything they deemed conservative
of society and wished to be held sacred by the multitude. A religion
which taught there was only one true God, the common Father of
all, in whose sight all men were equal,—that this God was no
respecter of persons or of classes, but would judge all alike, without
regard to rank, family, or condition,—that His worship demanded
the practice of all the virtues, and a renunciation of pride, lust,
covetousness, ambition, injustice—in short, of all the vices inseparable from tyranny and slavery,—that, to be acceptable in His sight,
men should be as brothers, loving Him above all things, and their
neighbours as themselves,—a religion which told masters and rulers
that whoever would be foremost should be the servant of the rest,
and which enjoined upon all that whatsoever they would have others
to do unto them, even so should they do unto others,—a religion of
this (till then) new and singular character must of necessity have
appeared a medley of abominations to masters and rulers. And

such, in good sooth, it did appear to them. Indeed, so utterly atrocious and "subversive of all law and order" did Christianity appear to the world at its first introduction, that, but for the obscurity and seeming insignificance of its first propagators, it is impossible it ever could have been established by mere human agency. Contempt and pity were the true safeguards of its first missionaries. Had they, at the outset, exhibited any signs of strength or importance, it is certain they would have been extirpated at once. No slave-owner would tolerate a system which went to deny him a property in his fellow-man. No ruler, no magistrate, would spare innovators whose doctrine went to revolutionize the entire social system as then constituted. No nation as a notion, no people as a people, would, for an instant, endure a religion which went to deprive them of *their* gods—the accredited protectors of their liberties and laws. For in those days, be it observed, every particular State or people had its peculiar form of worship, and its own peculiar gods; and every religion being particularly united with the laws which prescribed it, there was no way of converting a nation but by subduing it—no possibility of any system of proselytism proving successful but what could enforce its dogmas at the head of a victorious army. In other words, the only system of religious propagandism known in the old pagan world was the propagandism of the sword. And here let us note, for the benefit of certain shallow philosophists who declaim against Christianity on the alleged ground that before its introduction religious wars were unheard of, that political and religious wars amongst pagans were one and the same thing; and consequently, to make good their case, they should prove that political wars were unheard of. Rousseau exposes this philosophic error effectively in his "Social Contract," when showing the inseparable connection that subsisted between religion and politics under the pagan system. "The reason," he says, "there appear to have been no religious wars in the days of paganism was, that each State, having its peculiar form of government as well as of religion, did not distinguish its gods from its laws, and the political was also a religious war; the jurisdiction of their gods being, as it were, limited by the boundaries of the nation, and the gods of one country having no right over the people of another." Under an order of things like this, it is manifest no progress could have been made by the first Christians had they appeared in sufficient numbers, or of sufficient importance in the way of rank and station, to attract the notice of governments. As already observed, it was to their insignificance and obscurity alone they owed their preservation and first successes. For, as we shall presently see, the moment they grew strong enough to invite public vigilance, from that moment their persecutions began, and a torrent of execration and vengeance was let loose upon them the like of which was never witnessed before, nor will, we trust, ever be again. What we shall say of these persecutions will abundantly prove the horror which the doctrine of equality inspired in rulers and slave-owners, and, at the same time, show what miracles of *bearing* and *forbearing* the martyrs of the faith had to achieve before those great principles, which all true Christians and democrats now hold sacred, could ever obtain recognition in the world.

A third difficulty, as formidable as either of the others, although of a negative kind, also obstructed the early Christians. It was the absence of a numerous poverty-stricken, destitute class, corresponding with our modern proletarians, and having, like them, no guarantee for regular subsistence from day to day. Had such a class as this been in existence in St. Paul's time, his missionary labours amongst the Gentiles would have been immeasurably lighter and more successful. The millions would have been everywhere, as it were, predisposed for the new doctrine. Life being a burden to such people, they would have flung themselves with enthusiasm into the movement. But all history goes to show that hardly any such class existed till a century or two later. Speaking on this subject, an eminent French writer (M. de Cassagnac) observes:—" We have no certain means of determining up to what period of history pure slavery continued, *i.e.*, slavery without any enfranchisements or manumissions."

Although we find early mention made of *freedmen* in the Bible and in the "Odyssey," yet it is certain that in the primitive times of slavery there were no beggars. One is, in effect, a beggar only though lack of other means of subsistence. Now, a slave is not a beggar, he being found and provided for by his master. There were no beggars in our colonies during the early period of their settlement; and there are but few still, notwithstanding the people of colour have been set free. Blackstone judiciously observes, in his "Commentaries on the Laws of England" (without being apparently aware of the value and importance of the fact in a moral and social point of view), "that the vast numbers of destitute poor which had already, in his time, overspread England—and for whose subsistence the government had found it necessary to make some provision, ever since the reign of Henry IV., by an eleemosynary contribution levied with the regularity and permanence of an ordinary tax—arose chiefly from the manumission or setting free of large bodies of serfs during the middle ages, who were suddenly and without forethought thrown upon society." The monasteries, with their magnificent hospitals and well-organised system of charity, supported these poor outcasts as well as might be for a considerable period. But at length came the Reformation, which, pitilessly closing the monasteries, changed the workpeople into paupers, and the destitute poor into robbers. Following up this argument, M. de Cassagnac, after showing why there are fewer destitute poor in France than in England, concludes thus:—"But whether we regard France, England, or any other country,—whether we consult ancient history or modern history,— we shall find it everywhere and at all times to hold good, as a general rule, that *the emancipation of slaves is the first and universal cause of pauperism and mendicity all the world over.*" Our pseudo-philanthropists and saints of Exeter Hall—our abolitionists and humanity-mongers, who sentimentalize so blandly and edifyingly upon the evils of negro-slavery, will not, mayhap, be much gratified by this piece of historic intelligence. It is not the less true, however. Living experience adds the weight of its testimony to that of ancient history to confirm M. de Cassagnac's conclusions. For, to this day, we find that wherever direct or chattel slavery is the normal condition of the mass of the labouring class—as, for instance, in sundry Asiatic nations and in the Southern States of America till recently—there pauperism and mendicity are comparatively unknown. A few beggars and destitute persons may be found, here and there, amongst such people; but, besides that their number is hardly noticeable in the general mass, it will also be found that even these few are decayed freedmen and their offspring, or else the descendants of slaves who had purchased or otherwise obtained their freedom.

M. de Cassagnac mentions another fact confirmatory of this conclusion. It is, that the first great irruption of beggars, prostitutes, thieves, and paupers which overran Europe after the fall of the Roman Empire is ascertained to have taken place from the second to the sixth century—a period which corresponds exactly with the time when the mass of pagan slaves set free was added to the mass of enfranchised Christians ; and this irruption made itself manifest at once by the regular organisation of hospitals which then took place, but which were altogether unknown to the ancients, whose custom it was to provide for their sick and infirm slaves in private infirmaries, to which dispensaries were attached, within their own premises. Indeed, wherever we find the word " beggar " or " pauper " occur in primitive writings, we may make sure that those writings belong to an epoch when a great many slaves had already been emancipated—that is to say, to a secondary epoch in the civilization of the country the writings may refer to.

The same remark applies to mercenaries or wages-slaves ; for the ancient mercenary is no other than a manumitted slave, who is allowed to sell his labour when he can no longer be sold himself, he being no longer any one's property. There is an allusion to this class of persons in Leviticus xxv. 6: there are a few also in the "Odyssey.", Plutarch, in his " Life of Theseus," cites a verse of Hesiod, in which also allusion is made to mercenaries or wages-slaves. In the same poem of Hesiod there is mention made of beggars. These several allusions, however, are made in such a way as to show that the class referred to was insignificantly small. Moreover, it is far from certain that in some of them the word " mercenary " does not refer to a class of slaves corresponding with those modern ones in America, whose masters allowed them, as it were, to farm themselves out to other employers, accepting a fixed sum for themselves, and permitting the slaves to appropriate the overplus ; just as a modern London cabman is allowed to pocket all he can make in the day, over and above what he pays his " governor " for the use of his horse and vehicle. It is remarkable that Homer's " Iliad," which was written before the " Odyssey," does not contain a single hemistich having reference to paupers or beggars ; from which it has been inferred that the period intervening between the two works was one of those periods of transition when, manumissions occurring with unusual frequency, a small mercenary class was formed, to which allusion is made in the later poem. At all events, it is quite certain that no large class of mercenaries or wages-slaves existed at the time the Gospel was first propagated ; and this was one of the main difficulties in the way of its progress. A destitute proletarian class would have hailed the doctrine of equality with joy and gladness To well-fed, contented, ignorant slaves, who had neither hunger nor tuition to sharpen their intellects, it was all but incomprehensible : besides, the relation in which they stood to their owners made it perilous to tamper with them.

In the face of these formidable difficulties, it may well be asked what means, short of the miraculous, could have secured such amazing successes for Christianity so soon after its foundation ? We are not *divines*, and therefore shall leave the miraculous to those who prefer accounting in that way for the truly marvellous progress made by the first Christians in the propagation of their doctrines. Suffice it for us to say that nothing like it was ever before known in the world, nor since. Of the rapidity and multiplicity of its early triumphs we have abundant evidence in the history of the Acts of the Apostles. In Judea, where the Gospel was first preached (and where, no doubt, the labours of bygone martyred prophets, the preachings of John the Baptist, and, mayhap, the example and secret propagandism of the Essenes had prepared the ground for the seed), the new mission was, as might be expected, most successful. On the fiftieth day after the Crucifixion, it is said, three thousand persons were converted in Jerusalem by a single sermon of the Apostles. A few weeks after, five thousand true believers were present at another sermon preached in Jerusalem. Within less than ten years after Christ's death, the disciples and followers had become so numerous throughout Judea, particularly in and about Jerusalem, that they were objects of jealousy and alarm to Herod himself. About the twenty-second year after the Crucifixion they had so multiplied themselves that their name was legion. These facts may be collected from the Acts themselves.

Nor was it amongst the poor only that the doctrines of fraternity and equality gained ground; they penetrated all ranks of the population; they were ardently espoused by men in high stations and of responsible offices, whose countenancing of such a creed was at the moment a most perilous adventure. Amongst those early proselytes we find Joseph of Arimathea and Nicodemus, both members of the Jewish sanhedrim or council ; Jarius, a ruler of the synagogue ; Zaccheus, the chief of the publicans at Jericho ; Apollos, a distinguished orator; Sergius Paulus, a Roman and governor of the island of Cyprus; Cornelius, a Roman centurion; Dionysius, a judge and senator of the Athenian Areopagus; Erastus, treasurer of Corinth; Tyrennus, another Corinthian and professor of rhetoric; Paul, learned in the Jewish law ; Publius, governor of Melite (now Malta) ; Philemon, a man of great rank and influence at Colosse; Simon, a sophist of some note in Samaria; Zenas, a lawyer; and, we are told, even some of the emperor's own household.

F

For, as may be inferred from some of these names, it was not in Judea only the new faith triumphed: it spread with almost equal celerity and success throughout Asia Minor, Greece, Africa, and the islands of the Archipelago; indeed, everywhere in the countries bordering the Mediterranean.   There was hardly a province of the Roman empire that was not visited by its missionaries, even in the lifetime of the Apostles. Some of its earliest and most marked triumphs came off in the heart of Greece itself, at that time reputed the most polished nation in the world, and to whose schools and academies (as being the choicest nurseries of learning, art, and science) the aristocracies of Rome and elsewhere sent their sons to be educated and trained for public employments. Indeed, long before the last of the Apostles disappeared, we read of churches founded at Ephesus, Corinth, Thessalonica, Berœa, Philippi, and other Greek cities.   Rome herself, the seat of empire and mistress of the world, was not proof against the contagion of spiritualized democracy.   Before the end of the second century there were Christians to be found in almost every department of the imperial service— Christians in the senate, in the palace, in the camp, in the public offices,—in short, everywhere, it is said, except in the temples and the theatres, from which, of course, their religion debarred them.

But, it will be readily imagined, this amazing progress was not obtained without paying the cost which is paid for all reformations, in the blood and calamities of the principal actors. A religion of such unheard-of character, ushered into a world such as we have described, could not but excite the fiercest opposition and call forth the most malignant passions. It was so with Christianity, despite all the miracles alleged to have been wrought in its favour. The very term "Christian" was first heard of as a term of reproach. The new believers are said to have got that name at Antioch, where the people "were given to scoffing," but afterwards adopted it themselves as a term of honour, and gloried in it, just as we have seen the Chartists of England adopt that title (first given them in derision by their enemies), and glorify themselves in it; or as the French revolutionists of 1793 adopted and converted into an honorary title the nickname of "Sans Culottes," contemptuously given them by Lafayette; or as our democratic brethren in America converted "Yankee Doodle" into a national air, by way of revenge for the insult originally intended by their enemies in its use.

That the word Christian was, indeed, originally used as a term of reproach cannot be doubted. Christ or his disciples never used the term.   It is nowhere to be found in the Gospels; and if made use of twice or thrice in the Acts, and in one of the Apostolic Epistles, it is evidently used as a term borrowed from others, and not as one voluntarily adopted by the sect itself. But the best proof that the term was used in an offensive sense, and that the sect itself was held in detestation (mitigated only by contempt), is furnished by Tacitus's "Annals," in the only passage in which that historian deigns to notice them.   It occurs where, speaking of the Christians persecuted by Nero, he describes them as believers in a " deplorable and destructive superstition," which had its origin with one Christ; and then, as if for want of a name to give them, he adds, " *Vulgus Christianos appellabat,*" *i.e.* the vulgar or common people called them Christians.

At the period referred to here, the Christians were too few and too weak to cause much alarm out of Judea. Hence the air of contempt with which Tacitus wrote of them. Not very long after, however, the score was altogether changed. From a handful of obscure and unnoticeable sectarians, having scarcely any feelings in common with the rest of mankind, they grew into a gigantic community, having their missionaries, their churches, and even their political agents, spread throughout every corner of the empire. It was then their persecutions began to assume those forms and proportions which are necessary to attract history; it was then the pagan priesthoods, pagan magistrates, and pagan aristocracies found it necessary to check the tendencies of the new heresy, and to rouse and infuriate the superstitious prejudices and passions of the populace against the innovators. Nor was this a difficult task. At all times it is easy enough to influence ignorant mobs against reforms they understand not, and against men they comprehend not. It was peculiarly so in the case of the pagan rabble, let loose against the early Christians. For, be it observed, this new religion, which never ceased proselytizing, was a singularly exclusive one. It denied dogmatically, and rejected contemptuously, every alleged fact and article of heathen mythology, and the existence of every article of their worship. It would hear of no compromise, no amalgamation. If it prevailed at all, it must prevail by the subversion of every altar, statue, temple, consecrated to pagan uses. It pronounced all other gods false; all other worship sinful and an abomination. With these peculiarities engraved on it, it was impossible for the new religion to escape persecution from the pagan priesthood and superstitious rabble. And when we combine with this the consideration that the pagan magistrates and rulers regarded the doctrines of Christ as subversive of governmental authority, of the subordination of classes, and of the institution of property itself, as well as of religion and of the protection of their gods, we shall be at no loss to appreciate the nature of the feelings about to be roused into action against the Christians. We shall see, as we proceed, how these feelings showed themselves in the struggles and prosecutions which ensued.

CHAPTER XI.

THE FOUR GREAT PERSECUTIONS.

Obscurity and Insignificance of Early Reformers their best Protection—Christians the Great Levellers—Nero's Persecution—The Blood of the Martyrs the Seed of the Church—Persecution of Domitian—Martyrdoms under Trajan—Tortures under Antoninus.

WE have seen, in the preceding chapter, why Christianity must, upon its first introduction, have been universally and virulently opposed by the established powers of the world; and how, but for the lowliness and obscurity of its first propagators, it must, by attracting the notice of the wealthy and powerful, have been crushed at once, instead of making the amazing progress it did, before its persecutions began.

When the interests of wealth and power adjudged it necessary to crucify the Founder, their comparative insignificance could alone be a protection for his disciples and followers. And the supposed cause of their being spared so long is the fact of their appearing to the Roman governors only as a sect of Jews who had seceded from their brethren on account of some non-important item of worship or doctrine, not worth inquiring into. It was a part of Roman policy, as we have seen, to tolerate all religions, and even to incorporate the gods of their subjects or allies along with their own. The Jews, like all other people subject to the empire, enjoyed this toleration; and so long as the Christians appeared to be only a sect of this singular people, they participated with them in the imperial protection. We have a remarkable proof of this in the case of St. Paul. When he returned to Jerusalem from his third apostolic mission, the favour with which he was received by his Christian brethren there, and the joy they manifested at the great success of his mission in Macedonia, Achaia, &c., roused the ire of his countrymen. It is related that some Jews of Asia (who had probably witnessed the fruits of his zeal and ability amongst the Gentiles in their own country), seeing him one day in the temple, gave instant vent to their bigoted or conservative rage, by pointing him out as the man who was aiming to destroy all distinction between Jew and Gentile. They charged him with teaching things contrary to the law of Moses, and with polluting the holy temple by bringing into it uncircumcised heathen. The effect of this was to enrage the multitude against St. Paul. They seized him, dragged him out of the temple, brutally maltreated him, and were on the point of putting him to death, when he was rescued out of their hands by Lysias, a Roman military tribune, and the then principal army-officers at Jerusalem. This conduct of Lysias towards the great apostle, taken in juxtaposition with the previous well-known efforts of Pontius Pilate to save Christ himself from the hands of his Jewish enemies, shows clearly enough that the early Christians had little to fear from the Romans, so long as they were deemed to be only a religious sect of the Jews, and to be aiming at a kingdom which "is not of this world."

It became otherwise, however, as soon as the pagan priesthood and pagan magistracy began to discover that Christ's kingdom would very materially affect this world, as well as the next. The priests, trembling for their revenues and estates, the magistrates and rulers for their power, and the rich generally for their wealth and station, became *very* Jews from the moment that discovery was made. A religion which proclaimed *spiritual* equality was, to the priest and rulers, undistinguishable from one that, if it did not proclaim, would very speedily lead to *temporal* equality as well; and the principle of *community of goods*, which so notoriously prevailed in some of the early churches, was point blank evidence of the levelling tendencies of the sect. Indeed, examining it philosophically, the religion could not be otherwise than *social* in its effect. For, as its main doctrines went to condemn riches ("lay not up for yourselves treasures," &c.), to make power a *trust* for the governed, and not a profitable *monopoly* for governors ("let him who would be foremost amongst you be the servant of the rest," &c.), and to exhibit this life as a mere probationary state for another and eternal one, in which the poor of this world were likely to fare better than the rich ("it is easier for a camel to pass through the eye of a needle than for a rich man to enter the kingdom of heaven"),—as these and the like were amongst the vital doctrines of the new religion, it is impossible that such as embraced it with a firm belief in its ordinances, and promises of future rewards and punishment, could dare to rob and enslave their fellow-creatures, or peril their eternal salvation in another world for the sake of enjoying the mammon of unrighteousness in this for the brief space of a few years. These conclusions being but strictly logical deductions from Christian premises, it is no wonder that a people, whom one of their own historians (Sallust) represents as valuing riches, honour, and empire as the greatest goods the immortal gods could vouchsafe to man, should regard with an evil eye a religion which threatened them with the loss of all, by bringing them into contempt, and making the possession of them a peril to salvation.

At all events, such was the impression made upon the pagan mind. Had they regarded Christ's kingdom as pertaining only to another world, they would have cheerfully made his followers a present of it, on condition that they did not meddle with this. But in the face of such levelling doctrines, and in presence of a faith so lively and ardent, which made hosts of men renounce their temporal possessions in order to render themselves worthy of the new dispensation, the higher and wealthier orders of the empire soon became convinced that they would lose their kingdoms in this world if they allowed any further scope to that new and strange religion which promised so much in the next.

Hence originated that series of persecutions so well known in the history of the Christian church, and which lasted upwards of three hundred years. According to the best accounts, it began about A.D. 64, in the reign of Nero. Although the mummeries and monstrosities of polytheism were openly derided by St. Paul and others from the first starting of their missions, yet it does not appear that any public acts of legislation or administration were directed against Christianity till this period, when it had acquired such extension and stability as to make it truly formidable. It was then the Roman authorities began to blame themselves for their toleration, and to wonder that the Jews had found it so difficult to infuse into the breasts of Roman magistrates that rancour and virulence so conspicuous in the Jews themselves. Moreover, the open attacks upon paganism continually made by the Christians rendered them extremely obnoxious to the populace, who considered their understandings as well as their gods insulted by every sermon directed against them. They retorted upon the Christians by stigmatising them as *atheists*, and at the instigation of their priests, secretly backed by the rich, called loudly upon the civil magistrates to suppress them by force, as a body of seditious conspirators whose object was to destroy the politico-religious constitution of the empire. As happens in the suppression of all popular movements, lies and inventions the most horrid, imputing to them all manner of abominations, were circulated all over the empire, and, by these and like circumstances, the minds of all classes of pagans were prepared to regard with pleasure or indifference any amount of cruelty and wrong that interested vengeance might wreak upon them. In short, the sort of feeling that was got up against the Socialists and Red Republicans of France, before and after the June insurrection, will convey the best idea of the public opinion which was manufactured in Nero's time to prepare men's minds for the terrible proscriptions that followed. Indeed, many of the designations of horror applied to modern Socialists are little else than translations of the Latin terms so copiously lavished upon the poor Christians.

Besides the private persecution which never ceased (and which is always more galling and unbearable than the public), there were at least ten great imperial crusades directed against Christianity. When we say directed against Christianity, we wish to be distinctly understood as meaning against *liberty* and *equality*. About the *spiritualism* of Christianity the pagan rulers cared not a straw, more than they did about their own gods. Religion was a mere pretence in the matter, as it is in all such matters. It served their purposes with the multitude (who alone are sincere on such occasions) ; and that is all they cared for. It is by viewing persecution in this light —the only true light—that modern reformers can profit by our remarks on this head.

The first great persecution (which took place under Nero, about A.D. 64) is noticed by Tacitus in his "Annals." From the language used by that historian, it is manifest that the wealthier classes of

Rome regarded the Christians of that period as a most dangerous combination against not only the government, but (to use a *doctrinaire* phrase) against " society " itself. Tacitus—himself an aristocrat—regarded the aristocratic orders of his day as constituting *society ;* and finding these orders to be no favourites with the Christians, he roundly accuses the latter of " hatred towards the human race," and describes them as followers of *one* Christ, who was the founder of a " deplorable and destructive superstition " ! In the same way, the Bonapartes, the Thiers, and the Guizots of [the present day represent their own plundering class as *society*, and describe such men as Ledru Rollin, Mazzini, Louis Blanc, Proudhon, &c., as enemies of all law and order—as enemies of family, property, and religion, —in short, as warring against " the very existence of society itself " (their own words), because they preferred the rights and happiness of the great majority to the usurpations of a criminal and contemptible minority. It is now an established fact—a fact as well attested as any in history—that the insurrection and bloody carnage in June, 1848, was preconcerted and with great pains elaborated by the friends of " law and order," in order to purge " society " of Red Republicanism and Socialism, or (to use their own phrase) *pour en finir—i.e.* to make a finish of the democratic and social republic by drowning it in the blood of its authors and most heroic defenders.

It is not so well known how the great fire originated in Rome, which Nero and his myrmidons charged upon the Christians. History had no historians for the poor of those days. There is but too much reason, however, to believe that the burning of Rome in Nero's time was as much the work of the friends of " law and order," and for a similar purpose, as the June insurrection was notoriously the work of the same description of gentry in Paris. Times and circumstances change, but not human nature ; it is always the same, and will ever develop itself in the like way under like circumstances. Nero is said to have fiddled when Rome burned. The friends of " law and order," the defenders of " society," were never in brighter ecstacies than when Cavaignac announced the demolition, by shells and cannon, of the houses of the insurgents, and the massacre of their brave defenders. If setting fire to Rome, and reducing three-fourths of it to ashes, could have been made available for the destruction of the Christians, the aristocracy of that day would no more have scrupled at it than did Rostochin the burning of Moscow, Cavaignac the demolitions in Paris, or General Oudinot the bombardment of Rome. Aristocrats have never been aught but robbers since the birth of their order ; and all history proves that they invariably become murderers, burners, devastators, and hirers of assassins the moment the people attempt to recover their own. It was so, most likely, in the burning of Rome. To this day, Nero himself is suspected of the deed, though we think it far more likely to have been the work of his aristocracy, with whom he was no favourite, because he made himself too familiar with the common people.

But whether the atrocity was Nero's work, or that of the aristocratic enemies of Christianity, it is certain the unfortunate Christians were made to bear the odium and penalties of it. Without any evidence on the matter, the best and bravest of the Christian party—those publicly known as such—were openly seized and accused of the act. Through these, others were discovered and laid hold of, till the imperial net was full of victims. They were condemned to a variety of cruel deaths, and they perished in the midst of all manner of insults and execrations. Some were sewed up in the skins of wild beasts, and then thrown to hungry dogs, to be torn in pieces and devoured. Some were nailed to crosses, like their Divine Master. Others were burnt alive, in a manner which ought to cause aristocracy and vulgar intolerance to be abhorred till the crack of doom. The victims were first sewed up in pitched clothes or coverings ; these were then set on fire, and, being lighted up at night, they served as torches to illuminate Nero's own gardens, which were given for the purpose.

These barbarities were followed by edicts published against the Christians, which enjoined upon the authorities to repress them by every means placed at their disposal by the law. Of course, many martyrs suffered, especially in Italy. St. Peter and St. Paul are generally supposed to have been of the number. The former was crucified, it is said, with his head downwards, at his own request. St. Paul was beheaded. Such, at least, is the tradition preserved by the early Fathers, who are all unanimous that their martyrdom was a consequence of this persecution ; though it is not precisely known whether it was the burning of Rome that was made the pretence of killing them, or a revolt of the Jews from the Romans, which took place a year or two later, through a successful insurrection in Jerusalem. The former is the more likely and accredited, though the latter is not improbable, seeing the Christians gave the Romans some trouble at the time in Judea, where their garrison in Jerusalem was put to the sword, and one of their generals, who came to besiege it, was ignominiously repulsed and defeated in his retreat. Such events would naturally exasperate the Romans against both Jews and Christians ; and as the populace hated both sects alike, the martyrdom of Peter and Paul might be easily enough accounted for under the circumstances.

It is needless to say, Nero's persecution was unsuccessful. It only made the Christians more cautious.. Their numbers and zeal but multiplied in despite of it. And if, to men of their principles, it could be any satisfaction to hear of their enemy's death, they had abundant occasion for it when it became known that Nero fell by his own hand—thus atoning for his injustice to them by at last doing justice to himself. If we mistake not, the Red Republicans and Social Reformers of the Continent will have cause to rejoice at many such acts of self-retribution on the part of their oppressors before many years elapse.

The second general persecution of the Christians took place in the reign of Domitian, towards the close of the first century. In this persecution many Christian teachers of great eminence suffered, but with no better success to the cause of paganism than the first. It appears to have ceased at the death of Domitian.

The third great persecution commenced in the third year of the Emperor Trajan, A.D. 100. Without going into the causes alleged by divines and churchmen for this persecution (which they would have us think was a purely spiritual affair), let us at once say that every feature of it known to us in these days shows clearly enough that it was the *temporal* and not the *spiritual* tendencies of Christianity the Emperor Trajan directed his force against. Indeed, the charges recorded against them are precisely the same as those made against Chartists in England, Red Republicans in France, or democrats anywhere in the present day. One churchman, treating of it, says, "Under the plausible pretence of their holding illegal meetings and societies, they were severely persecuted by the governors of provinces and other officers, in which persecutions great numbers fell by the rage of popular tumult, as well as by laws and processes." Is it not under a similar "plausible pretence of holding illegal meetings and societies" that most persecutions take place against the political and social reformers of the present day? And wherein are the doctrines professed by the latter different from those recorded of the Christians in Trajan's time? In no one essential particular. What a pity that our modern divines and churchmen cannot be got to see the persecutions of Chartists and Socialists, now-a-days, with the same eyes with which they look upon those of our predecessors, in religion and politics, who suffered under Nero, Domitian, and Trajan! The Trajan persecution continued several years, and made an immense number of martyrs; amongst others the famous Clement, Bishop of Rome. But as Trajan was an emperor famed for his liberality, justice, and moderation, some of our modern parsons are at a loss to account for his severity to the Christians. Unless it be the chastening hand of Providence, they know not what to see in it. Sweet innocents! Did they ever hear of any *liberal* persecutors in England, or of any *moderate* mitrailleurs in France? Know they not that the authors of all the late massacres, transportations and dungeonings in France call themselves *moderate* reformers and liberals, and declare they will have only *la république des honnêtes gens*—the republic of honest men? Know they not, too, that the really honest men who are their victims get the very identical names, in France, that Trajan's judges gave the victims of his persecution—viz., brigands, malefactors, and traitors? Yes, let modern churchmen and parsons pretend what they may, the authorities they now uphold are the exact counterpart of the Trajans and Domitians of old; and the political victims of the present day are as exactly the counterpart of those early Christians whose martyrdom they so affect to deplore, and which (to blind their flocks) they would have us believe was purely the consequence of their opinions touching a future state.

In this persecution under Trajan, and in another which ensued under his successor Adrian, it is as well known as anything in history that the great bulk of the martyrs suffered for the *political* and not the *spiritual* dogmas they upheld, and that in the eye of public opinion they passed not so much for blasphemers and atheists (names given to them to please the superstitious rabble), but as seditious disturbers of the peace, enemies of the emperor, malefactors towards society, and traitors to the imperial government.

The fourth great persecution took place under Antoninus the Philosopher, and, with different degrees of severity in different places, continued throughout the whole of his reign. In this persecution perished the famous Polycarp, Bishop of Smyrna, said to have been the friend and companion of St. John. Thus the poor Christians fared no better under a philosophic emperor than under the "moderate" and "virtuous" Trajan. Indeed, we have at this moment shoals of "philosophers" in France and England who, for absurdity and hard-heartedness, throw churchmen entirely into the shade. Parson Malthus's divinity may have been bad enough ; we aver it was not worse than his philosophy. Many of the unfortunate sufferers in this philosopher's reign were devoured by wild beasts; others were tortured to death in an iron chair, made red-hot for the purpose. Even women were not spared. The names of two are preserved—Biblia and Blandina—whose sufferings and heroic courage contrast nobly with the cowardly cruelty of the philosophic scoundrel-emperor who gave his sanction to their death. Singularly enough, France, the "eldest daughter of the church," was the scene of the worse persecutions which took place in this reign, when false philosophy *versus* real Christianity was the order of the day ; and, singularly enough, France is now the country where, *par excellence,* real Christianity is taking the field in right earnest against both philosophism and false Christianity. What France failed to do in the first and second centuries, and failed again to do in the eighteenth, she is now labouring to accomplish for all the world in the middle of the nineteenth.

CHAPTER XII.

PROGRESS OF PROPAGANDA TO THE TENTH PERSECUTION.

Seven Years' Persecution of Equalitarian Innovators—Seventh Great Persecution—Christians charged with Sorcery in Eighth Persecution—Tortures of Ninth and Tenth Persecutions—Pretended Conversion of Constantine—Lives of Early Christians Exemplars to the Pagan World.

THE persecutions under the "moderate" Trajan and the "philosophic" Antoninus had no effect, as we have seen, in stopping the progress of Christianity. On the contrary, they but served to extend it, by causing the multitude to interest themselves more in examining a religion which excited so much alarm amongst those orders of men who, from their power and riches, they could not but regard as their natural oppressors. The discreet conduct and humane character of the early Christians was another, indeed, the chief cause of their success. Those pagans who had relations with them in private life, and who had thereby opportunities of judging them as men and citizens, could not be brought to regard with horror a religion which had produced such characters, nor to sympathise with the atrocious spirit which consigned them to the fate of malefactors. Up to the reign of Severus, then, Christianity went on conquering and to conquer, in despite of edicts and persecutions.

It was in this reign that the fifth great persecution took place. In the early part of it no additions were made to the severe edicts already in force against them; and history preserves but few cases of their suffering from the application of the old. This was partly owing to the greater caution imposed upon them by the laws against illegal meetings and societies passed under Trajan and Antoninus, and partly, it is said, to the interest at court of a celebrated Christian, named Proculus, who, by an extraordinary application of his medical art, had cured the emperor of a dangerous distemper. This precarious lenity, however, did not endure long. After having been partially interrupted by an occasional execution of the old laws in force, it was effectually terminated by an edict of Severus (A.D. 197), which prohibited every subject of the empire, under severe penalties, from embracing the Jewish or Christian faith.

This edict would appear, at first sight, designed only to prevent the further growth of Christianity; but as, in one of its clauses, it urged the magistracy to enforce the laws of former emperors, still in force, it gave rise to a frightful proscription. For seven years the Christians were exposed to all manner of persecution and prosecution, not only in Rome and Italy, but in Gaul, Greece, Asia Minor, Palestine, Syria, Egypt and the rest of Africa. Amongst the celebrated martyrs in this persecution fell Leonidas, the father of Origen, and Irenæus,

Bishop of Lyons, in Gaul. It was on this occasion Tertullian composed his well-known "Apologetica," or apology on behalf of the victims—a work from which a great deal may be learned of what the early Christians had to endure in this persecution, more particularly at Alexandria in Egypt, where the violence of pagan intolerance was most felt.

The sixth persecution, under the Emperor Maximinus, which began about A.D. 235, does not appear to have been so severe as the preceding ones. Maximinus's predecessor, the Emperor Alexander, was rather favourable to the Christians, he and his family having given shelter and patronage to many of them. This excited the envy and hatred of the party favourable to Maximinus's interests, and, at their instigation it is supposed, the latter prince rekindled the flames of persecution against the Christians. Celsus was the literary champion of the pagans on this occasion; and Origen, that of the Christians. The latter gained great credit and influence amongst his own party, by the zeal and energy with which he supported the Christians in the fiery ordeal they had to pass through in the trials of this period.

The seventh persecution is considered by many the severest that ever befell the Christian world. It took place during the short reign of Decius, and was ushered in by an imperial edict, couched in the strongest terms, and issued A.D. 249. One of its first effects was the putting to death of Fabianus, Bishop of Rome, with a number of his followers. Immense numbers of the Christians were publicly destroyed in almost every province of the empire. The Bishops of Jerusalem and Antioch died in prison. Tortures the most excruciating were resorted to, to extort confessions of guilt, the betrayal of accomplices, or a renunciation of their faith. These were, for the most part, endured with heroic fortitude; but many sank under the trial, and, to save their lives, consented to burn incense upon the altars of the gods; others purchased safety by bribes, or secured it by flight. The poor, as usual, fared worst. Unable to secure themselves by patronage or bribery, they were seized before they had time for flight, and put to death with every refinement of torture, and in a variety of ways. Some were publicly burnt in the market-places; others were whipped, branded, and then impaled or crucified. Many were thrown to wild beasts to be devoured; and not a few were stoned to death by an enraged populace, whose "wild justice" was too impatient to await magisterial decisions. At Alexandria in particular, they anticipated the emperor's edict, and in their blind fury put many to death who were not Christians at all, mistaking them for such on account of their connections, real or supposed. Political bias had much to do in embittering this persecution. The leading Christians were known to be attached to the family of the Emperor Philip, who was supposed to be secretly favourable to their sect. This aggravated the rage of the opposite faction, and superadded political passions to fanatic zeal in the proscriptions under Decius. Upon the whole, no other pagan persecution cost the Christians more lives than this, nor entailed upon them a greater variety of sacrifices and sufferings.

The eighth general persecution was not upon so large a scale; but it had its distinguishing barbarities to bear witness to the truth of a celebrated saying of Plutarch, namely, that rage and rancour stifle all sentiments of humanity in the human breast, and that "no beast is more savage than man when he is possessed of power equal to his passions." We may conceive to what excess these passions were carried under the Emperor Valerian (A.D. 257), when we find that potentate and his aristocracy employing an Egyptian magician (named Macrinus) to give out, as the result of his occult science, that he had discovered that the peace and prosperity of the Roman empire were incompatible with the "wicked spells" and "execrable charms" practised by the Christians. This, of course, was a mere pretence to infuriate the rabble and the distressed of all classes against them. To counteract the pretended "spells" and "charms" of Christianity, Valerian is said, by the advice of Macrinus, to have performed many impious rites and sacrifices, amongst which was the cutting the throats of infants, &c. All this jugglery was intended to disguise from his subjects the true nature of the struggle between Christianity and pagan despotism, namely, the struggle of humanity to vindicate its inherent rights against arbitrary power and the barbarism of superstitious ignorance. At any rate, fresh edicts were promulgated in all places against the Christians; and, with the emperor's sanction, they were exposed without protection to the common rage. Amongst the noble army of martyrs sacrificed under this brutal emperor, history makes honorary mention of St. Lawrence, Archdeacon of Rome, and of St. Cyprian, Bishop of Carthage, said to have been two of the most learned and distinguished men of their age.

The ninth general persecution took place under the Emperor Aurelian, about the year 274. So little, however, is recorded of this persecution, that we may safely infer it gave but little interruption to the peace of the church. Indeed, by this time the Christians were, in many places, as numerous as the pagans; and many of their body were opulent subjects, possessed of great local and general influence. One more great persecution, and we shall find them upon an equality with their proud oppressors. We shall next find them, in political parlance, "masters of the situation;" we shall find them established in power, and corrupted with riches and luxury. A portion of them, at least, we shall find in that position; and then, agreeably to the laws of human nature, we shall find them no longer Christians, but practising the same vices, and committing the same crimes of tyranny and wrong, they so much condemned in the old pagans. One great persecution more, and lo! Christianity will be enthroned in power; and then farewell to Christian progress and Christian principles! One great persecution more will give to "Christians" the ascendancy; and in that ascendancy will be the death of Christianity itself!

The tenth and last great persecution of the early church took place under the Emperor Diocletian, and broke out in the nineteenth year of his reign (about the year A.D. 303). Diocletian himself does not appear to have been animated by any bigoted zeal or political hatred against the Christians. Galerius, whom he had declared Cæsar, and the mother of Galerius, who was a zealot in the pagan interest, vehemently urged him to promulgate edicts for their suppression. To this end, the philosopher Hierocles prepared public opinion for them by violent writings against the Christians; and the pagan priesthood, as in interest bound, supported Hierocles.

This persecution began in the city of Nicomedia, and thence extended into other cities and provinces, till at last it became general all over the empire. Though, doubtless, the historians of the church have exaggerated this as well as other persecutions, yet there is a sufficiency of well-authenticated facts to show that, however the wealthy and intriguing Christians might have contrived to secure lenity and even impunity for themselves, it was far otherwise with the majority, who were poor, ardent, and enterprising. As in the seventh persecution under Decius, the diabolical ingenuity of man was racked to discover new modes of punishment, new refinements of torture. Some were roasted alive at slow fires till death put an end to their sufferings ; others were hung by the feet, with their heads downwards, and suffocated by the smoke of dull fires. Pouring melted lead down the throats of the victims was one variety of torture ; another was tearing off the flesh from their quivering limbs with shells. Some of the sufferers had splinters of reeds thrust into the most sensitive parts of their persons—into their eyes, for example, or under their finger-nails and nails of their toes ; others were impaled alive. Many had their limbs broken, and in that condition were left to expire in protracted agonies. Such as were not capitally punished were scourged or branded, or else had their limbs mutilated and their features disfigured. Altogether, the victims were as numerous as in the persecution under Decius. Amongst the more noted ones we read of the Bishops of Tyre, Sidon, Emesa, and Nicomedia. Very many matrons and virgins of unblemished character passed through the flames of martyrdom. And as to the plebeian or poorer classes, they perished literally in myriads. At length, upon the accession of the Emperor Constantine the persecution slackened. He declared in favour of the Christians, and soon after, openly embracing the new religion, he published the first law in their favour. The death of Maximian, Emperor of the East, soon after put an end to all their tribulations at the hands of pagans.

It was then that, for the first time, Christianity (or rather a something worse than paganism which usurped its name) took possession of the thrones of princes. The religion of the court, it became the fashionable religion. Aristocrats, military men, the leading professions, men of the world, became converts to it in a twinkling. We speak, of course, only of the *name*—not of the *thing*. It was the *name* only that was established by Constantine : the *thing* itself he knew and cared nothing about. The religion as taught by Jesus and his disciples is not a religion for courts and courtiers ; it flourishes not in presence of emperors and praetorian guards.

Constantine's conversion was but a *coup d'état*, or political *ruse*, to destroy Christianity by itself; *alias*, to make its votaries (all true believers) ashamed of its very name, through seeing it professed by base hypocrites—its natural and irreconcilable enemies. Its immediate effect was to neutralise the force of Christianity as operating against the abuses of government and against social injustice. It became henceforward impossible to know who were Christians and who were not—at least, who were sincere and who were not; the false ones bearing the same name as the true ones, and, in proportion to their hypocrisy, more emphatic and ostentatious in their profession of faith than the true believers. As a matter of course, the rich, the ambitious, the low intriguer, the bustling man of the world, adhered publicly to the name or profession of Christian for the sake of the good things attached thereto in church and state. The honest, the simple-hearted, the oppressed many saw they were foully tricked, but were powerless to right themselves. Between the pagans, who still adhered to the old system, and their hypocritical betrayers in high places, their fate was a deplorable one. After all their struggles and sacrifices for Christianity, they had the mortification to find that, just at the moment they counted upon victory, they found discomfiture and shame; and that what 300 years of pagan torturings, dungeonings, and terrorism had failed to accomplish against their religion, was effected at once by an " organised hypocrisy " of *soi-disant* Christians supposed to belong to their own church and party.

Most people date the triumph of Christianity from the accession, or rather from the conversion, of Constantine. In our opinion, it is the *decline* of Christianity, or the *reaction* against it, that ought to date therefrom. During the first three centuries the progress of Christianity was one continued series of triumphs—purchased, it is true, by the blood of countless martyrs, but not the less real and effective on that account; but from the moment it became a state religion, under Constantine and his successors, it ceased to be the religion of Christ and his apostles, and became a figment of forms and ceremonies worthless as the ceremonialism of the Pharisees. Many, it is true, continued sincerely attached to the real thing—the religion of Jesus; but, discountenanced and discouraged by their own priests and rulers, they soon fell into discredit, and their numbers diminished with every succeeding reign, till at last Christianity (as at first taught) was nowhere to be found.

In this present century, and in this present year 1850, it is reviving again under new names and forms. It is allying itself with a philosophy which has nothing in common with the hollow philosophism of the last century, but much in common with the natural instincts and primitive feelings of man. The Christianity which is being now revived in France, Germany, and elsewhere on the Continent approaches nearer to the Christianity of the first and second centuries than most people are aware of. At bottom it is the same; but in form and garb it must necessarily partake of the science and civilization of the times we are in. Its object, like that of

Christ and his disciples, is to banish sin and slavery, crime and misery, from the world, but without pretending to any extraordinary mission, or to any other light than the revelations of Scripture interpreted and explained by reason. The *Christianisme* and the *humanité* of Pierre Leroux may be taken as samples of this modern revival of Christianity.

As a general rule, the early Christians exemplified in their lives the charity, the purity, and the disinterestedness enjoined by the Gospel ; it was therefore they were so successful with the people. The persecutions of the pagans did not make them retaliate. They were too wise, too discreet, to rebel against laws or governments that could have crushed them at once ; and for the unfortunate, deluded populace they had nothing but pity in the midst of their worst excesses. They knew it was ignorance alone that made the populace so furious against them : they knew they were the true friends of this populace ; and that this populace would be their friend, if they could but understand each other. Hence the tolera-tion preached and practised with such good effect in the early ages of the church. It is true, there were disputes and occasional intolerance amongst Christians from the first,—we have sundry proofs of it in Paul's Epistles, the Acts, and in the writings of the early Fathers ; but it was not till after the legal establishment of Christianity that the guilt of intolerance or persecution could be charged against Christians as a body. Though corruption had been making way amongst them long before that, and though there were symptoms enough in the Church prognosticative of the dire effect that power and the mammon of unrighteousness might have upon them, yet the main body remained sound. What they suffered from the pagans naturally made them hold together for mutual aid and counsel ; it also cemented in them habits of mutual love and tenderness for each other's feelings : above all, it confirmed them in their aversion to tyranny and intolerance, and enamoured them more and more of that Gospel which everywhere enjoins charity, tenderness, mercy, and self-denial for the sake of others. They remembered Christ's sermon on the mount, his unbounded compas-sion for sinners, his forgiveness of all, his love of little children, his humility, his readiness to be the servant of his followers, his teach-ings, fastings, prayers, and sufferings for all. These were ever present in their minds. They knew and felt that, guided by the spirit and precepts of the Gospel, by the conduct of its Author, and by the preachings and examples of his apostles, true Christians could not be otherwise than tolerant, forgiving, just, and affectionate to-wards one another.

The general conduct of Christians before the age of Constantine was in conformity with those maxims. They believed what they professed ; and they practised what they believed. Upon this head the writings of the early Fathers are all but unanimous. We could cite a volume-full of exemplifications ; but the fact, as an historical one, is notorious beyond the necessity for proof.

Up to the time of Constantine the progress of Christianity was one continued series of triumphs over the principles and practices of human slavery—one earnest, uninterrupted protest against those vices and passions in which the subjection of man to his fellow-man has its origin. In the minds of the early Christians, the Gospel dispensation was no other than a divine protestation against the abasement of the human race by tyranny, upon the one hand, and slavery upon the other. Not one of the sublime virtues so beautifully pourtrayed and so authoritatively enjoined by Christ and his disciples could flourish and bear fruit in a world of tyrants and slaves. Either that divine Gospel must, therefore, ever remain a dead letter, or the system of human slavery, with all its violence, vice, and crimes, must be overthrown. Every act, every institute, every martyrdom, of the early Christians goes to show they were impressed with this belief. Hence their marvellous labours, their still more marvellous sufferings (voluntarily incurred and borne), and, most marvellous of all, their extraordinary successes. Everything goes to prove their fixed determination to subvert, from its foundation, that anti-social structure of society which made man the slave of his fellow-man; their every act and discourse tended accordingly to its overthrow. It cannot be overthrown by an outbreak, a *coup de main*, a surprise, or onslaught of brute force. Its existence being the work of opinion, it can be overthrown only by opinion. The world must therefore be made to believe differently. The minds and hearts that uphold it must be enlightened, softened, refined, exalted, reformed. Behold the mission of the early Christians—the means and end of their godlike labours.

Up to the age of Constantine, we repeat, the Christian revolution gained ground incessantly, if not uninterruptedly. It progressed not only in despite of, but actually *by means of* every one of the ten great imperial persecutions we have sketched. Like the Antæus of mythology, it gathered fresh strength from every fall.

With its *establishment* under Constantine ended its triumphant progress! What churchmen call its final victory, its crowning glory, was in reality its first decisive check—the cause and forerunner of its downfall; in other words, it was the beginning of the counter-revolution or reaction which soon afterwards rendered null and void all the martyrdoms and triumphs of three hundred years.

CHAPTER XIII.

DEBASEMENT OF THE NEW POWER WHEN SEIZED BY RULERS.

Cost of making the New Ideas triumphant—Change in Character in the hands of Kings, Courtiers, and Profitmongers—Emancipations become a matter of Policy and Profit—Repudiation of Principles of Fraternity and Equality—Horrors of Introduction of Proletarianism.

WE have seen, in the two last chapters, what terrible tribulations it cost the early Christians to obtain admission into the world for the doctrines of liberty, fraternity, and equality,—we ought rather, perhaps, to say, for the more comprehensive doctrines of justice and humanity, upon which the others must be based to be real and enduring. For upwards of three hundred years these poor Christians were the victims of an untiring persecution, which smote them without pity and without remorse, in every part of the wide-extended Roman empire. We have seen how, at ten distinct epochs, by the edicts of as many emperors, this persecution burst upon them with such signal and surpassing fury that, to this day, it seems almost a miracle that the sect was not utterly extirpated. More marvellous still, we find them growing and extending themselves after every persecution, till at length, under Constantine, they have become so numerous and formidable that persecution may no longer be safely tried. Indeed, force would no longer prevail; so fraud must be resorted to. The sham conversion of Constantine and his courtiers was the fraud had recourse to. Those hypocrites suddenly pretended to a new light. Constantine made his own conversion quite a supernatural affair; he pretended to have seen a brilliant apparition in the heavens, presenting a cross with this inscription, " In hoc signo vinces,"—" In this sign thou shalt conquer." His courtiers and expectants, of course, partook of the imperial illumination ; they discovered with miraculous haste, if not by miraculous agency, the divine authority of the Christian religion. By embracing it in *name* and *profession* they wisely calculated they could more easily extinguish it in *substance* and in *practice* than by any other means. In the first place, it would detach the mere *political* Christians— *i.e.*, the selfish and ambitious ones—from the real ones, the honest, unsuspecting mass. In the next place, it would conciliate the former by throwing open to them the offices and honours of the state ; and, at the same time, flatter the multitude by the seeming conversion of an emperor and his court to their religion. Above all, it would have the advantage of pricking up the Christian organization (which, up to that epoch, was a veritable democratic organization) by detaching from the multitude all their leading spiritual and political chiefs, who would thenceforward be sure to have one doctrine for the rich and another for the poor, in order to keep the doors of preferment open for themselves. Such, at least, was the effect of the legal establishment of Christianity; and they know but little of men and of politics who would attribute that event to other motives or causes.

In truth, the progress of real Christianity—the Christianity taught by Christ and his disciples—received its death-blow from its legal establishment by Constantine. As long as it had the enemies of human rights for its foes, it attracted to itself the friends of human rights; but the moment it became a state religion—the religion of courts and courtiers—the religion of emperors and aristocrats—the religion of ambitious priests and sanguinary soldiers—the religion, in short, of the rich and powerful,—from that moment it repelled sincere believers from all communion with the church. It either plunged them into despair for humanity, or else forced them, by their necessities and passions, to become servile and hypocritical professors of what in their hearts they despised, as being a libel upon the Redeemer and a fraud upon humanity. It was, in effect, paganism under a new name and with somewhat new forms.

Altogether the propagation of Christianity assumed a new aspect after it became the religion of the Roman empire. Pride and hypocrisy took the place of humility and zeal. Ambition, corruption, and servility entirely supplanted in the hearts of men the virtues which the Gospel had hitherto consecrated in the eyes of Christians. Not a shred of democracy, not a vestige of fraternity nor of the love of liberty and equality, could survive in a religion patronised by courts, professed by its parasites and prostitutes, made a stepping-stone for the purposes of lucre and ambition, guarded and defended by prætorian bands, and surrounded with the munificence and corruption of imperial power.

The effects of the change soon became visible and palpable to all. During the three first centuries every extension of the Christian propagandism was followed by the most beneficial social consequences. It brought rich and poor, gentle and simple, high and low, learned and unlearned, Jew and Gentile, into terms of the closest and most cordial communionship. All distinctions of wealth and talent, of rank, station, office, intellectual and personal endowments—all, all sank before the beneficent spell of a religion which declared all men equal and brothers, and which promised to all a heaven both here and hereafter, upon the sole condition of keeping its commandments and carrying into effect its precepts. In the face of such a religion, no man who believed in it could be a tyrant; no man would be a slave a moment longer than he could help. "My service," says Christ, "is perfect freedom." Thus was it understood by the Christians of the first three centuries. Under the Heaven-bred influence of the new dispensation, masters manumitted their slaves in thousands. The slaves so manumitted loved their masters to distraction, and would die rather than betray or disoblige them. The rich converts divided their substance freely with the poor; the poor as freely bestowed their services, and administered comforts to the rich, renouncing or losing all feelings of envy and distrust towards them. Everywhere collections were made amongst the brethren for distressed members—for members even of churches or congregations in far-off countries; and these collections were always superabundant, because from the heart, and inspired by a power greater than the power of pelf. In many of the primitive congregations a real equality prevailed amongst all the members—a veritable reciprocity of benefactions and sacrifices—a *bona fide* community of goods and of friendly offices.

This it was which gave such an extraordinary impulse to Christianity at its first outset:—the total absence of selfishness; the perfect sincerity of the members; their unbounded faith in their new religion and in one another; their sovereign contempt for worldly advantages obtained by trickery and fraud; and their firm belief that it needed only their example and precept to change the face of entire humanity, and assimilate the rest of the world to themselves in virtue and innate happiness. In a word, they abounded and superabounded in the three cardinal virtues—

FAITH, HOPE, AND CHARITY!

faith in their principles—a perfect hope of seeing them realised—and a charity prepared to make the most unbounded allowances for the weaknesses and follies of all who might oppose themselves to the new dispensation. No wonder, with such principles, they accomplished such marvels.

But all was changed with the change that took place under Constantine. Masters, it is true, still continued to manumit their slaves; but, alas! it was in a very different spirit, and for very different purposes from those which actuated the true or early Christians. It appears from the concurrent testimonies of the Fathers of the church, and of legal documents still extant, that vast numbers of slaves were manumitted, in the first three centuries, through the pious zeal of their masters; and that those slaves and their progeny fell into great poverty and want through the absence of any legal provision for them, to compensate for the loss of their masters' protection and support. The early Christian missionaries, who caused their liberation from slavery, never, of course, contemplated such a result. They looked to a complete renovation of society, which would dispense the blessings of creation to all God's creatures alike, according to their services and deserts. They never imagined a state of things in which *to be free* would imply *freedom only to starve.* Yet such, unfortunately, was the result they unconsciously brought about. The myriads of manumitted slaves, once deprived of their masters' homes and protection, had thenceforward no other means of providing a subsistence, but to betake themselves to one or other of the four courses indicated in our first and second chapters. They must either find work as hired labourers, or they must beg, or they must steal, or they (if females) must turn to prostitution. They must, to repeat the Guizot classification of proletarianism, become

LABOURERS, BEGGARS, THIEVES, OR PROSTITUTES

And that is just what happened. All that could find work, and were inclined to work, became labourers for hire; others took to begging; a third class became thieves and robbers; and the unfortunates of the weaker sex as naturally and as necessarily betook themselves to prostitution.

The majority of both sexes, of course, took to hired labour, when they could get it, as the safest occupation. Having no land nor capital wherewith to turn their freedom to account for their own advantage, they had no alternative but to find employers, or else die of hunger, unless they betook themselves to the other courses adverted to.

Here began that frightful system of wages-slavery, so often adverted to in the progress of this inquiry—that desolating system which has since extended itself all over the civilized world, and which has converted three-fourths of Christendom into more degraded and unhappy beings than were the ancient chattel-slaves of the pagans or the negro-slaves who were in the Southern States of the American republic.

Constantine's courtier-" Christians " and capitalists were not slow in availing thamselves of this new form of slavery. They soon discovered that it was (to them) a *cheaper* slavery than the old one. They discovered that an "independent labourer" might be made, by the fear of starvation, to do more work than a chattel-slave ever did under the fear of the lash; and with this advantage in their own favour, that he might be turned off and left to starve when there was no work for him; whereas they would have to *keep* the chattel-slave, and *keep him well* too, whether there was work for him or not.

But as we have already, in a former chapter, so largely dwelt on the comparative merits of the two kinds of slavery, it is unnecessary to repeat here the signal advantages which landlords and capitalists derive from wages-slavery in comparison with the other. At any rate, the capitalists or proprietors, under Constantine and his successors, must have been well aware of them; for we find that, instead of compelling the manumitted slaves and their progeny to return to the condition of chattel-slavery, they greatly added to their numbers by still further manumissions, only accompanying them with very stringent laws and regulations to keep them, now " independent labourers," as effectually under their thumb as when they had been nominal bondsmen.

Had the primitive Christians foreseen the terrible abuse their benevolent labours were destined to give rise to, it may be questioned whether they would not have abandoned their mission, rather than risk the superinducing of proletarianism, with all its horrors, upon the system they sought to explode—the system of chattel-slavery. It was not in order to fill the world with famishing beggars, with necessitous thieves and prostitutes, and, above all, with myriads of honest producers starving in the midst of their own productions,—it was not for such unholy purposes that the early Christians divized the *régime* of fraternity and equality; yet all the traditions that remain to us of Christian propagandism prove unmistakably that such were its effects, even before the downfall of the Roman empire, to which event it, in our opinion, in no small degree contributed.

Indeed, Rome was already overrun with paupers and fugitive slaves, and Italy with thieves and vagabonds, before Constantine found it politic to make Christianity a state religion. But, lest we might be suspected of giving scope to invention, or of indulging in idle imaginings, on a subject so fraught with interest to mankind, we shall here use the authority of a profound antiquarian to illustrate this critical period of history, when the great transition from chattel-slavery to proletarianism was effected. Let our readers fail not, in perusing it, to compare it with what we have previously laid down in respect of the condition of slaves under the old pagan system. We quote from the learned work of M. Granier de Cassagnac, entitled " Histoire des Classes Ouvrières et Bourgeoises " :—

" Things remained in this state, that is to say, the poor, still far from numerous, had no hospital or asylum in which to take refuge during the first ages of the vulgar era. The Christians dispensed alms freely and bountifully, nourishing the necessitious poor out of their substance. But they were not yet masters ; they were still a minority of the population. They could not act collectively, publicly, or in a corporate or legal capacity, but only individually and in an isolated manner, each on his own account. The pagan clergy, on the other hand, who were in possession of immense territorial estates, which proceeded partly from permanent grants or donations disbursed from the imperial treasury, and dating as far back as the age of Numa (who had originated them), and partly from innumerable inheritances and legacies which had subsequently fallen to them, never had any idea of succouring the poor, or of organizing any system of public charity; and when, towards the close of the fourth century, Symmachus addressed to Valentinian II., to Theodosius, and to Arcadius those two celebrated letters on the pagan worship which was falling into decay, in which he complains so bitterly of the emperors having confiscated the property of the priests and the vestals, St. Ambrose, in the first of his two answers to Symmachus addressed to Valentinian II., contrasts with the avarice of the pagan clergy, who kept all their riches to themselves, the self-denial of the Christian church, which possessed nothing (as St. Ambrose expresses it) but its faith, and the whole of whose goods were the property of the poor.

"However, although it is certain the number of permanent poor or professional beggars was not very numerous up to the beginning of the third century, there occurred terrible epochs when this number was fearfully augmented. It was in years of famine—in years when the harvests failed in Sicily or in Africa, or when the two corporations of shippers and bakers—one charged with superintending the importations and the other with the distribution of bread and flour—were suddenly brought to a standstill, that occurred those horrible famines from which the superior administration of modern times preserves the people of our times; it was then that all the slaves of Italy, no longer fed by their masters, were seen flocking to Rome to demand bread; but as this increase of population soon threatened Rome itself with starvation, they were expelled the city upon a given day, to go and die where they might. This was the ordinary course adopted by Roman administrations in critical times; and Symmachus, who was prefect of Rome about the year 383, wrote thus:—' We fear the total failure of provisions at Rome, even after having chased away all the stranger-population which took refuge amongst us, and which the city subsisted.'

" On their side, the Christians inveighed loudly against the burgesses of Rome for refusing to divide their superfluity with the strangers who sought relief within her walls. St. Ambrose, who makes mention of this expulsion in several parts of his works, inveighs indignantly against this want of feeling on the part of the pagans. 'Those,' says he, 'who banish the poor strangers from Rome are much to blame. It is inhuman to repulse a fellow-creature at the moment he craves succour at your hands. Brute beasts do not treat their kind so : 'tis only man that behaves so to man.' Sometimes the pagans themselves protested against the expulsion of strangers when famine threatened the towns they had fled from."

This, it will be observed, took place after the legal establishment of Christianity under Constantine. M. de Cassagnac continues :—

" For the rest, it is manifest from divers writings of the third and fourth centuries that, as soon as the charity of the early Christians became known, the poor gathered in groups around the churches. At Rome they congregated near the church of the Apostles, in the Vatican. It was there they received a diurnal distribution of alms, as may be seen (amongst other proofs) in the works of Ammian Marcellinus, and in the poem of Prudentius against Symmachus. Moreover, it seems all manner of imposition used to be committed by loose characters to surprise the compassion of the Christian bishops. Here is the way St. Ambrose expresses himself on this subject, in the second book of his treatise on the duties of ministers: —' We must fix bounds to our liberality, that it may not be abused or rendered useless. The priests, in particular, ought to be very circumspect on this head, that they may proportion their alms to the justice of the case, and not to the importunity of the claimant. Never did the greediness of beggars reach such a pitch. Able-bodied men present themselves, strolling about for the mere pleasure of vagabondizing, and who would absorb the relief due only to the veritable poor. There are some of them who feign to be in debt : let this point be strictly verified. Others declare they have been despoiled by robbers : let exact information be taken of these persons,' &c. The scandal given by these fraudulent beggars and their impositions went to such a length, that the Emperor Valentinian II. made a law, dated from Padua, in 382, expelling from Rome all who were not beggars really incapable of gaining a livelihood.

" The law of Valentinian is very curious, in so far as it contains certain data and precise details illustrative of the state of pauperism in Italy towards the close of the fourth century. We see by it, for example, that the greater part of the beggars congregated at Rome were either runaway slaves or serfs whom the culture of the fields could not supply with employment. They precipitated themselves into Rome, which was then the largest city in the world, and where, better than anywhere else, they might escape the vigilant search of their masters. . . . . Justinian re-enacts pretty nearly the same law as Valentinian—only with this difference,—that he condemns all sturdy beggars to labour on the public works.

The whole of this vast redundancy of beggars took place in the third and fourth centuries. It seems they had interpreted literally St. Jerome's character of Christians, when he calls them, in his 26th Epistle to Pammachius, the *subordinates and candidates of the poor*. The predominant historic and social fact of the fourth century is the outrageous multiplication of proletarians, and (after innumerable failures of private charity) the creation and organization of a grand system of public charity to relieve the wants of the poor, and to provide asylums for old age, for the infirm, and for deserted children. This eleemosynary system, which the lapse of time has but more largely developed, and which is still the only palliative resorted to by modern societies to cure, or rather to bandage, the wounds of civilization, thus owes its origin to Christianism.

" Seeing that antiquity, during a period of more than 4,000 years, had not emancipated so many slaves as to produce any noticeable or considerable mass of proletarians, and that in less than 400 years Christianism had so multiplied them, that regular society was, as it were, choked and perilled by them, one would be tempted to believe that Christianity made a dead set against slavery, and went to work by grand essays of systematic enfranchisement. That, however, would be an error. In general, Christianism did not meddle with the positive law : it left to Cæsar what belonged to Cæsar. St. Paul wrote to the slaves of Ephesus that the new religion made no change in their duties as slaves. Nevertheless, Christianity created, alongside the old moral world, a new moral world, into which it admitted all who volunteered to accept its conditions. It was by this attractive power that Christianism drew over to it, in succession, all the members of pagan society; and the magnificent application that it gave to its ideas of charity, fraternity, and love was the principal cause which indirectly determined so many emancipations, and which gave birth to such a host of proletarians."

CHAPTER XIV.

SERVICE OF CHRISTIANITY IN BREAKING CASTE-BONDS.

Division of Emancipated Slaves into two Classes of Proletarians—Equality and Fraternity gave the desire for Liberty—Inveteracy of Caste-Prejudice—Perversion of Christianity under Constantine—Antagonism of Wages-Slavery and Christianity.

OUR last chapter concluded with an instructive passage, translated from the work of M. Granier de Cassagnac, showing how the pure spirit of primitive Christianity had operated the manumission of slaves in such masses that the Roman empire was soon overrun with proletarians of the several conditions described. What four thousand years of paganism had not effected, to any sensible extent, was the work of less than three hundred years of Christian propagandism. But, alas! how different was the result aimed at by Christ and his successors! Those emancipations, which the early Christians had fondly hoped would bring about the reign of universal liberty and fraternity, but introduced a new form of slavery infinitely worse than the old, became, under Constantine and his successors, a curse to the emancipated, whose fatal consequences have never since ceased to be felt by three-fourths of Christendom. A few of the manumitted prospered, in the old Roman guilds or corporations, as burgesses, employers, or administrators; and a similar class, more extensive and more opulent, still obtains in our own times. But the vast majority, being without land, capital, or the patronage of masters, had to seek a precarious subsistence by casual labour, or else by theft, beggary, or prostitution. The passage from Cassagnac, quoted in the last chapter, shows how fearfully those unhappy proletarians had multiplied before the end of the fourth century. Immediately following it, there is another which bears so authoritatively upon the subject-matter of our inquiry, and which so strongly corroborates what has been advanced, in this work, on the relative merits of chattel and wages slavery, that we cannot forbear giving it a place here. We translate from pages 304 and 305 of the work referred to:—

"In pagan society few slaves desired to become free; and the reason is very simple. As slaves, they had, in their masters' homes, all the necessaries of life; they were sure of never having to suffer cold, nor hunger or thirst, and to be comfortably housed and well taken care of, in old age as well as in youth, in sickness as well as in health. As freemen ('independent labourers'!) they would have to provide not only for their own wants, but also for those of their wives and children; and this not only during the vigour of life, but also in old age and during their infirmities, without taking into the account that, poor and weak as they must necessarily be when emerging from slavery, they would have to encounter all the chances of a perpetual struggle with society—a struggle in which even the rich and the strong not unfrequently succumb."

This account of the ancient pagan slaves corresponds exactly with Mr. Edward Smith's account of the slaves he met with in the Southern States of America. The latter would not give you "thank ye" for their liberty, "feeling the protection of their masters to be an advantage," and because the "mere hirer has not the attachment for the hired that the master naturally feels for his slave."

It may be asked, then, how came the ancient pagan slave to appreciate the boon of liberty when gratuitously given to him by his Christian master? M. de Cassagnac, we think, answers the question with great force and truth. "But in the new Christian association the slave felt a new motive and attraction towards liberty. In the first place, the enfranchised Christian was not, as in pagan society, repulsed by the remorseless prejudices of caste. Without refusing to take nobility of race into account, it showed no extravagant preference for it, as paganism did. The Apostles and the early Fathers had freely extended the hand of fellowship to the enfranchised and to the lower orders in general—a race of men whom the Gentiles, that is to say, the genteel society of paganism, had, up to that time, scornfully flouted. St. Paul wrote to the Romans, that before God there is no exception of persons; and St. Gregory and St. Ambrose have filled their works with philosophical as well as Christian raillery levelled against the pride of pedigree, and the right of domination founded upon it, which was a direct onslaught upon the pagan nobility, whose principle was the tradition of power and rank according to blood. The enfranchised slaves and their offspring were always welcome amongst the Christians, to share with them every social advantage. They might pass through all the degrees of clerical ordination— become deacons, priests, bishops,—in short, leap that hitherto impassable gulf, which, under the old pagan régime, completely separated the humble from the higher ranks of society. Accordingly, the Christian slaves who became free were sure to have no moral prepossession or prejudice against them, while all religious ones were in their favour. They were certain not to be insolently scouted as of the lower orders, and also to be succoured and relieved, in case of need, as fellow-Christians. It was on this account they precipitated themselves into the régime of liberty, and that so imprudently and in such immense masses that, suddenly becoming their own masters, and responsible for their own maintenance, the vast majority were soon overtaken and overwhelmed by misery of which they had had no foresight—a misery till then unheard of—an appalling misery, the recollections of which, as handed down to us from the fourth century, present a veritable picture of horrors."

It is only those who have felt the insolence of rank and power who can appreciate the motives which impelled the slaves and the lower ranks of citizens to embrace the new Christian code of liberty in the days to which the foregoing passage refers. One more passage, illustrative of this view, we shall translate from another part of

Cassagnac's work. And, in this passage, what a true but frightful picture is presented to us of the wrongs inflicted by the self-privileged few upon the despised many—wrongs as old as the world, and yet as green in the present day as though they were but of yesterday's growth! It is a fearfully significant passage :—

"The proletarians are, then, the progeny of the ancient slave-class—of the ancient junior branches of families, given, bartered, or sold by the *fathers* of the *heroic* period—the age of gods and heroes. This great, active, terrible, poetic, and calamitous race has been marching onwards since the beginning of the world, struggling to conquer repose for itself, like Ahasuerus, and mayhap, like him, will never attain it. It has still the old malediction on its head, which dooms it to move incessantly without making progress. All it has gained from its fatigues of ages is, that Homer and Plato say to it, ' March on !—you will never reach your destination in this world ;' and that St. Paul says to it, ' You will reach it in the next world.' It marches on, then, and has been so marching for sixty centuries; covered with obscurity, opprobrium, and contempt; obtaining no credit for its virtues or talents, none for its labours, none for its sufferings. It is not accounted more beautiful for having produced an Aspasia, more illustrious for having given birth to a Phedon, more brave for having turned out a Spartacus from amid its ranks. Whatever may have been its intelligence, its patient endurance, its wisdom, its parts, it was never honoured with the title of ' sons of the gods,' like the noble race; and Plato himself, though he had felt what slavery was under King Dionysius, cast in its teeth the famed Homeric verse, in which it is told that the slave has but the half of a human soul. Singular fatality ! In vain did manumissions and enfranchisements break the chains of this doomed race. The mark of the collar is still on their necks (as with the dog in the fable) ; and one of their own caste, Horace, the son of a *freed* man, in the very golden age of antique philosophy, poesy, and civilization, threw in their face the eternal aspersion, ' Money alters not the race—changes not the blood.' Though they had gained this money by fatigues of body or fatigues of mind, by manual or by intellectual excellence,—though they had been merchants or soldiers, senators or philosophers,—still was the cry rung in their ears, ' Money alters not the race.' This malediction of race or blood was implacable. In vain had Ventidius Bassus become a consul : he was told, ' You have been a scavenger and a muleteer.' In vain had Galerius, Diocletian, Probus, Pertinax, Vitellius, Augustus himself, become emperors. Galerius was told, ' You are but an upstart ;' Diocletian, ' You have been a slave ;' Probus, ' Your father was a gardener ;' Pertinax, ' Your father was an enfranchised bondsman ;' Vitellius, ' Your father was a soap-maker ; ' and they were very near writing upon the marble statue of Augustus, ' Your grandfather was a mercer, and your father was a usurer or a money-lender.'

"If this eternal and universal reprobation of the slave and enfranchised caste did not spare the most exalted heads and the most illustrious, imagine what the wretched proletarian was to expect in his lowly, poverty-stricken, and degraded state. The gentlefolk repelled him from the family hearth; civil society made him an outcast from all its prerogatives. He was born, and he lived and he died, apart from other men. And as we are told of certain rivers which flow together in the same bed or channel without once commingling their waters, so proletarianism and gentility, enfranchised slavery and nobility, touched and elbowed each other, and even lay down in the same bed, but without ever combining or losing themselves in each other by amalgamation."

Had Christianity operated no other good in the world than breaking down the barriers of rank and pedigree—those barriers which up to Christ's advent had effectually divided the human race into two irreconcilable castes—it would have done enough to entitle it to be regarded as the most important event that had till then occurred in the world. Until that most stupid and inveterate of all prejudices, the prejudice in favour of race or blood, was effectually rooted out, no real progress could have been made by humanity. The early Christians felt this, and so did the few freed-men and proletarians of their day. The latter, ousted from the family circle and from the rights of citizenship, rejected at once from private and from public society, must naturally have yearned for some new society in which their wounded feelings might find a refuge from the barbarous pride of their fellow-men. Such a society they found in the new Christian brotherhood. Hence the ardour with which the slave and proletarian class embraced the new dispensation ; and hence its first fatal but unforeseen consequence—the myriad pauper-population which soon after overran Italy and the whole Roman empire.

But no sooner was the character of Christianity altered and debased—as it became after its legal establishment under Constantine—no sooner did the wealthy and ambitious portion of the Christians abandon their religious obligations for worldly advantages, and lose all sympathy with their poorer brethren, than the latter found themselves in a worse condition, in respect of social intercourse, than was the lot of the old slaves, their forefathers. They had then to endure the pangs of destitution, superadded to the insolence and pride of race and riches.

Before the epoch of Christianity, the only refuge society offered to the few manumitted slaves and proletarians from the withering pride of social disparagement was what Frenchmen call *communes,* or what we in England would call *municipal institutions*. All ancient history goes to show that *communes* or *municipalities,* of some kind or other, existed from a very remote period. In these communes or municipalities the progeny and descendants of slaves formed a sort of society amongst themselves, in which they were governed by their own bye-laws, according to the charters they held, or the amount of privileges conceded to them by the governments under which they found shelter. The enormous mass of proletarianism caused by Christianity necessarily enlarged and greatly altered the character of these municipal bodies: one portion of the members became in time opulent burgesses, growing rich by manufactures, commerce,

and the professions allied with them; the remainder—the vast
majority—became wages-slaves, or else fell into the other degraded
sections of proletarianism already described.

In our modern society, the pride and exclusiveness of the upstart
burgess-class towards their proletarian brethren is not less insulting
and obdurate than were the same qualities in the ancient nobles
towards the slave-class from which these burgesses are derived. If
our modern middle-classes have still to endure an occasional humili-
ation from aristocratic *morgue*—from the exclusive pretensions of
noble blood and ancestral honours—they take care to indemnify
themselves largely by similar insolence at the expense of their less
fortunate brethren, the working-classes. Indeed, were the latter to
be asked which of the two classes, the higher or the middle, they
ordinarily experience most courtesy from, they would unhesitatingly
make answer, from the higher.

Nor is this class-insolence, this two-fold pride of blood and riches,
confined to monarchical countries. It is as rife in republican
Americas as in purse-proud, aristocratic England. In Spanish
America both kinds of pride exist in full vigour; but that of caste,
or blood, is carried to such excess as must render the excluded
classes perfectly miserable all their lives. In the Free States even of
republican America a man of colour dared not sit in the same part
of a church or a theatre with the whites. Intermarriage between
the two races was regarded with horror, and with difficulty could a
clergyman be found to officiate at such a ceremony. In travelling,
the people of colour must not enter the same carriages, nor (if in
a steamboat) must they be seen in the same cabin as the whites.
The negro-class, male and female, must travel in inferior trains by
land, and sleep in inferior berths or upon deck when at sea or in
excursions up and down the rivers. At places of public amusement
they have their "coloured" seat and in the house of God their
"coloured" gallery. In New Orleans and other cities in the South
there are great numbers of coloured ladies of excellent education —
ladies highly accomplished, and possessed, too, of great wealth, who
lived in concubinage with white men, because they could not be
legally married to them. There was a distinguished American
general in the States who had several children, the offspring of such
concubinage; and, with all his influence, he could not find admission
into society for the members of his family. They and their like find
barriers everywhere opposed to them.

It is true, these are not so much distinctions of wealth and
pedigree, as distinctions of blood and race. But the principle of
exclusiveness is the same. It is the exercise of injustice by the
strong against the weak—the oppression of one class by another—
a particular form or phase of slavery, which under any and every
phase is anti-Christian and anti-human. Liberty and Christianity
do not require a black man to marry a white woman, nor *vice versâ;*
but both liberty and Christianity forbid coercive laws against such
marriages, and more especially do they repudiate and reprobate the
system of exclusiveness and unnecessary insults so universally exer-

cised by the whites against the people of colour. Had the Christianity which overthrew paganism, in the three first centuries, continued to prevail in the world, and succeeded in assimilating the laws and institutions of nations to the law of the Gospel, it is certain slavery must have long since become extinct. Christianity knows no distinction between black men and white men—between noble and peasant—between proletarian and millionaire. Wages-slavery is as incompatible with its spirit as is chattel-slavery. Were that spirit to prevail, our laws and institutions would be such that neither form of slavery could for an instant raise its head anywhere.

It is true, great efforts are being made by a certain class of *soi-disant* Christians to procure the abolition of chattel-slavery. We must, however, regard all such efforts as the fruits of folly or hypocrisy, so long as we find no efforts made by the same parties to abolish *wages-slavery*—a slavery which we have shown to be immeasurably worse for white slaves than is chattel-slavery for the blacks. If it be said that to abolish wages-slavery would be impossible, we answer, No! We shall show, before we dismiss this inquiry, that wages-slavery is wholly and solely the work of tyrannical laws which one set of men impose upon another by fraud and force, and which they have no more right to impose, nor necessity for imposing, than they have to traffic in human flesh, or the black king of Dahomey has to make war upon his neighbours that he may conquer and sell them for slaves.

As long as these infamous laws (the laws alluded to) continue to be in force, we hold it to be disgustingly absurd and even infamous to agitate the world for the abolition of chattel-slavery. If we attempt to alter the condition of slaves we should do so for their own benefit, and not for *ours*. We should do so to ameliorate their condition, and not to make it worse. The ranters of Exeter Hall have no idea of ameliorating the condition of the negroes they so yearn to "emancipate." Their whole and sole object is to "proletarianize" them for the benefit of employers and usurers. Their object is, in fact, to reduce them to the level of the Irish peasantry, or of the labourers in Dorsetshire or the weavers in Lancashire. The planters themselves did not deny that they would have preferred "independent labourers" to slaves, if they could have got them. They acknowledged that white labour would have been more profitable to them than slave-labour—even in cotton and sugar planting—if they could only have made sure of a constant supply of it when wanted. But they said the white labourer was too independent to render it safe for the planters to trust to his services in seasons of pressure, as during the time of cane-pressing, sugar-boiling, and cotton-picking. Assure him of a supply of such labour—only give him a "surplus population" of starving proletarians to be ever ready at his hand, like so many sheep in a crib, and you will make him an abolitionist at once. And why? Because wages-slavery would be then cheaper and better for him than chattel-slavery. On no other principle would he emancipate them. Upon no other principle did any emancipations ever take place in the world, save in the three first ages of Christianity. And no sooner did the pagan masters and hypocritical *Christians* discover, under Constantine, that more work could be got out of "free" proletarians than out of chattel-slaves, and that the former *need not* while the latter *must be* kept, than they, too, became abolitionists upon the same principle.

CHAPTER XV.

FORM OF SLAVERY UNDER MODERN CIVILIZATION.

Persistence of Chattel-Slavery in Eastern Countries—Assumption of Form of Wages-Slavery under Modern Civilization—Creation of Millionaire Capitalists by Present System—Result in Ruin and Starvation of the Labouring Class—Necessity of Repressive Armies and Police—Measures necessary to secure Social Reform.

HAVING seen how human slavery originated in parental despotism—how it expanded by war, commerce, indebtedness, marriage, &c.—how it continued to be *direct* or *chattel* slavery all over the world till the advent of Christianity—how it, in consequence of the workings of the Gospel, gradually assumed the form of *wages*-slavery, and generated modern proletarianism throughout Western Europe and America—having also seen how the system of chattel-slavery *worked* in the ancient world and in the slave-states of America, and compared, or rather contrasted, that system with its more hideous successor, wages-slavery—let us now inquire what are the forms and conditions of human slavery as it exists under modern civilization, and by what means and appliances it may be effectually and for ever banished from the world.

As already stated, direct or chattel slavery is still the normal condition of the labouring classes in most Eastern countries, and of the black population in South America. In Russia and other countries a species of serfdom, until quite recently, obtained, which partook of the nature of both chattel and wages slavery, but which was probably, on the whole, less objectionable than either. The serfs of such countries correspond with our *villains* of the Anglo-Saxon and Norman times, and are clearly a remnant of the old feudal system which grew up in most parts of Europe upon the dissolution of the Roman empire. Wherever this serfdom prevails, proletarianism is confined to the cities and towns, the serfs being, like chattel-slaves, provided for out of the lands to which they are attached.

In the principal states of Europe and America, in our colonies generally, and indeed in most modern countries called " civilized," wages-slavery is the normal condition of the labouring classes. This latter kind of slavery is, *cæteris paribus*, more or less intensely severe according to the degree of perfection to which civilization is carried. Thus, in our United Kingdom, which is accounted the most civilized country in the world, wages-slavery is attended with greater hardships, and subject to more privations and casualties, than anywhere else. Nowhere else do we find employment so precarious ; nowhere else such multitudes of people overworked at one time and totally destitute of employment at other times ; nowhere else do we see such masses of the population subsisting upon pittances wholly inadequate to sustain human beings in health and strength ; nowhere else do we find jails and workhouses so overcrowded ; nowhere else do we hear of whole districts depopulated by famine, nor of upwards of 1,500,000 out of eight millions of people being cut off by actual starvation and forced expatriation in the course of twelve months, as has happened in Ireland in our own times. All this, too, we find to be contemporaneous and in juxtaposition with granaries, warehouses, and shops teeming with a superabundance of the choicest produce of all climes—with cries of over-production and glutted markets ringing in our ears wherever we pass—and with the most opulent and numerous aristocracy, territorial and commercial, that was ever known to be congregated in any country of seven times the extent— to say nothing of a still more numerous middle-class, in whose ranks may be found some thousands far surpassing German counts or German princes in command of wealth and luxury. Hence, no doubt, it was that Sir Robert Peel, not many years since, accounted in Parliament for our distress by assuring the House that "the occasional distress and destitution of great numbers of people was a necessary consequence of our advanced civilization, and was there- fore a thing naturally to be expected in such a country as England."

We remember, some years ago, when an address was presented to this same Sir Robert Peel by some 6,000 or 7,000 of the merchants, bankers, shipowners, &c., of the City of London, to console him for his temporary expulsion from office by the Whigs,—we remember how the *Times* (which was then *ratting* from the Whigs) boasted, by way of demonstrating the respectability of the addressers, that the list contained the names of 1,500 citizens whose aggregate wealth would suffice to redeem the National Debt, and still leave enough to support the owners in opulence. We remember having seen it stated, about the same period, in a City article of the said *Times*, that so prosperous was trade that ironmasters in Staffordshire and Wales were known to have realised £200,000 in one year. We remember hearing, on the best authority, of the house of Baring & Co. clearing £650,000 by the speculations of a single year. We know a banker died, a few years since, in Liverpool whose estate was com- puted at from £5,000,000 to £7,000,000. Peel's father is said to have died worth £3,000,000; and old Arkwright worth twice that much. Soames, the late shipowner, was worth several millions. Rentals varying from £20,000 to upwards of £200,000 a year are numerous in England. The Duke of Westminster's property will, it is said, be now worth half-a-million per annum of income. London, Liverpool, Manchester, Leeds, and other towns abound in millionaires worth from a *plum* to twenty, thirty, and even fifty *plums*. A year's rental of some of our dukes would pay the wages of some 20,000 Irish labourers for a whole twelvemonth, at sixpence per day each, which is more than thousands of them can earn by a hard day's work. A single bargain on the Stock Exchange will realise, for a Rothschild, a Baring, a Gurney, or a Goldsmid, more than 30,000 needlewomen in London could possibly earn in two

H

years at present wages.   Were a few of our great landowners and
millionaire capitalists so inclined, they might, by clubbing together,
keep an army of 100,000 fighting men about them, whose maintenance, at their present wages, would actually not be missed out of
their enormous revenues.   At £15 per man, the annual cost would
be only a million and a half, which, divided amongst Sir Robert
Peel's 1,500 city addressers, would weigh less heavily upon them
than a penny a week subscription upon a poor Chartist weaver.

And while this monstrous hell-begotten opulence stares us in the
face wherever we go, what find we to be the condition of the men to
whom we owe the very bread we eat, and without whom England
would be a howling wilderness, namely, the agricultural labourers?
We find them, in order to escape death from starvation, driven to
the very brink of rebellion, as may be collected from paragraphs like
the following, which may be seen in almost every agricultural
journal we may chance to take up.   We quote from a Wiltshire
paper :—

"RIOTS IN THE AGRICULTURAL DISTRICTS.—The farm-labourers
of the district round West Lavington, Devizes, have been resisting
an attempt to reduce wages from seven to six shillings a week, by
forcibly stopping farm operations.   The men having got a hint of
the contemplated reduction, a number of them waited upon the
steward of Lord Churchill, the owner of the principal farms, with a
view of inducing him to intercede in their behalf.   This led to no
beneficial results ; and the men finding that their masters were
determined on reduction, about a hundred and fifty of them assembled
in front of the house of a Mr. Spencer, and stopped men, horses, and
agricultural implements that were proceeding to work by that road.
Having persuaded other labourers to join them, they went round to
all the farms and completely stopped all operations.   They took
horses from ploughs, opened sheep-pens, and prevented all labour
being proceeded with.   On the following day some of them returned
to work ; but warrants being issued for the ringleaders, more than a
hundred men formed themselves into a band and paraded the streets,
armed with staves.   The assistance of the constabulary was then
obtained, and something like order restored.   The next day a man
named Kite was taken before the magistrates and committed to
prison.   He had not been long in custody before a large body of his
fellow-labourers, armed with sticks, came into the town for the purpose of rescuing him, but were deterred by the presence of a strong
military detachment."

Here we find soldiers and policemen (whose keep costs for each
man more than double the labourer's pay) employed to force
Englishmen to choose between starvation and toiling all the week
round for six shillings.   Supposing these unfortunate labourers to
work every day in the year (Sundays excepted), their wages, at six
shillings a week, would be just £15 12s. for the whole year!   Here
is a sum wherewith to keep a wife and, mayhap, five or six young
children !   Mr. Edward Smith has told us how common it is to see
nigger-slaves in America making and spending from 50 to 150 dollars

per annum by the labour of their leisure hours—that is to say, exclusive of the maintenance provided for them by their masters in exchange for their regular work. Take the mean—100 dollars. This, at 4s. 2d. per dollar, is just £20 16s. 8d. If he saves or spends 150 dollars, it is upwards of £30. Here, then, we find a nigger-bondsman so far superior in condition to the free-born Englishman, that he can actually afford to throw away upon luxuries (by the earnings of his leisure hours) one-third more than, or even double, the entire sum that a Wiltshire labourer is paid for the whole of his time, though he drudge all the year round, and is never sick a single day. If facts like these do not make the blood of Englishmen rush to their cheeks, and the very cravenest of them take the field for their social rights, they are past redemption.

Sir Robert Peel calls all this "civilization;" and the House of Commons cried, "Hear, hear," and cheered and supported him, when he declared that the remedy for such a state of things lay not within the compass of legislation; that Parliament depended, itself, upon the people, and not the people on Parliament; and that the only and proper remedy for the distressed classes was for them "to take their affairs into their own hands"! Well, in the foregoing paragraph from the Devizes newspaper, we see them essay to take their affairs into their own hands; and we see also, that no sooner do they attempt to do so—no sooner do they proceed to act upon Sir Robert's advice—than soldiers and police are brought down upon them, and warrants issued for their apprehension. If this be not the perfection of human slavery, as well as the perfection of inhumanity and injustice, we really know not what is.

But is it true that no Parliamentary cure is findable for the disease? —that the evil is one beyond the reach of legislative control?—that, after all, the boasted "omnipotence of Parliament" (which, Blackstone tells us, can do anything and everything not naturally impossible)—is it true that this boasted omnipotence cannot secure for an Englishman the food he has raised, the bread he has earned—nay, doubly, trebly, quintuply, decuply earned? Is this true? No, no; a thousand times no! What Parliament has done, it can undo; what Parliament ought to do, and can do, it ought to be made to do, or else to abdicate. There is not a member in either House of Parliament that does not know, as well as we know, that our *land* and *money* laws are at the bottom of all the distress in the country, and that the repeal of bad laws, and the enactment of good ones, are all that is wanted to make England a paradise. There is not a member in either House that does not know that all the slavery in the world, or that has ever been in the world, is, or has been, the work of landlords and money-lords; and that, consequently, the only true and proper way to put an end to slavery is to make laws to deprive landlords and money-lords of the power to enslave and rob their fellow-creatures. If it be said, this cannot be done without interfering with the rights of private property, we answer emphatically that it is laws against robbery, and not against property, that are wanted. We assert emphatically (because we know we can prove satisfactorily) that the repeal of unjust laws, and the enactment of a few just and salutary ones, upon Land, Credit, and Equitable Exchange (the latter including Currency), is all that is needed to terminate poverty and slavery for ever; and that it is perfectly within the compass of Parliament to enact such laws without violating the rights of private property, or confiscating to the value of one shilling of any man's estate, or otherwise dealing with it than in the legitimate way of taxation and commutation, which the laws of all countries recognise and practise, and none more than our own.

But, before going a step further in this inquiry, we beg to submit here the following resolutions which were proposed to a crowded public meeting by the author of this work, and carried by acclamation without a single dissentient, although the meeting was composed of reformers and philanthropists of all shades and sects :—

" This meeting is of opinion that in addition to a full, fair, and free representation of the whole people in the Commons House of Parliament, upon principles the same, or similar to those laid down in the People's Charter, the following measures, some of a provisional, the others of a permanent nature, are necessary to ensure real political and social justice to the oppressed and suffering population of the United Kingdom, and to protect society from violent revolutionary changes :—

" 1. A repeal of our present wasteful and degrading system of poor-laws, and a substitution of a just and efficient poor-law (based upon the original Act of Elizabeth), which would centralise the rates, and dispense them equitably and economically for the beneficial employment and relief of the destitute poor ; the rates to be levied only upon the owners of every description of realized property ; the employment to be of a healthy, useful, and reproductive kind, so as to render the poor self-sustaining and self-respecting. Till such employment be procured the relief of the poor to be, in all cases, promptly and liberally administered as a right, and not grudgingly doled out as a boon ; the relief not to be accompanied with obduracy, insult, imprisonment in the workhouses, separation of married couples, the breaking up of families, or any such other harsh and degrading conditions as, under the present system, convert relief into punishment, and treat the unhappy applicant rather as a convicted criminal than as (what he really is) the victim of an unjust and vitiated state of society.

" 2. In order to lighten the pressure of rates, and at the same time gradually to diminish, and finally to absorb, the growing mass of pauperism and surplus population, it is the duty of the Government to appropriate its present surplus revenue, and the proceeds of national or public property, to the purchasing of lands, and the location thereon of the unemployed poor. The rents accruing from these lands to be applied to further purchases of land, till all who desired to occupy land, either as individual holders or industrial communities, might be enabled to do so. A general law, empowering parishes to raise loans upon the security of their rates, would greatly facilitate and expedite the operation of Government towards this desirable end.

"3. Pending the operations of these measures, it is desirable to mitigate the burdens of taxation and of public and private indebtedness upon all classes who suffer thereby,—the more especially as these burdens have been vastly aggravated by the recent monetary and free trade measures of Sir Robert Peel. To this end, the Public Debt and all private indebtedness affected by the fall of prices should be equitably adjusted in favour of the debtor and productive classes, and the charges of Government should be reduced upon a scale corresponding with the general fall of prices and of wages. And, as what is improperly called the National Debt has been admitted, in both Houses of Parliament, to be in the nature of a *bona fide* mortgage upon the realised property of the country, it is but strict justice that the owners of this property, and they only, should be henceforward held responsible for both capital and interest. At all events, the industrious classes should not be held answerable for it, seeing that the debt was not borrowed by them, nor for them, nor with their consent, and that even had it been so, they have had no assets left them for the payment of it. Moreover, the realised property of this country, being estimated at eight times the amount of the debt, the owners or mortgagers have no valid excuse or plea to offer on the score of inability, for refusing to meet the claims of their mortgagees.

"4. The gradual resumption by the State (on the acknowledged principles of equitable compensation to existing holders or their heirs) of its ancient, undoubted, inalienable dominion and sole proprietorship over all lands, mines, turbaries, fisheries, &c., of the United Kingdom and our Colonies; the same to be held by the State, as trustees in perpetuity for the entire people, and rented out to them in such quantities and on such terms as the law and local circumstances shall determine;—because the land, being the gift of the Creator to ALL, can never become the exclusive property of individuals; because the monopoly of the land in private hands is a palpable invasion of the rights of the excluded parties, rendering them more or less the slaves of landlords and capitalists, and tending to circumscribe or annul their other rights and liberties; because a monopoly of the earth by a portion of mankind is no more justifiable than would be the monopoly of air, light, heat, or water; and because the rental of land (which justly belongs to the whole people) would form a national fund adequate to defray all charges of the public service, execute all needful public works, and educate the population, without the necessity for any taxation.

"5. That, as it is the recognised duty of the State to support all those of its subjects who from incapacity or misfortune are unable to procure their own subsistence, and as the nationalization of landed property would open up new sources of occupation for the now surplus industry of the people (a surplus which is daily augmented by the accumulation of machinery in the hands of the capitalists), the same principle which now sanctions a public provision for the destitute poor should be extended to the providing a sound system of National Credit, through which any man might (under certain conditions) procure an advance from the national funds arising out of the proceeds of public property, and thereby be enabled to rent and cultivate land on his own account, instead of being subjected, as now, to the injustice and tyranny of wages-slavery (through which capitalists and profitmongers are enabled to defraud him of his fair recompense), or being induced to become a hired slaughterer of his fellow-creatures at the bidding of godless diplomatists, enabling them to foment and prosecute international wars, and trample on popular rights, for the exclusive advantage of aristocratic and 'vested interests.' The same privilege of obtaining a share of the national credit to be applicable to the requirements of individuals, companies, and communities in all other branches of useful industry, as well as in agriculture.

"6. That the National Currency should be based on real, consumable wealth, or on the *bona fide* credit of the State, and not upon the variable and uncertain amount of scarce metals; because a currency depending on such a basis, however suitable in past times, or as a measure of value in present international commerce, has now become, by the increase of population and wealth, wholly inadequate to perform the functions of equitably representing and distributing that wealth; thereby rendering all commodities liable to perpetual fluctuation in price, as those metals happen to be more or less plentiful in any country; increasing to an enormous extent the evils inherent in usury and in the banking and funding systems (in support of which a legitimate function of the law—the PROTECTION of property—is distorted into an instrument for the CREATION of property to a large amount for the benefit of a small portion of society belonging to what are called vested interests); because, from its liability to become locally or nationally scarce or in excess, that equilibrium which should be maintained between the production and consumption of wealth is destroyed; because, being of intrinsic value itself, it fosters a vicious trade in money and a ruinous practice of commercial gambling and speculation; and, finally, because, under the present system of society, it has become confessedly the 'root of all evil,' and the main support of that unholy worship of Mammon which now so extensively prevails, to the supplanting of all true religion, natural and revealed.

"7. That in order to facilitate the transfer of property or service, and the mutual interchange of wealth among the people, to equalize the demand and supply of commodities, to encourage consumption as well as production, and to render it as easy to sell as to buy, it is an important duty of the State to institute, in every town and city, public marts or stores for the reception of all kinds of exchangeable goods, to be valued by disinterested officers appointed for the purpose, either upon a corn or a labour standard ; the depositors to receive symbolic notes representing the value of their deposits, such notes to be made legal currency throughout the country, enabling their owners to draw from the public stores to an equivalent amount, thereby gradually displacing the present reckless system of competitive trading and shopkeeping—a system which, however necessary or unavoidable in the past, now produces a monstrous amount of evil, by maintaining a large class living on the profits made by the mere sale of goods, on the demoralizing principle of buying cheap and selling dear, totally regardless of the ulterior effects of that policy upon society at large and the true interests of humanity.

"It is not assumed that the foregoing propositions comprise all the reforms needed in society. Doubtless there are many other reforms required besides those alluded to; doubtless we want a sound system of national education for youth, made compulsory upon all parents and guardians; doubtless we require a far less expensive system of military and naval defence than now obtains; doubtless we require the expropriation of railways, canals, bridges, docks, gas-works, water-works, &c.; and doubtless we require a juster and more humane code of civil and penal law than we now possess. But these and all other needful reforms will be easy of accomplishment when those comprised in the foregoing propositions shall have been effected. Without these, indeed, justice cannot be done to humanity; society cannot be placed in the true path of improvement, never again to be turned aside or thrown back; nor can those natural checks and counter-checks be instituted without which the conflicting passions and propensities of man fail to produce a harmonious whole, but with which, as in the material world, all things are made to work together for good, reconciling man to his position in the universe, and exalting his hopes of future destiny."

We shall treat the subject of these propositions in the following chapters; and meanwhile the reader will please observe that similar resolutions have also received the sanction of numerous meetings, large and small, throughout the country.

CHAPTER XVI.

REFORMS AS MUCH NEEDED IN AMERICA AND IN COLONIES AS IN EUROPE.

Answer to question, "How is Human Slavery to go out?"—Insufficiency of mere Political Freedom—Accessibility of Public Lands in new Countries their chief Advantage—Inadequacy of Universal Suffrage without a Knowledge of Social Rights—America falling into same Abyss as Europe.

BEFORE resuming the subject of the foregoing propositions, we pray the reader to bear in mind, that we are now arrived at that all-important branch of our inquiry which proposes to answer the question, "How is human slavery to be made to go out of the world?" To have shown how it came in,—how it was propagated,—the varied phases it has assumed, and the hideous, wide-spread proletarianism to which the conversion of *chattel*-slavery into *wages*-slavery has given rise,—to have shown all this, without at the same time essaying to show how the fell monster is to be eradicated from the face of the earth, would be a mere idle literary dissertation—a contemptible parade of erudition, without object, without end. A higher purpose will, we trust, be found to have dictated this inquiry. An earnest, heartfelt desire to contribute our quota towards rescuing humanity from oppression and sorrow is the motive we lay claim to. This motive it is which impelled us, on the part of the National Reform League, to propose the resolutions embodied in the last chapter. In those resolutions we profess to answer the question, "How is human slavery to be made to go out of the world?" It is true, their immediate application is intended only for our own country; but they are equally applicable to France, Germany, and every other "civilized" country—America itself not excepted. America is comparatively free from most of the political anomalies and exclusive privileges which disgrace Europe, and degrade the vast numerical majority of its people. There are no crowned heads there; there is no State Church. Some of the States have public debts, but they are comparatively light, and, for the most part, in course of easy liquidation. Moreover, there is no titled aristocracy claiming, by hereditary right, to legislate for or govern any of the States. In this respect, men of all grades and conditions are equally eligible for office, and for places of trust, honour, and emolument. Universal suffrage may be said to be the general rule, and property qualifications the exception, for the election of members of the legislature and officers of government. Treason works no corruption of blood in America. There is no law of primogeniture or entail; there is no religion established and maintained by law, and consequently no legal bars to religious freedom. Taxation is, generally speaking, equal, uniform, and direct. It was, before the civil war, comparatively light, too; and when otherwise, the remedy lies with the people themselves; for, as restrictions upon the suffrage by property and tax-qualifications exist but in some few of the States (and in these are not very onerous or stringent), the basis of representation may, for all practical purposes, be considered *numerical*, and not territorial or financial. Add to these advantages the fact that the old common law of 'England is the common law of America; and that where any departure from it is made by statute, it is invariably in a democratic sense. Thus, in Texas and other States, for instance, that part of the old common law which considers a married woman as dead in law is abrogated by statute in favour of the gentle sex, and so as to give her more power than she possesses under the civil law. Thus, any property possessed by her before marriage remains at her sole disposal after marriage, as also any property she may become entitled to during coverture. She may receive from and give to her husband a deed of conveyance whilst under coverture. And any deed of conveyance made by the husband requires for its full validity the joint signature of the wife. In some of the States, too, the homestead can never be taken in execution of debt; and, at the moment we write, a powerful movement is going on throughout the States to secure a similar exemption of the homestead through-out the entire Union. These and other privileges—the result of her political constitution—America fully enjoys. No European state can compare with her in these respects—not even Norway or Switzerland. In a word, America is already possessed of every political amelioration contended for by the old Radicals of this country, or by the financial or mere middle-class reformers of the present day. Indeed, to assimilate us to America is their *summum bonum*—the *ne plus ultra* of their reforming aspirations.

Far be it from us to undervalue the political rights secured to the Americans by their general and State constitutions. Nevertheless, we unhesitatingly affirm that the foregoing propositions are no less necessary for the extinction of slavery in America than in England, France, or any other European country. ⊱

Our position is this : It is the land and money laws of a country that must ever mainly determine the social condition of its people. ✻ In other words, without just agrarian and commercial laws—laws that shall establish for all classes equal rights in the soil and equal advantages from the use of money and credit (so as to secure equit-able exchange in trade)—no country can be prosperous, be its form of government what it may. Now, in these respects America has but little to boast of over England, France, or any other European country. If she does not exhibit the wide-spread distress that these countries exhibit, she owes it not so much to the superiority of her political institutions (for of these she has as yet but little availed herself), as she does to her unbounded resources (in the extent and fertility of her soil), and to the comparative exemption she enjoys from public and private indebtedness owing to her being a new country. But for these causes—but for the facility with which un-appropriated land may be had, and but for the fewness of her territorial and commercial aristocracy as compared with those of older countries—her citizens would very soon exhibit the same hideous extremes of rich and poor as are to be found in Europe. Indeed, New York and some of the New England States (where most of the land is appropriated, and the population crowded) have already, on more than one occasion, exhibited all the worst features of British " civilization "—that is to say, wholesale squalor and destitution (with their necessary consequences) in close proximity to teeming granaries and warehouses ; otherwise, an unemployed labouring population, in rags and hunger, within sight of merchant-princes and master-manufacturers worth some hundreds of thousands of dollars each.

And why should it be otherwise ?   The social system is the same there as here.   Rents are higher in New York, Boston, Philadelphia, &c., than in London, Edinburgh, and Dublin.   Competition is the same or worse.   Wages-slavery is as rife in Massachusets, Pennsylvania, and New York as in any part of the British Isles ; and if wages be not quite as low in Philadelphia and Lowell as they are in Manchester and Birmingham, it is partly owing to the high protective duties laid on foreign manufactures, partly to the comparative scarcity of hands, but chiefly to the facility with which the victims of competition can escape from the mills and factories to the backwoods of Indiana, Missouri, &c.

In other words, the Americans owe whatever advantage they have over us not to any superiority in their *social* institutions,—not to better agrarian and commercial laws,—nor even to the acknowledged superiority of their civil and religious system of polity,—but to the territorial and other local advantages to which we have referred, and which no more distinguish them than they do the people of Sydney, Adelaide, Port Phillip, Natal, New Zealand, or any other new country in which land is abundant and labour scarce.   But let America (with her present social system) come to be peopled as England is,—let her now unappropriated land be made private property of, and her agrarian and commercial laws remain what they are,—and we venture to say that not one jot better off will her labouring population be than ours now is.   Universal suffrage might stem the aristocratic tide for a season (as it has done in other new countries); but the men of land and money would sweep away universal suffrage there, as they have ever done elsewhere, the moment they found it incompatible with landlordism and usury.   All the principal States of Europe had universal suffrage a few years ago; France alone possesses it now, and that with a tenure so insecure that it can hardly be said to be established.   In all the other States the men of land and money destroyed universal suffrage by brute force; they dispersed diets and national assemblies at the point of the bayonet, and made rights and constitutions to disappear before the cannon of disciplined assassins.   It may be the same in France before six months. It would have been the same long ere now, but that some two millions of *social* reformers were known to be ready to take advantage of the event, in order to wreak vengeance upon the landed and commercial villains who have defrauded them out of the fruits of three revolutions purchased with torrents of blood.

In truth, universal suffrage is no guarantee at all for liberty, unless it be accompanied, on the part of the working classes, with a knowledge of their social rights, and a consequent determination to use political power for their establishment. The Romans, the Spartans and Athenians, the Sicilians, and many other ancient peoples had universal suffrage—at least, a vote for every citizen who was not a helot or a bondsman; but it proved of no use to them, for want of knowing their social rights. For the like reason, the Irish made no good use of their forty-shilling freehold vote, when they had it; and, for the same reason, they offered no resistance when it was taken away. The French people had universal suffrage in 1793. Their Convention of that period was elected by universal suffrage; and the constitution it made was far more democratic than the French constitution of 1848. But, not understanding their social rights then so well as they do now, they suffered their landlords and money-lords to rob them of it, just as the old Romans, Athenians, &c., had allowed *their* land and money lords to do in their day. After the Convention had succeeded, with the aid of the Parisian shopocracy, in murdering Robespierre and in striking terror into all who, like him, loved justice and the people, they not only abolished the democratic constitution of 1793 and put a middle-class constitution in its place, but they actually decreed that they (the Convention members) should constitute *two-thirds* of the next Legislative Assembly, and that the nation should be at liberty to choose only the remaining third! Strange to say, too, the people submitted to this, as to every other abomination of the times; they submitted because the great mass of them were too profoundly ignorant of their social rights to take much interest in the franchise question. It ever was so, it ever will be so, with a people ignorant of their social rights: they will never risk life or limb in defence of their *political* till they comprehend their *social* rights.

In America there is less danger than anywhere else of the people losing their political rights. This is owing partly to the greater equality in property which subsists there, but chiefly to the agitation of *social* questions which has been forced upon the working classes of late years by the continuous arrival of European emigrants competing with them in the labour-market, and alarming them, by their example, as to what might prove their own fate hereafter, should they suffer a powerful territorial and commercial aristocracy to grow up amongst them. Hence the springing up of the "Free Soil" and "National Reform" movements in the United States; hence an attempt to radicalize the constitution of Rhode Island; hence the numerous publications which denounced the sale of the public lands—especially to foreigners and companies; hence the hatred of national debts—especially if they arise out of foreign loans—and the determination of the working-classes to repudiate them; and hence, above all, the cheering fact, so well deserving of our notice, that every new revision of an American constitution—whether it be that of a State or of the entire Union—is invariably distinguished by an increase of strength or latitude given to the democratic principle. This is particularly observable in the new States, where the settlers, consisting in great part of exiles forced from Europe by poverty and tyranny, have carried out with them an intense hatred of the systems they fled from, and therefore take all the democratic precautions they can to keep down the aristocratic leaven.

But not even America herself, we predict, will escape the *régime* of Europe, unless she reform her social institutions while she is yet young and healthy. Her agrarian laws are not a jot better than those of France or England ; and her commercial spirit is even more ravenous and unscrupulous. In one respect she is worse than either. We allude to her preference of metallic money to symbolic money ; which is a result of the fraudulent paper-systems she has so often smarted under. There is no subject upon which the American working-classes are so lamentably at fault as the subject of money. They fancy that an honest paper-system is impossible, because they have been so often cheated by the worthless rags of fraudulent usurers ; and in this suicidal delusion the bullionists and usurers take good care to confirm them. Next to their want of sound views upon the Land question, this delusion as to the real nature and proper functions of Money is the greatest foe to American progress. On the subject of *Credit*—that most potent of all levers of modern production—the same ignorance prevails in America as here and in France. In truth, were it not that universal suffrage is the fundamental law in France and America, while it is scouted in England, we should be at a loss to know what advantages the French and Americans possess over us, so deplorably similar are the three countries in respect of social rights.

But we shall better comprehend these matters when we come to analyze the propositions of the National Reform League, and to test their value by showing their equal applicability to, and desirability for, all three countries,—indeed, for all civilized countries under the sun.

CHAPTER XVII.

RELIEF TO UNEMPLOYED OR DESTITUTE A RIGHT, NOT A CHARITY.

Inability of a People ignorant of Social Rights to choose Representatives—Duties of a wise Democracy—Omnipotency of a Knowledge of Social Rights—Facility of Application of Social Reforms—Exposition of the three Provisional Measures necessary.

WE have stated, in a former chapter, that the repeal of unjust laws, and the enactment of a few just and salutary ones, upon Land, Credit, and Equitable Exchange (the latter including Currency), are all that is wanted to terminate poverty and slavery for ever; and that nothing is easier than for Parliament to enact such laws without infringing the rights of private property, without confiscating to the value of a shilling of any man's estate, or otherwise dealing with property than in the legitimate way of taxation and commutation which the laws of all countries recognise and practise, and none more so than our own.

The resolutions which we have before cited show clearly how it may be done. An honest Parliament is of course presupposed; for, without an honest legislature to begin with, reform is all moonshine. The first article of the League's creed is, therefore, a full, free, and fair representation of the whole people. To that end it demands the enactment of the " People's Charter "—not because it regards the Charter's plan of representation as perfect, but because that plan is sufficiently so for all practical purposes, and because, having already received the sanction of millions of the population, it would be unwise and mischievous to risk dividing the people by the pro-pounding of any fresh scheme, the more especially as any defects in the " Charter " may be easily enough remedied hereafter by a parliament or convention elected upon Chartist principles.

But although the " People's Charter" is a *sine quâ non* with the League, it is, after all, but a machinery for providing the means to an *end*. The *means* is parliamentary reform; the *end* is social reform, or a reformation of society through the operation of just and humane laws. The " Charter," in fact, but aims at restoring to the people the undoubted right of self-government—the right of making the laws according to which, and to which only, they are to be ruled. It leaves to the people themselves to do all the rest. It gives them the power to elect what sort of representatives they choose, and to exact from them what pledges they like in the way of social and political reform. With the people themselves, however, it must ultimately rest whether even the " People's Charter " shall give them veritable political and social rights.

If they know how to choose their legislators, and are resolute to enforce the law, they will have both. But if, from ignorance, corruption, or other causes, they know not how to make a proper choice, they will but have escaped Scylla to fall into Charybdis, and, mayhap, make bad worse. The very men they elect to save them may prove their direst enemies. These, with the aid (out of doors) of the ignorant and depraved of all classes, may accomplish the ruin of their best friends, and then (as the French Convention did, after murdering Robespierre) destroy universal suffrage itself, under pretence that it had led to nothing but folly, blood, and crime. These are no imaginary suppositions. We are but supposing for England, and the present time, what has heretofore occurred in most other countries and in all times under similar circumstances. A people ignorant of their true political and social rights will never elect a Parliament of real political and social reformers ; they will only elect declaiming demagogues and crafty adventurers, who will promise everything and perform nothing,—who, professing to be doing everything for the people, will, in reality, do nothing for them but make them stepping-stones to their own aggrandisement, and who, as usual, beginning with frightening the aristocracies of land and money, will end with compromising and going shares with them for the public spoil, after establishing a reign of terror over the people for their own conjoint security. How easily might we demonstrate this by à priori reasoning, were it necessary. The history of all past revolutions, however, dispenses with any such necessity. Indeed, the bare fact that universal suffrage is nowhere to be found now-a-days amongst those ancient states and communities where it formerly flourished is proof sufficient. A truly intelligent people would ever remain a self-governing people. A people fully conscious of the value of their political and social rights could never lose the franchise. In the first place, they would so use it as to remove or prevent the growth of those unnatural interests and institutes which are incompatible with its free exercise and permanent security. In the next place, they would use it to establish the social rights of the people upon a basis as broad as the population itself. And, lastly, they would so know how to appreciate the blessings of self-government, from a consciousness that they owed their liberties and happiness to no other source, that they would fight like lions, and die to a man, rather than surrender their franchises. Such a people might be exterminated ; it could not be enslaved or disfranchised. Xerxes, with his innumerable hordes, was not a match for a few thousand Greeks inspired with the love of freedom. A Persian army could not force the pass of Thermopylæ against three hundred freemen under Leonidas, till treachery leagued with numbers for his overthrow ; and even then the handful of freemen had to be exterminated, because they could not be taken alive, nor subdued to slavery. We have a still more striking example of this in the present day. Of all the European States that enjoyed universal suffrage a few years ago, France is now the only one in which it survives. And why? Because France is the only one of them in which a large proportion of the working-classes are imbued with a knowledge of their *social* rights, and consequently the only one in which the working people are determined to maintain the right of self-government by fire and sword, if necessary. In Prussia, Austria, and in most of the German and Italian States the mass of the people had heard little or nothing of their *social* rights, and consequently attached too little value to them to fight for them, or for the political power through which alone they could be securely established. Hence their comparative non-resistance to the overthrow of their respective constitutions. It is otherwise in France. There, at least two millions out of eight millions of adult males understand so well the value of their political and social rights that Louis Napoleon and his *bourgeoisie* dared not overthrow universal suffrage by their *coup d'état*. The upper and middle classes hate universal suffrage quite as much in France as their feudal and money-grubbing brethren hate it in England, Germany, and Italy. Nevertheless, they dared not strike the blow, lest it should recoil fatally upon themselves. There are full two millions of *social* democrats in France who are resolved to set the whole country in flames, and, if needs be, perish in the conflagration, rather than suffer a traitorous conspiracy of landlords and money-lords to put down their constitution by force. It is in the stern determination of these two millions that rests the sole real security for universal suffrage in France. The number of these social democrats increases, too, every day with the spread of knowledge, and with their greater experience of the baseness and perfidy of the commercial villains who seek to eject them from the constitution, and at whose instigations the present government is continually persecuting their party, and seeking to goad it into premature insurrection in order to create an occasion for establishing a pitiless military despotism. With the increase of social democracy, increases the security for universal suffrage. Every Social Democrat is essentially a freeman in heart and soul, in conviction and sentiment. Such men will fight when slaves would not. They were the freemen of Athens and Sparta that overthrew the hordes of Xerxes. Had the helots and bondsmen been sent against them, they would have succumbed to the barbarians, even as they had to their own masters. The helots of Sparta and the bondsmen of Athens knew nothing of *political* and still less of *social* rights. Hence did they all die, as they had lived, bondsmen and slaves. For the same reason did the chattel-slaves of the ancient world live and die in bondage for forty centuries before the Christian era. For the same reason the serfs and *villains* of the middle ages suffered themselves to be *adscripti glebæ*, and quietly transferred from lord to lord as estates changed hands, just the same as the other live stock on the lands. For the same reason, and no other, were the modern serfs of Russia, Poland, &c., no better off than their predecessors of mediæval times; and precisely for the self-same reason are the wages-slaves of modern "civilization" so tractable under a system which, for real though disguised savagery, throws Oriental barbarism and chattel-slavery completely into the shade.

Impressed with these convictions, the National Reform League sees no hope for the successful establishment of the "Charter," and for the permanent enjoyment of its legitimate fruits, but in the diffusion, amongst the people at large, of sound political and social knowledge. Real *political* they believe to be inseparable from real *social* power, and the converse. To make the people appreciate universal suffrage, we must teach them what they lose by the want of it, and what they may fairly expect from a wise and legitimate use of it. In answer to Sir Robert Peel and the House of Commons, we repudiate their doctrine that legislation is not responsible for the sufferings of the people; and the terms of our repudiation are made good in the seven resolutions or propositions of the League.

What is, then, demanded in those seven propositions that is not within the easy compass of a few acts of Parliament? What is there in them incompatible with the acknowledged rights of individuals or with the public peace or public security? In what respect can they endanger, ever so remotely, life, liberty, property, religion, family, home, or any other thing held sacred amongst men? On the contrary, do they not go to secure all these with stronger guarantees than they can ever derive from coercive laws or from the corruption of public opinion?

The "People's Charter," unaccompanied by the social reforms we demand, might possibly prove a danger for all classes, through the poor, in their ignorance, demanding what they had no right to, and through the rich, in their selfishness, refusing everything to an enfranchised people armed with power to take more than their own. But we challenge the world to prove that the "Charter," accompanied with the social reforms we ask, could be a danger or an injustice to any class, or that it could fail to work out the complete emancipation of the whole people, politically, socially, morally, and intellectually.

What are the social reforms we demand? They may be classed under two heads. The three first propositions demand reforms of a provisional kind, to meet temporary evils. The remaining four are of a permanent kind, to cure permanent evils. Resolution I. is as follows:—

"A repeal of our present wasteful and degrading system of poor-laws, and a substitution of a just and efficient poor-law (based upon the original Act of Elizabeth), which would centralize the rates, and dispense them equitably and economically for the beneficial employment and relief of the destitute poor. The rates to be levied only upon the owners of every description of realized property. The employment to be of a healthy, useful, and reproductive kind, so as to render the poor self-sustaining and self-respecting. Till such employment be procured, the relief of the poor to be, in all cases, promptly and liberally administered as a right, and not grudgingly doled out as a boon; the relief not to be accompanied with obduracy, insult, imprisonment in the workhouses, separation of married couples, the breaking up of families, or any such other harsh and degrading conditions as, under the present system, convert relief into punishment, and treat the unhappy applicant rather as a convicted criminal than as (what he really is) the victim of an unjust and vitiated state of society."

What is there unjust or impracticable in this proposition? Who ought, by right, to support the poor? Clearly, those who have most profited by their labour, and whose enormous revenues (derived from the aggregate labour of the people every year, without yielding any equivalent) are the main cause of so many labourers falling into pauperism. And who are these? Clearly, the owners of *realised* property,—the owners of lands, houses, mines, collieries, turbaries, fisheries, docks, wharfs, canals, bank-stock, railway-shares, consols, and every other description of property yielding an annual income independently of any labour or service or risk on the part of the proprietor. It is not upon mechanics, tradesmen, or professional men who have but their own exertions to trust to for a living, and who may or may not be worth a groat, that the burden should fall. These parties are supposed to render to society an equivalent for what they get, and consequently ought not to be made responsible for keeping others whose poverty they have not caused. At all events, it will be time enough to tax them when they have realised something by their respective callings. But as the others render to society no equivalent for their incomes, as their incomes are purely and wholly the *creation of law*, and not of their own labour or services, and as they are therefore the parties who *make* the poor, both common sense and common justice demand that they should be made to *keep* the poor, or at least enable the poor to keep themselves by remunerative labour. Moreover, it was upon these classes, and these only, that the original Act of Queen Elizabeth contemplated the levies should fall. The 43rd Elizabeth extended the rate to every other description of *realised* property, as well as mere *real* property; but owing to the comparatively small amount of *realised* property (other than what falls within the legal description of *real*) which existed in Elizabeth's time, and for 150 years after, and owing to the difficulty of ascertaining it for assessment purposes, it escaped its due share of the burden; and, indeed, until about eight years ago most people fancied that it was *real* property only, and not *realised*, that was contemplated in the original Act. The enormous strides, however, that other descriptions of *realised* property (besides lands and houses) have made of late years have opened people's eyes to the true intent and purport of the Act; and hence moneymongers, scrip-holders and annuitants must no longer expect to escape and throw their burden upon shopkeepers, mechanics, and needy professionals.

In truth, it is not their interest to do so, unless they choose to risk their all for the sake of a beggarly saving of a few pounds a year, which they, of all others, ought least to begrudge the poor, their especial victims. As to centralizing the rate, the selfish conduct of landed proprietors and others has made such a step almost inevitable. By preventing the building of cottages on their respective estates in town and country, and by working the law of settlement to their own selfish ends so as as to debar the poor from having

I

any legal claim in their respective townships, they have so effectually overcrowded some parishes with paupers, to spare their own, that nothing but a centralised rate (to be dispensed according to the number of claimants in each) can now restore justice as between parish and parish and union and union.   But let those who may entertain any doubt as to the expediency or necessity of centralization but read Mr. Hutchinson's admirable work on the subject, and we think they will at once admit that such an arrangement ought no longer to be deferred.

As to the liberal and kindly treatment we demand for the unemployed and destitute poor, it is no more than a fraction of their right.   If they had *justice* done them they would need no *charity*, and, till justice is done them, we demand that their treatment shall be what our resolution describes, and that it shall be considered their *right*, and not grudgingly doled out as a boon.

Thus far for Resolution No. 1.   In the following chapter we shall show cause for Resolution No. 2.

CHAPTER XVIII.

GRADUAL RESUMPTION OF PUBLIC LANDS BY THE STATE.

Necessity of Agrarian Reform—Crown Lands, Church Lands, and Corporation Lands to be immediately resumed, and their Rent applied to the relief of Taxation—The Rich have no right to meddle with them—Needed, by the exploited Millions, as a Fulcrum to raise them from the Earth.

THE first three resolutions of the National Reform League affirm (as already observed) only provisional or temporary measures to redress temporary grievances. They apply to pauperism, public and private indebtedness, and to onerous and unequal taxation, which, though great and oppressive evils, are nevertheless but natural and inevitable consequences of the gigantic social wrongs they emanate from, and which are grappled with in the four last resolutions. But for radically bad agrarian and commercial laws, there would be no pauperism, no overwhelming public and private debt, no oppressive and unequal taxation. It is these laws that are at the bottom of all the mischief; it is these laws that have produced the pauperism, the indebtedness, the taxation, and that would produce them again were they extinguished this hour. Therefore, to have a permanent cure of our social evils we must radically reform our agrarian and commercial systems. Resolutions 4, 5, 6, and 7 show how this may be done. But, meanwhile, the evil consequences of our agrarian and commercial systems cannot brook delay: they must be dealt with provisionally and summarily before the permanent remedy can be applied. Paupers cannot be left to starve, debtors to be overwhelmed with usury and law expenses, and struggling millions to be ground down with oppressive rates and taxes, while our agrarian and commercial systems are being reformed by the slow operation of the measures suggested in Resolutions 4, 5, 6, and 7. These several classes must have speedy relief; else relief will come too late. The effect of Peel's monetary and free-trade measures in aggravating the burdens of debts and taxes while it diminishes the means of meeting them, and in multiplying paupers while it impoverishes ratepayers, renders it absolutely necessary to deal speedily and summarily with the evils of pauperism, indebtedness, and taxation. Hence the three first resolutions of the League. By perusing them attentively, the reader will find that they, at one and the same time, go to mitigate the evils of pauperism, indebtedness, and taxation by just and efficient provisional measures, and to prepare the way for those larger and permanent measures by which Resolutions 4, 5, 6, and 7 seek to extirpate social evil altogether.

In the preceding chapter we have shown cause for Resolution No. 1; we now proceed to show cause for Resolution No. 2, which is as follows :—

" In order to lighten the pressure of rates; and, at the same time, gradually to diminish, and finally to absorb, the growing mass of pauperism and surplus population, it is the duty of the Government to appropriate its present surplus revenue, and the proceeds of national or public property, to the purchasing of lands, and the location thereon of the unemployed poor. The rents accruing from these lands to be applied to further purchases of land, till all who desired to occupy land, either as individual holders or industrial communities, might be enabled to do so. A general law, empowering parishes to raise loans upon the security of their rates, would greatly facilitate and expedite the operation of Government towards this desirable end."

If it be but an act of justice to paupers and ratepayers that the rates should be levied and dispensed as Resolution No. 1 suggests; it is no less an act of justice to both that the rates should be expended in the most beneficial manner for all parties, and finally dispensed with altogether when no longer necessary. Resolution No. 2 has this end in view. It asks the government and ratepayers to use the *public* money in the most advantageous way for the *public*. It does not ask them to take money from one class to give to another, nor to relieve the pauperism *that is* at the risk of what may be elsewhere. All surplus revenue in the hands of government is clearly public property : it is raised from the whole body of the public. The proceeds of crown lands, corporation lands, church lands, and various other descriptions of public property are also clearly amenable to public uses, without infringing the rights of private property or vested interests. The seven or eight millions of rates raised annually for the relief of the poor are also *public* property,—only with this important distinction, that being a legal substitute for the share which the poor formerly enjoyed of the tithes and other ecclesiastical revenues, their destination for the poor has *equity* as well as *law* for its sanction. The celebrated William Cobbett estimated that, if everything that was titheable formerly were titheable now (that is, if lay-impropriators had not converted to their own use the " great tithes," and if they had not also taken possession of the abbey-lands at the time of the Reformation), the poor's share of the tithes, &c., would be now upwards of ten millions sterling per annum. For this, which was their ancient patrimony, the present poor's rate is but a substitute. Surely, then, it is not asking too much for the poor to ask that the eight millions arising from this rate should be appropriated to the best advantage for them.

And how could it be better appropriated than by purchasing land, whereon to employ them productively, and locate them in comfortable habitations ? At present their lives are a burden to themselves and others. Upon the land they would enjoy independence and happiness—the natural result of their own industry and thrift. After the first year or two they would be able to subsist themselves in comfort. The rents paid by them would, in the first instance, go to liquidate the loans contracted on the credit of the rates ; and, these discharged, they would be afterwards available for the purchase of other lands as they came into the market. Thus paupers and ratepayers would be both benefited,—the former made independent, the latter relieved permanently from a grievous and growing burden on their respective parishes. Then, as to the surplus revenue and the proceeds of public property, to what better use could the public possibly apply them than to the location of the industrious poor on the land? Talk of repealing the duty on bricks! talk of a sinking fund to reduce the National Debt!—no sensible man has any faith in these schemes. Every such man knows that no reduction of taxes can possibly benefit those who cannot command employment, or an adequate remuneration for it when they have it. Every such man knows, too, that as long as landlords and capitalists can create what "surplus population" they like, by keeping the people from cultivating land *on their own account*, there can be no security either for regular employment or adequate wages. Farmers and manufacturers will employ only those they want—those they can make a profit by. The rest will be left to the union bastile or to starvation. But let the surplus revenue and the proceeds of public property be applied in the way we speak of, and, from that moment, the surplus population diminishes with every fresh location on the land; the food of the country is increased in amount and cheapened in price; employment and wages are augmented for the unlocated; and a new and never-failing home market is created for the benefit of all, through the conversion of unemployed paupers (half-starved upon workhouse diet) into substantial husbandmen able to give agricultural produce in exchange for manufactures. There is a vast deal of public property in this country, a portion, at least, of whose proceeds a universal-suffrage parliament would be sure to employ in this way. There are the crown lands; there is still a good deal of unenclosed common (though not less than 6,000,000 acres have been filched from the people during the reigns of the 2nd and 3rd Georges); there are the lands belonging to the church, the universities and the colleges; there are the tithes, too; there is a deal of property in the hands of corporate bodies, and attached to various educational and eleemosynary establishments, and most of these endowments have been altogether perverted from their original destinations.

A universal-suffrage parliament would secure to the poor their full share of benefit accruing from the revenues of all this property. What belongs to the whole public ought to be applied for the advantage of the whole public; and it is only a majority of the whole public that is competent to decide how corporate bodies elected upon property qualifications have a right to dispose of property which equitably belongs to the non-electors as much as to the burgesses having votes. The same remark applies to schools, charities, and other endowments, the original founders of which intended them principally for the benefit of the poor. The crown lands do not belong to the higher or middle classes, more than they do to the working-classes or to the paupers in our union workhouses. Yet the aristocracy and their retainers alone derive any benefit from them. The lands and revenues of the church are *public* property.

A parliament which represents only a fraction of the public has no right to appropriate these lands and revenues to the Established Church, or to any church, if the vast majority of the population desire they should be differently applied. And who can doubt that such majority is totally averse to their present appropriation? Many, like ourselves, might not like to dispossess the present incumbents. But why should not their revenues, as they die off, revert to the public for public uses, and their successors be left (like the ministers of other churches, and like all other professional men) to their own congregations and their own resources? Suppose this had been done twenty or thirty years ago—the revenues of bishopricks and livings, as the incumbents died off, thrown into a common fund for the purchase of lands, and the rents of these lands again applied in the same way—what a goodly slice of the soil, and what a goodly revenue, would be now in the hands of the public! And who would be wronged by such appropriation? Clearly not the then clergy, for the reform would not have taken effect till after their death. Clearly not their present successors; for these would have no legal title to a property which the public and the law had chosen to appropriate otherwise. Indeed, the majority of them— the poor curates—would have been even benefited by the change; for, if left to the voluntary principle, their congregations would provide better for them than does the present Establishment. At all events, they could not be said to have lost what they never had; and even if they fared worse than they do now, they could not blame the public for having " done what it liked with its own." What was not done twenty or thirty years ago ought to be done now: the public should now insist that church property and every other description of property belonging to the public, should be henceforward devoted only to such public uses as a majority of the public may sanction. Any other application of it is robbery. A parliament has no more right to rob the public for the benefit of individuals, than it has to rob individuals for the benefit of the public. This is their own maxim, and they should be held to it.

The proceeds of public property and the poor's rate would, if honestly applied, be amply sufficient to locate the unemployed poor upon the land. Estates are every day coming into the market for sale. To the owners it matters not a straw who buys their lands, so long as the full price is paid for it. They are willing to sell, and the public are willing to buy. The funds wherewith to buy are the surplus revenue, the proceeds of public property, and some £8,000,000 of poor's rate. Assuredly, here is ample means of restoring their own to the people, without robbing anybody. All that is wanted is an honest parliament to legalize the work.

If it be said that such application of public property would benefit the poor only, and be an injustice to the rich, the answer is that the lands so purchased would not be the property of the poor, but the property of the whole nation—rich and poor; and that, inasmuch as the rents accruing therefrom would be applicable to public uses only, the whole public, and not the poor alone, would have the benefit in the remission of rates and taxes. The only disadvantage the rich would suffer from such reform is that it would gradually emancipate industry from their iron grasp. Now that disadvantage is its best recommendation. The rich *may* have a right to use their own *private* property as they like (though with respect to *land* they have no such right), but they can have no right to use the *public* property otherwise than as a majority of the public may decide—much less to use it for the enslavement and degradation of the great majority.

As to the present parliament doing anything like what is here recommended, it would be madness to expect it. A parliament which represents only those who thrive by labour's wrongs will never recognise labour's rights, nor legislate for labour's emancipation. Such a parliament will never apply public property otherwise than to the injury and enslavement of the industrial classes. If it had a surplus of twenty millions, these classes would not derive a shilling benefit from it. Indeed, not even the distressed portion of the middle classes can command its sympathies where aristocratic interests stand in the way: of this we have a remarkable instance in the result of a motion for the repeal of the window-tax—the tax on air and light. At the same time there was an opportunity of saving about a million a year by calling home the African anti-slavery squadron. But no; the precious House would neither repeal the tax on air and light nor disband the anti-slavery armament. Everybody is now aware that this blockading squadron on the Gold Coast was the veriest humbug that ever provoked derision.

In the next chapter we shall treat of the 3rd Resolution. We are on the eve of great changes, and nothing but a clear understanding by the people of their social rights can enable them to profit by what may occur.

CHAPTER XIX.

NATIONAL DEBT A MORTGAGE ON REALISED PROPERTY.

Necessity for Adjustment of Public and Private Debts—Their overwhelming
Burden must result in Civil War—Third Resolution the only Remedy—
Opinion of Cobbett—Enormous Increase of Debt through Improvements in
Manufactures—Only just Claims of Public and Private Creditors.

RESOLUTION No. 3 of the League proposes an equitable settlement
of questions of grave moment—of questions which will ere long be
settled by force out of doors, unless Parliament adjusts them within
by fair legislation.   It is to the following effect :—

"Pending the operation of these measures, it is desirable to
mitigate the burdens of taxation and of public and private indebtedness upon all classes who suffer thereby—the more especially as these
burdens have been vastly aggravated by the recent monetary and
free-trade measures of Sir Robert Peel.   To this end, the Public
Debt and all private indebtedness affected by the fall of prices should
be equitably adjusted in favour of the debtor and productive classes,
and the charges of government should be reduced upon a scale
corresponding with the general fall of prices and of wages.   And as
what is improperly called the National Debt has been admitted, in
both Houses of Parliament, to be in the nature of a *bonâ fide* mortgage upon the realised property of the country, it is but strict justice
that the owners of this property, and they only, should be henceforward held responsible for both capital and interest.   At all events,
the industrious classes should not be held answerable for it, seeing
the debt was not borrowed by them, nor for them, nor with their consent ; and that, even had it been so, they have had no assets left
them for the payment of it.   Moreover, the realised property of this
country being estimated at eight times the amount of the debt, the
owners or mortgagers have no valid excuse or plea to offer, on the
score of inability, for refusing to meet the claims of the mortgagees."

The questions here dealt with are those which, in all probability,
are destined to involve England in the great European revolution.
If not adjusted somehow in an early session of parliament, we predict they will cause a civil war between the agriculturists and the
town "interests"—between the men of acres and the fund and
money lords.   And should that war ensue, it will merge into a general
social war of classes, in the progress of which all will be losers, but
the final issue of which will be the extinction of "vested interests"
and the proscription of all who would maintain them.   Resolution
No. 3 is intended to avert such a catastrophe for the sake of all
parties.   Let us see if we are just in our demands.

The Public Debt is estimated, in round numbers, at £800,000,000.

The private indebtedness of the country is calculated at more than three times the amount of the Public Debt—say £2,500,000,000. The interest of the Public Debt is at least £30,000,000 per annum, including the expenses of collection. The annual interest of private debts is believed to exceed £100,000,000. Here is a fearful deduction to be made from the aggregate earnings of the people every year, before a shilling can be set aside for wages or profits. This mass of £130,000,000 per annum is all sheer usury—a sheer plundering of the productive classes. Yet it is only a part, and by no means the major part, of the annual sacrifice entailed upon the industrious orders by our agrarian and commercial systems. There is acknowledged to be upwards of £700,000,000 of property insured with our several insurance companies, who of course receive premiums on the whole, varying in the per-centage charged, according to the nature of the property insured, but amounting in the aggregate to an enormous annual sum. This sum, like the interest of the public and private debts, must be provided for every year before wages and profits can begin. Then there is the unmortgaged portion of the incomes derived from lands and houses. Then there is the public and private taxation of the country (not included in the £30,000,000 set aside for the payment of the interest of the debt). There are the tithes; the losses accruing from bad debts; the revenues of railway companies, canal companies, water companies, gas companies, dock companies, mining companies, banking companies, cemetery companies, and countless other companies; the whole of which must be deducted from the annual production of the country before the mechanic and labourer can receive a farthing of wages, or before the mere employer and tradesman can enter upon that margin to which wages and profits must look for their share of the general produce. If we assume our present annual production to be £630,000,000, one-third of this, or some £200,000,000, must be set aside for the interest of public and private debts, the revenues of companies, the claims of taxation, &c. The capitalists and tradespeople may be supposed to pocket some £300,000,000 more, and the miserable remnant, some £130,000,000 per annum, is probably the *maximum* of what the working-classes receive for producing the whole. At all events, the latter do not average above 10s. per week for each family; and supposing the number of working families to be about 5,000,000, this would give them a gross income of about £130,000,000 per annum.

We pretend not to perfect accuracy in these figures: we profess to deal only with round numbers. An approximation to the actual state of things is all we aim at; for that is all we require to elucidate our position. But if we deviate from arithmetical exactness (as must needs be in such calculations), the deviation will be found to be rather *in favour* of the producer than against him; and therefore our argument must be held so much the stronger, the less exact we are in figures.

That the producer does not, upon the average, receive a fourth of his produce is a certain fact. If the producers got back £125,000,000 out of a gross annual produce of £600,000,000 and odd, it is the very extreme of their good fortune. Some of them, we know, get far more than in this proportion—more than a fourth or than a third,—nay, mayhap one-half. But the majority, on the other hand, get less than a fourth; and millions of them less than a sixth or even an eighth of their produce. An Irish labourer or a London needlewoman does not, probably, receive a tithe of the value of their labour. Estimating in this way—striking a balance between all the various descriptions of producers—we do not understate their income when we average it at 10s. per week for each family, or at from £125,000,000 to £130,000,000 for the whole, out of a gross annual production of, say, from £600,000,000 to £630,000,000 sterling. Small as is this proportion allotted to the producer out of his own earnings, it is becoming smaller and smaller every year, as prices and wages decline under the operation of Peel's monetary and free-trade measures. The reason is obvious. To make money scarce, on the one hand, and to invite foreign competition on the other, must of necessity lower prices. Whatever lowers prices swells the burden of debts, taxes, and of all other fixed money obligations. In the same ratio it must reduce the aggregate of profits and wages; for the more the producers (employers and employed) have to give out of the common stock to pay taxes and the interest of public and private debts, the less there must be left for themselves.

Peel's monetary laws of 1819 and 1844-45 have made money scarce, and will keep it permanently so while they remain in force. His free-trade measures of 1846 go to aggravate competition in our home markets, and tend directly to the lowering of prices and wages in favour of the mere annuitant or idle consumer. The effect of both measures, conjointly, is to increase the pressure of debt and taxes to a degree that is already felt to be unbearable. If persevered in, the inevitable result is revolution—violent revolution. Under the conjoint effects of his measures, wheat has already gone down below 40s,—nay, as low as 36s. Bankruptcies have reached an appalling figure; and estates are rapidly changing hands (passing from mortgagors to mortgagees), and not a few of them are going out of cultivation altogether. The Encumbered Estates Commission was sitting hardly three months in Dublin before one-twelfth of the landed property of Ireland, measured by rental, came within its jurisdiction. Scores of Scotch landlords and hundreds of Irish are no longer able to pay interest on their mortgages, owing to the reduced prices of agricultural produce. For the same reason, farmers cannot pay rents, nor the interest of borrowed capital. In England they are universally reducing, or threatening to reduce, wages. In Ireland they are throwing up their farms, or falling into arrears with their rent. In Scotland the same may be said. In all three countries the poor labourers are ground down so low that lower they can hardly be. Hence the agricultural risings and incendiarisms in England; hence the midnight outrages and murders in Ireland; hence the unprecedented tide of emigration from all three countries. No farmer can possibly pay rent, taxes, tithes, and interest of capital with wheat below 40s. No landlord, having his estates encumbered, can make head against his liabilities with existing prices. No labourer can have any other prospect before him but starvation and crime under such a system. To have to pay some £200,000,000 a year (out of £600,000,000) to usurers and tax-eaters would be a dire enough infliction even with wheat at 60s. and all other commodities at proportionally high prices. But to be saddled with such a liability in the face of wheat at 36s., and of the like downward progress of prices and wages in every other department of industry, is what the country cannot bear. No country on earth could stand it: England will not stand it. A furious civil war—a downright revolution—must, we repeat, be the inevitable consequence of perseverance in such a system.

Our third resolution offers the only just and feasible way of averting such revolution. We cannot restore corn-laws; we cannot go back to Protection: it is too late for that. The country has no more sympathy with the landlords than it has with the money-mongers. It wants not to bolster up one interest at the expense of the other, but to compel both to adjust their conflicting claims without robbing the public. If parliament will insist upon "keeping faith with the public creditor," let it do so at the expense of the parties properly liable. Let the owners of *realised* property be the only parties responsible for the "National" Debt. Sir Robert Peel and Lord Brougham declared, amid the cheers of both Houses, that this debt is a *bonâ fide* mortgage upon the whole realised property of the country. Very well. Let the mortgagors, then, be made to do as all other mortgagors do;—let them either redeem the mortgage (as they may do), or pay the interest till they do. And if they will not pay interest or capital, let the mortgage be foreclosed, and their estates sequestered. This is but common sense and common justice. It is only the most shameless and hardened dishonesty that could saddle such a liability upon the non-propertied classes, seeing they never borrowed the money, had no advantage from its expenditure, and have had no assets left them wherewith to pay that or any other debt. Speaking of this monstrous injustice—the injustice of taxing the working-classes for the interest of this debt—the late Mr. Cobbett indignantly asked, " What would be said of a law that should compel the children to pay the debts of the father, he having left them nothing wherewith to pay?—of a law that should make the children work all the days of their lives to clear off the score run up by a profligate and drunken father?—of a law which should say to the father, ' Spend away; run in debt; keep on borrowing; close your eyes in the midst of drunkenness and gluttony; imitate the frequenters of Bellamy's all your life; and your children and children's children shall be slaves to pay Bellamy and others, with whom you have run up the score?' Would not the makers of such a law be held in everlasting execration? And in what respect does this case differ from that of a prodigal and borrowing nation which would make its working-classes responsible for debts they had no share in borrowing or spending?"

There is no getting over this. Cobbett's reasoning is the reasoning of every just and honest man who knows anything of the subject. The case is even stronger than he puts it. The bulk of the debt was contracted to force unjust taxation on the American colonies and to force back Bourbon royalty upon France. These are the very last objects upon which the working-classes would expend money or incur liabilities. It is, in fact, making them pay for crime and murder, as well as for their own impoverishment and enslavement!

These views, we rejoice to say, are making way in all quarters, high and low. Mr. Isaac Buchanan (formerly President of the Boards of Trade of Toronto and Hamilton in Canada, and who represented the metropolis of Upper Canada in the Canadian parliament) has boldly demanded that all connection shall cease between the National Debt and her Majesty's Exchequer, in a pamphlet issued by him, entitled " The Moral Consequences of Sir Robert Peel's Unprincipled and Fatal Course," &c. The same view is taken by the democrats of Ireland, and has been successfully pro mulgated at sundry Chartist meetings in town and country. By-and-by it will be the creed of all classes, as well as of the Chartists and National Reform League.

But while we insist that the owners of realised property shall be held solely responsible for the National Debt, we assert that justice to them demands that the debt be equitably adjusted for them before they are called upon to liquidate it. Peel's monetary and free-trade measures have more than doubled the debt. We say nothing of the £27,000,000 which our " reformed " parliament has added of late years to the debt; let that pass. We speak of the change made in the value of money by the Act of 1819, restoring cash payments; and of the complete revolution in prices effected by the tariff and corn-law repeal. These measures have more than doubled the value of the pound sterling, and more than trebled the original value of Consols. For example, the average price paid for £100 stock in the 3 per Cents. during the war was £60 of depreciated bank paper, worth then only £40 in silver. The holder of that stock is now entitled to receive ninety-seven sovereigns for it. Every individual pound of the £60, at the time it was lent, would only buy one-fourth of a quarter of wheat. Every pound paid back now will buy more than half a quarter—more than twice as much. It will buy more than three times as much of London or Birmingham goods, and more than four or five times as much of Manchester and Glasgow goods. Here, then, we have the value of the pound more than doubled, on the one hand; and, on the other, we find the fundholder entitled to receive £97 for every £60 he lent in rags! Combine these two alterations : mark their conjoint effect in favour of the public creditor. Observe the difference to him of going into market with ninety-seven sovereigns wherewith to buy wheat at less than 40s. and going with only sixty rags to buy wheat at upwards of 80s. (the average price during the war, when he lent his money) ; and then bear in mind that what is clear gain to him is so much clear loss to us, the taxpayers. The difference is, in fact, so much downright plunder taken from the industrious and given to the idle and useless.

Not even at the expense of the owners of realised property are the fundholders entitled to any such advantage. They are entitled to their own (to receive it from the proper parties, the borrowers), but they have no just claim for more than their own. What was borrowed should be paid back, and no more. Peel's measures give them thrice their own, while they work in an opposite direction against land and labour. Let there be a fair adjustment, then. Let the £800,000,000 of capital be reduced according to the change in the value of money and the fall in prices, and let the owners of every description of property be made to pay their equitable share of the adjusted burden; but on no account let another shilling of taxes be raised on account of the debt. No doubt the Chartists will have an eye to this when their day comes; and it is coming fast.

Private obligations affected by Peel's measures should be adjusted upon the same principle as the public debt. Not to do so is to rob one class to enrich another: to persevere in such a course is to invite convulsion. Law is intended to *protect* property for all; not to *create* property for any. To pervert it from this, its legitimate function, into an instrument of rapine for the injury and ruin of those it should shield is to arm the nation against the law. This is the very effect Peel's measures are now producing. Hence the necessity for a timely adjustment. The Act of 1819 ought to have provided against any such necessity; and when he introduced his free-trade measures in 1846, he ought to have made provision in his Acts that all public and private liabilities, involving fixed money payments, should be dischargeable only upon a reduced scale to be calculated upon the general fall of prices. Upon this principle all mortgages, leases, contracts, &c., would be open to easy readjustment, and the whole of our taxation might be reduced upon a scale corresponding with the fall of prices, without any necessity for a fresh enactment on the subject. If prices fell *one-third*, upon the average, all salaries, pensions, &c., would be reduced one-third; and the same in respect of public and private debts, mortgages, leases, &c. As it is, we see no remedy for the mischief but what is pointed out in our third resolution. We said so before Peel's measure became law; and some of the ablest and most experienced men in the kingdom have since publicly expressed a similar opinion.

But enough on the *provisional* or *palliative* measures that are needful ere the four resolutions, embodied in the succeeding chapters, shall have had time to operate a full reform of our present iniquitous agrarian and commercial laws and institutions.

CHAPTER XX.

NATIONAL LANDS AND CREDIT FOR THE USE OF THE PEOPLE.

Unjust Laws to enable the Few to deprive the Working Class of their Earnings—. Private Property in Land the Basis of Wages-Slavery—Raw Materials of Wealth belong to all—Land and Money Lords govern the World—Right of Working Class to the Use of Credit—Surplus of Earnings of Working Class beyond Consumption the Source of all Capital.

To provide a full, adequate, and permanent remedy for the manifold and all-pervading ills that are the consequence of land-monopoly and usury, the people must reclaim their right to the National Territory, which has been gradually and surreptitiously usurped by private and sinister interests ; the enactment of laws to secure for all, co-ordinately therewith, the mighty engine of Credit, which must be utilized for the industrious orders of society, who are the strength and mainstay of the nation, and therefore the most entitled to its benefits.

The fourth and fifth resolutions of the League run as follows:—

" The gradual resumption by the State (on the acknowledged principle of equitable compensation to existing holders or their heirs) of its ancient, undoubted, inalienable dominion and sole proprietorship over all the lands, mines, turbaries, fisheries, &c., of the United Kingdom and our Colonies, the same to be held by the State, as trustee in perpetuity for the entire people, and rented out to them in such quantities as the law and local circumstances may determine ; because the land, being the gift of the Creator to ALL, can never become the exclusive property of individuals ; because the monopoly of the land in private hands is a palpable invasion of the rights of the excluded parties, rendering them, more or less, the slaves of landlords and capitalists, and tending to circumscribe or annul their other rights and liberties ; because a monopoly of the earth by a portion of mankind is no more justifiable than would be the monopoly of the air, light, heat, or water ; and because the rental of the land (which justly belongs to the whole people) would form a national fund adequate to defray all charges of the public service, execute all needful public works, and educate the population, without the necessity of any taxation.

" That as it is the recognised duty of the State to support all those of its subjects who, from incapacity or misfortune, are unable to procure their own subsistence—and as the nationalisation of landed property would open up new sources of occupation for the now surplus industry of the people (a surplus which is daily augmented by the accumulation of machinery in the hands of the capitalists)— the same principle which now sanctions a public provision for the destitute poor should be extended to providing a sound system of National Credit, through which any man might, under certain conditions, procure an advance from the national funds arising out of the proceeds of public property, and thereby be enabled to rent and cultivate land on his own account, instead of being subjected, as now, to the injustice and tyranny of wages-slavery (through which capitalists and profitmongers are enabled to defraud him of his fair recompense), or being induced to become a hired slaughterer of his fellow-creatures at the bidding of godless diplomatists, enabling them to foment and prosecute international wars, and trample on popular rights, for the exclusive advantage of aristocratic and ' vested interests.' The same privilege of obtaining a share in the national credit to be applicable to the requirements of individuals, companies, and communities in all other branches of useful industry, as well as in agriculture."

What is it that creates poverty—the mother of slavery, ignorance, and misery—but unjust laws, by which the many are robbed for the benefit of the few? A poverty-stricken people can never be a free, a happy, a religious, or an educated people. No reform that will not give the people the means of acquiring property by honest industry—which will not enable them to be independent of wages-slavery—which will not enable them to live in houses of their own, and allow them free access to the soil of their country, is worth their serious attention.

We defy all the genius and statesmanship in the world to save a population from being the slaves of middle-class vampires so long as land is private property. We defy all the learning and ability in the United Kingdom to show me how we can be extricated from poverty and premature death in this country without a radical reform of our land and money laws. It is assumed that land, mines, rivers, &c., are fit and proper subjects of private property, like bales of cloth, pottery wares, or any other product of man's skill and industry; and that, accordingly, the works of God's creation may be bought and sold in the market, the same as if they were the works of human hands. This is a principle so utterly abhorrent to common sense and reason—it is, on the face of it, so gross a perversion of natural justice, that the rights of property cannot possibly be reconciled with it, nor coexist a moment in presence of it. Once allow the soil of a country, which God made for all its inhabitants, and for all generations born upon it, to be bought up, or otherwise monopolized or usurped by any particular section of any one generation (be that section large or small), and that moment your community is divided into tyrants and slaves—into knaves who will work for nobody, and into drudges who will have to work for anybody or everybody but themselves. No subsequent legislation—no possible tinkering or patchwork in the way of remedial measures—can sensibly affect a system based upon so hideous a foundation. You may talk of forms of government, or of reforms of parliament; but we hesitate not to say that no reform of parliament, no reconstruction of the government, can be of the slightest avail towards amelioration whilst that glaring and gigantic injustice constitutes the basis of private property; and for this simple reason, because the rights of labour and the rights of property, which ought to be really one and the same, are utterly irreconcilable under such a system. As long therefore as it shall prevail, so long must the rich be insecure, and the mass miserable, whatever may be the form of government, from monarchy to democracy the most pure and unlimited.

No man, not a fool or a knave, will deny that the *raw materials* of all wealth belong to all men alike in their natural state : to assert the contrary, would be to assert that God, like a capricious human despot, dispenses His favours regardless of justice or of the wants of His creatures. The only question is this—Can the lands, mines, turbaries, collieries, fisheries, &c., containing all materials of wealth in every country, be restored to its inhabitants without injustice or undue suffering to the present possessors, whoever they may be? If this could not be done, there might be some excuse for the present monstrous system. But no government need have the least difficulty on this point. Our own government, for instance, has only to do, in respect of landed property, for the benefit of the nation, what it does every day to promote the speculative interests of individuals and private companies. Owners of real estate are compellable now, by existing laws, to exchange such property for a money-compensation when the public interest requires such change. Does anybody consider that a wrong is done to the owners of such property so long as the money-compensation to them is sufficient to satisfy the public conscience represented by a sheriff's jury ? Now, if it be right to do this for the sake of a company or a few speculating individuals, how much more justifiable is it to do it for the just benefit of millions, and to produce thereby such a reformation, materially and morally, as no pen nor tongue could adequately describe ? Indeed, in order to restore its land gradually to the nation, it would not be necessary to go so far in expropriation or forcible dispossession as existing laws authorise in favour of companies chartered by parliament to make railways, canals, docks, barracks, or any other public works. There would be no need to dispossess any proprietor during his lifetime, nor even his successors, without their own consent; it would be quite sufficient for all useful national ends and purposes to buy up the land as it comes into the market in the ordinary course, either by the voluntary act of the seller or by due legal process, such as a decree of the Court of Chancery, &c., and then make the land so bought with the public money the inalienable property of the nation ever after, as it by right should be.

Unquestionably, land-usurpers and money-changers, taking both terms in their widest sense, must *in foro conscientiæ* be distinguished from all other sinners. We know of no great social evil in civilized life that is not clearly traceable, directly or indirectly, to these two classes. It is they that govern the world everywhere, and that have always governed it since the first dawn of civilisation; it is they that make all revolutions and counter-revolutions, all false systems of religion and education, all State-Church establishments, all standing armies of soldiers, constables, priests, and lawyers, and that impose on all peoples the burdens requisite for the maintenance of those armies; in a word, it is landlords and profitmongers that have everywhere organised society as we find it, and that uphold this organisation for their own advantage, at the cost of more wrong and wretchedness to mankind than tongue or pen ever did or ever will be able to describe. And amongst the greatest of their crimes against humanity is this, that, in addition to the machinery of brute force they keep in pay to uphold their domination, they have rendered an effectual exposure of their system next to impossible through the legions of venal journalists, mercenary orators, and unprincipled *littérateurs* they subsidise to corrupt public opinion and to mystify the people on every subject that bears upon their weal or woe, as also to hunt down by calumny, and to destroy by private persecution, any and every man that shall dare to lift the veil that hides from the millions their horrible policy.

We must *live* somewhere; and we must have the *needful things* to live on. But landlords and profitmongers claim to own every rood of ground in the kingdom, and every house on the land; and we cannot procure the commonest necessaries of life except through some profitmonger. We must therefore either go without homes and without meat and drink altogether, or we must have them from the landlord and profitmonger on their own arbitrary terms. To have them on *any* terms, too many persons are often obliged, in times of difficulty and danger, to connive at and even laud what they abhor. Again, the wrongs done by ordinary criminals are in general superficial and ephemeral in their effects. The man who steals my watch, or robs my house, does me only as much wrong as I may repair at the cost of earning the price of another watch or of the goods stolen from my house. But they who rob a people of their territory rob them of a priceless possession, for which all the labour and labour's worth in the world would be no adequate compensation. It is not only a robbery of the existing generation, but a robbery of all generations to come; for it is depriving the whole posterity of the disinherited of their fair legitimate share of the *raw materials* of wealth, which God made equally for the use of all, in order that the descendants of the wrong-doers, so far as human laws can determine it, may be able to grow richer and richer in every succeeding age, by letting out for rents that raw material which is by natural right the inheritance of all.

Perhaps the most extortionate system of legal robbery, in connection with private property in the soil, is found in what are called *ground rentals*. By virtue of this system, a man like the Duke of Westminster is enabled to realise an income greater than the queen gets for her services (and she does something for her money, but the duke does absolutely nothing for his), merely because the land on which certain houses are built is *said*, by a fiction in law, to belong to him; and, after a certain number of years, the houses themselves become his property, and he forthwith proceeds to grant fresh leases of them at increased rents.

As to the right of *occupation* of the land, we should make it the same for all, giving the tenancy to those who would pay most rent

K

to the State, only taking care that no man held more than one farm, or a larger one than he could cultivate himself whilst there were others in want of small ones. As a matter of course, we should guard against too great a subdivision as well.

Another false principle at the root of our politico-commercial system is, that Credit should exist only for the rich, and not at all for the poor. This is a most atrocious principle, both in theory and practice. As between citizen and citizen, or between subject and subject, the principle might be defensible enough on prudential grounds; but as between the citizen and his country it is wholly unjustifiable, and calculated to keep subordinates subordinate, and to fatten tyrants and usurers with the sweat and blood of slaves. If the *rents* of the country were public property, as they ought to be, no honest, industrious man should be refused a temporary advance or loan from them for productive purposes ; and it is not in the power of man to conceive a better security for the repayment of the same than the skilled labour of an industrious, sober freeman protected by laws made with his own consent. There is no other security *now* for the repayment of loans, public or private, than the known capacity of working men to produce a *surplus* over and above their own consumption. If they could not, or did not, do this, there would be no interest for fundholders, mortgagees, or money-lenders of any sort. Indeed, there is no other source than the said surplus for the payment of rents, taxes, dividends, premiums on insurance policies, and the interest of upwards of two thousand millions of private debts. Out of the same source, and no other, comes also the enormous income annually received by capitalists and traders under the name of Profits. Upstarts, who have made fortunes in trade, invariably make the worst landlords—the least social and hospitable, the most grinding and exacting. This is exemplified in every country in Europe, where rents are continually becoming heavier, and small farms more difficult of attainment by the poor, in proportion as the mercantile body and master-manufacturers increase in numbers and in wealth. In all such countries, national or public debts, provincial debts, and corporation debts are never-failing concomitants of increased commerce and manufactures, as are also banking and other joint-stock companies, which absorb so much of the produce of the soil for profits, discounts, dividends, and interest of money, that there would be nothing left for the landlords and cultivators, if it were not that the working-classes are dispossessed altogether both of their *proprietary* and their *occupancy* rights in the soil, and turned into mere drudges or wages-slaves to the landlords and tenant-farmers, who work them harder, and feed them worse, than their cattle. The difference between what the labourers and mechanics actually produce in value and the miserable pittance allowed to them is the plunder-fund out of which are kept in comparative ease and luxury the worthless classes that enslave and prey upon them. Yes, the whole and sole security for all is the labourer's capability to produce a surplus over and above what he consumes during the period of production. It were strange, then—passing strange, indeed—if that surplus, which is now sufficient security for everybody else, should not be as good a security for himself, when the very object of the advance or loan is neither more nor less than to furnish him with the means of repayment, by at once enabling him to produce, and by making him the master of his own products. Yet, in the teeth of this well-known capability on his part, the man whose surplus productions enable others to get loans, and repay both capital and interest, is the only man who can get no loan for himself, because, by our atrocious system, the Credit as well as the Land of the country is hermetically sealed against him. To support the system of the landlords and the profitmongers, it is absolutely necessary to place millions of the population in positions and situations wherein they cannot possibly earn their bread without breaking one or other of the Ten Commandments and running counter to the injunctions of the Gospel.

Partington tells us, in his Encyclopædia, that the history of every country in Europe goes back to the time when its land was public property. Did that state of things obtain now, all the mines, as well as all the land that covers them, would be the property of the public, agreeably to the old law maxim, " Cujus est solum, ejusdem sunt omnia quæ infra sunt, ad imam terram, et omnia quæ supra sunt, usque ad cœlum,"—" Whoever owns the soil, to the same belongs all that is beneath the soil, down to the bottom of the earth, and all that is overhead, even up to the sky." If this maxim prevailed now-a-days, the rents of mines would go to public uses only. After a due examination and survey by public authority, they would be let out to companies of actual workers by public tender, and all they realised above the rent to the State would go only to those who risked their lives in working them. There would be few accidents, we suspect, under such arrangement ; and if there were any, the workers alone would be to blame for their greed in not sinking more shafts and taking the other necessary precautions for their safe working.

In the manufacturing districts of England it has been ascertained that half the children born to the artisans die before they complete their fifth year, and that the average duration of human life amongst the working classes is only some 17 or 18 years, while it averages 38 years amongst the "better classes," *i.e.*, amongst the landlords and profitmongers who reap the best fruits of their toil. This is an arbitrary confiscation or squandering of human life not to be found, even in time of war, in any other country not manufacturing, mining, and commercial. The men composing the master-class in these callings are, with hardly an exception, open and even avowed enemies of the political and social rights of the working classes. They have literally expelled the people from every institution in the State. They and their accomplices, the landlords and tenant-farmers, have usurped and absorbed all the prerogatives of the Crown and all the rights of the people. They have turned the producers out of parliament, out of the corporations, out of the vestries,

out of the juries, out of the magistracy, out of the church, out of
the public press, out of all the public boards—in a word, out of
every department of the State, and left them without a single
legislator, magistrate, administrator, common-councilman, vestry-
man, or public organ of any kind to represent or protect their
interests. But it is not simply of what are called their organic or
political rights that these tyrants have despoiled the working
classes; they have also robbed them of all *proprietary* and *occupancy*
rights in the soil, combining for that purpose with the landlords
and the tenant-farmers, to whom the sight of an agricultural labourer
putting a spade or a plough into the land on his own account, or in
any other capacity than that of a wages-slave to some bull-frog
farmer, is the horror of horrors.   Just as farmers in the rural districts
will take vacant farms they do not want, and at rents by which they
know they must be losers, merely to keep out labourers or exclude
from occupancy the men they want for slaves, so will these mining
and manufacturing tyrants rent on long leases, or actually buy up
outright, lands in the neighbourhood of the towns where their
factories are, to prevent their toiling slaves from having the chance
of renting them, or any portion of them, however small, lest they
might be able to escape the slavery of the mill through comparative
independence.

We doubt if there be a single recorded instance in the whole
history of civilized society of any king, ruler, statesman, legislator,
prophet, philosopher, orator, or other public man, seeking honestly,
and with probabilities of success, the reign of justice, humanity, and
fraternity for his fellow-countrymen, that was not overwhelmed with
calumny, overpowered by faction, and ultimately either put to death
or forced to fly for his life and bury himself in poverty and obscurity
to escape the malice of the oppressors of his country.   But who
were those oppressors?   The same everywhere—the same now as
ever—the idle rich, who prey on their industrious fellow-creatures
through the inventions of rents, profits, interest of money, dividends,
taxes, and so forth—all arising out of usurpations of the soil, and
making money grow money.   The ancient prophets and apostles
suffered for causes not essentially different from those which
destroyed the Gracchi at Rome and Agis and Cleomenes of Sparta.
Romulus and Julius Cæsar were victims of the same spirit that
beheaded Paul and sawed Isaiah asunder.   Heraclides and Hippo
of Sicily perished through landlordism and profitmongering, in no
other sense than did John the Baptist under Herod ; St. Stephen, by
the Jewish rabble, let loose upon him by the middle-class Pharisees ;
and Socrates, by the hypocritical " property " classes of Athens ;
nay, the Saviour himself, whose crucifixion was perpetrated by like
influences on behalf of like interests.   All honest reformers, spiritual
or temporal, must necessarily be foes to landlordism and usury,
though not to the persons of landlords and usurers.   The latter,
however, have ever considered attacks upon their system to be
attacks upon themselves : and, accordingly, they have crushed or
murdered every honest reformer whose influence has hitherto

threatened to supplant their own with the millions. And so it ever will be—until the millions shall become wise enough, and moral enough, to be able to dispose summarily of landlordism and usury without further preaching or teaching. Any one who will take the trouble to read over a list of the laws proposed by Julius Cæsar, in any book of Roman antiquities (say Adams's "Antiquities"), will see by their titles that they were all essentially popular, and designed to protect the citizens from the cupidity of land-monopolists, usurers, and dilapidators of the public revenue. In this we have the true *secret* of his murder by the patrician conspirators, headed by Brutus, who, with all the stoic virtues attributed to him, was a rank aristocrat in grain, and a usurer to boot; for, according to the testimony of his friend Cicero, he used to charge interest for his money at the rate of 48 per cent., and gather it in, too, with the sabre's edge when necessary.

In a well-ordered state of society there would be neither land-usurpers nor money-changers; that is, no persons living by letting out land as *private* property (since all land would be public property solely, the rents going to the public for public uses only), and no persons living upon what Lord Bacon called "the bastard use of money," that is, upon profits, usury, dividends, &c. In other words, the whole people would be sole landlord, every individual of the people having the same *proprietary* and the same *occupancy* rights as every other individual; and with respect to money, it would be a mere *representative* of wealth or value, which would disappear altogether when the wealth or value it represented disappeared; money would not grow money, as it does now. In a just and rational state of society, all the money in the world could not purchase an acre of land, nor would it enable the owner to add one pound more to his heap, unless he earned it by producing a pound's worth of wealth, or doing a pound's worth of service for society, such as society would recognise. To speak downright, plain English, landlords and money-changers have no right to be in the world at all. Instead of governing society absolutely, as they do now, they have no right to form a recognised part of society at all, no more than wolves and crocodiles have to invite themselves to our Christmas parties that they may devour our children, or than wens, tumours, ulcers, cancers, running sores, or deformities of any sort have to constitute themselves parts of our natural bodies, and to claim to invade, overrun, and subject our whole systems to their pestilential domination. All the talent and all the sophistry in the world could not show any legitimate use for landlords or profit-mongers *as such*, or anything they do for society that could not be better done without them than with them, and at less than a hundredth part of their cost.

CHAPTER XXI.

NATIONAL SYSTEM OF CURRENCY AND EXCHANGE REQUIRED.

Inadequacy and Absurdity of present Medium of Exchange—Necessity for new National Currency for Home Trade—Example from Iron Currency of Sparta—Labour Notes of Guernsey—Gold and Silver mere Commodities —All four Reforms must be combined.

In this chapter we shall elucidate the remaining two propositions of the League, on the important complementary reforms necessary to be introduced for the expulsion of human slavery from the face of the land, and the full emancipation of industry from the trammels of a false and pernicious system of Currency and Exchange. The sixth and seventh resolutions read as follows :—

" That the National Currency should be based on real, consumable wealth, or on the *bonâ fide* credit of the State, and not upon the variable and uncertain amount of scarce metals ; because a currency depending on such a basis, however suitable in past times, or as a measure of value in present international commerce, has now become, by the increase of population and wealth, wholly inadequate to perform the functions of equitably representing and distributing that wealth ; thereby rendering all commodities liable to perpetual fluctuation in price, as those metals happen to be more or less plentiful in any country ; increasing to an enormous extent the evils inherent in usury, and in the banking and funding systems (in support of which a legitimate function of the law—the PROTECTION of property—is distorted into an instrument for the CREATION of property to a large amount for the benefit of a small portion of society belonging to what are called vested interests) ; because, from its liability to become locally or nationally scarce or in excess. that equilibrium which should be maintained between the production and consumption of wealth is destroyed ; because, being of intrinsic value in itself, it fosters a vicious trade in money, and a ruinous practice of commercial gambling and speculation ; and, finally, because, under the present system of society, it has become confessedly the 'root of all evil' and the main support of that unholy worship of Mammon which now so extensively prevails, to the supplanting of all true religion, natural and revealed.

" That in order to facilitate the transfer of property or service, and the mutual interchange of wealth among the people, to equalise the demand and supply of commodities, to encourage consumption as well as production, and to render it as easy to sell as to buy, it is an important duty of the State to institute in every town and city public marts or stores for the reception of all kinds of exchangeable goods, to be valued by disinterested officers appointed for the purpose, either upon a corn or a labour standard; the depositors to receive symbolic notes representing the value of their deposits, such notes to be made legal currency throughout the country, enabling their owners to draw from the public stores to an equivalent amount, thereby gradually displacing the present reckless system of competitive trading and shopkeeping,—a system which, however necessary or unavoidable in the past, now produces a monstrous amount of evil, by maintaining a large class living on the profits made by the mere sale of goods, on the demoralising principle of buying cheap and selling dear, totally regardless of the ulterior effects of that policy upon society at large and the true interests of humanity."

Add to the gigantic fraud of the land-usurpers the hardly less monstrous fraud of the money-changers in daring to make two particular metals (falsely called precious) the sole basis of that currency which is the life's blood of society, without which exchanges cannot be safely effected, and you see capped before you the climax of iniquity. These precious metals being articles of commerce— mere merchandise, like iron or cotton, at the same time that they are made the sole basis of our instruments of exchange, it follows, as a necessary consequence, that whoever can, by commerce, monopolise these precious metals can, by so doing, monopolise at the same time the basis of our currency, and so leave us without any instruments of exchange at all, but what may be convertible, upon their own fraudulent terms, into those two favoured metals, which their commercial wealth has enabled them to monopolise.

The false principle at the root of our present system is, that *money* or the *medium of exchange* should be itself a thing of intrinsic value. By this false principle there must be an expenditure of labour equal to what is required to produce the equivalents it exchanges for; and besides the absurdity of such misplaced, because wholly useless, labour, it is manifestly ridiculous to suppose that any one commodity (more especially an exceedingly scarce one, like gold) can ever be obtained in sufficient abundance to represent adequately all other commodities which may be produced *ad libitum*, to any extent demanded by consumption, and which, without the intervention of gold at all, might be interchanged from hand to hand, in one single week, to an amount equal to fifty times the value of all the gold in the country. It is like supposing a part of a thing to be equal to the whole. Gold may be a good measure of value, and, as such, is perfectly unobjectionable; but as an exclusive representative of value, or as the sole basis of representation (which our present laws have virtually made it, by constituting it the sole basis of our circulating medium), it is to our productive and trading population what a single blanket or a single suit of clothes would be, applied to the use of a whole family consisting of divers persons of all ages and sizes. The strongest and most important members of the political family get the best share of the blanket; the others get the least, and some get none at all. As well might the garments of a dwarf be expected to fit a giant, as well might our legislators attempt to restore a full-grown bird to the egg whence it was hatched, as attempt to tie down the population and commerce of this great country to the Procrustean bed of Peel's monetary system as established by his laws of 1819 and 1844. That system alone, were there no other causes in operation, *must sooner or later produce a convulsion in this country, if it be not speedily unmade by wiser and better men than its authors.* To pretend that the rights of property exist in a country where such a monetary system coexists with private ownership of the soil, is a monstrous perversion of language. It is not the rights of property, but the wrongs of robbery, that these land and money laws tend to conserve.

The prime necessity of man is to live : he cannot live without corn, unless in the lowest condition of the savage ; but he may not only live, but live in comfort, without gold or silver. They are not the "staffs of life," however in our ignorance we may bow the knee to them as to graven images. We invest them with supreme power, as superstition invests its idols. The ancient fabulist who sketched the character of *Midas* seems to have written, by anticipation, a satire on modern credulity. *Midas* enjoyed the fatal gift of turning all he touched into gold ; his food was transmuted into the precious metal, and starvation taught him that corn was the true standard of all that was physically valuable. *Midas* was the prototype of modern bullionists and moneymongers. The Bank of England can now pave its floors with gold ; but what does it avail to the people ? And yet was it not the industry of the people that raised the ore from the mines, and brought it hither by the sale or exchange of their labour, sustained by corn, the produce of labour in another form ? What was the *intrinsic* value of gold to *Midas ?*

We must not confound the *qualities* of a mineral with its *properties.* Undoubtedly, the precious metals possess durability, sameness, great value in small bulk, portability, resistance to wear and tear, in a greater degree than any other substances ; but these qualities *per se* do not constitute them *money,*—they do no more than recommend them to mercantile nations as the best instruments of their kind out of which money can be manufactured ; it is the act of the legislature, and that alone, which gives them the character and force of a *legal tender,* without which they would not form part of the currency of a nation. The legislature could confer the same power on any other material, even the most worthless, as Lycurgus did on iron, deprived of its malleability ; and yet Sparta flourished with that circulating medium ; nay, more, Sparta fell into ruin when the precious metals superseded the worthless iron, which its rulers were compelled to revive before the Republic was restored to prosperity. Some Eastern nations have used *cowries* (small shells) as money ; and the Russians, in the fourteenth and fifteenth centuries, employed the skins of squirrels and martens. We ourselves use paper, and have used it without the condition of convertibility. In fact, if gold and silver had never been deposited in the bowels of the earth, or had been suffered to remain there, the wealth of nations would not have been deteriorated one farthing. They are the *signs* of the thing signified, made such by Act of Parliament; they will neither feed us, nor clothe us, nor house us through their *own inherent qualities*. It is we ourselves who give them all their gigantic power; we make them a legal tender. Thus credulity set up graven images in the temples of old ; and Labour, having deposited all its earnings on the shrine, bent its knee before the shining metal, and implored food and raiment from the idol carved with its own hands. Common sense would have appealed to the *plough* and the *loom*.

We have said that the precious metals, when made a legal tender by the legislature, are still no more than signs of the thing signified; what, then, is the thing signified, whose value they measure, and in measurement represent ? We answer, all those things of value which, in return for a sufficient inducement, are capable of being transferred from one person to another. These are expressed by the terms Property, Capital, Stock. All these possess *intrinsic* value, for they represent accumulated labour; and accumulated labour is the result of a continuous consumption of corn—the standard of all values—the staff of life, without which neither property, capital, nor stock could be accumulated, without which, indeed, the race of civilised man could not be perpetuated. A granary full of corn, or a warehouse full of cottons and woollens, are examples of *real money*: they may exist while the proprietors of them have not an ounce of gold or silver in their coffers ; and, in a mercantile sense, they may be poor, nay, necessitous, with all this wealth in their possession; because corn, cottons, and woollens are not legal tenders according to Act of Parliament,—no man is *bound* to take them in acquittance of a debt,—they are not a satisfaction to the sheriff. It is idle to say that such persons may obtain relief through a banker : the very application shows a state of dependence into which the holder of real money ought never to be reduced : for he who produces the thing signified ought not to be under the control or caprice of him who merely deals in its sign. Moreover, the banker himself may be unable to give any accommodation : gold and silver may have left the country ; even the Bank of England may be so crippled as to have borrowed some millions of the precious metals from France : we may be within twenty-four hours of barter. Is this a picture of the imagination ? No ; it is a faithful sketch of what *has* happened ; and why should it not happen again, the same causes remaining in readiness to act ?

What is the lesson that such considerations ought to teach ? It is this, that a nation, rich in real money, may be thrown into bankruptcy, and perhaps revolution, by adopting a false representative of value, through the privation of that gold which its legislature recognises as the sole legal tender. Let the gold go, what remains? Our land, retaining its fertility ; our machinery, capable of continuing its work ; our vessels, as seaworthy as before ; our skilled industry, with its intelligence unimpaired ; our unskilled labour, not a whit enfeebled in its natural productive powers. These are the elements of real money.

In the island of Guernsey it was proposed to build a meat-market, and the estimates amounted to about £4,000. As all taxes in that island are raised by a direct assessment on property, the rich protested against the expenditure, though they desired the proposed accommodation. Here, then, was a dilemma, since they who willed the end would not will the means, and without the means the structure could not be erected. Had such an emergency arisen with us, our Chancellor of the Exchequer would unhesitatingly have thrown all the burden on the working-classes, by taxing the commodities they daily consumed; but the rulers of Guernsey have notions of honour and justice which do not permit them to relieve the rich at the expense of the poor, and they are too well instructed in the principles of commerce to crush trade by customs and excise; these contrivances, as iniquitous as they are bungling, would be disdained by the legislatures of the Channel Islands. How, then, did they proceed in building the meat-market? They issued paper notes, *guaranteed by the States of Guernsey*, this national paper *not bearing interest*; and the better to show the nature of this currency, the words " Meat-market Notes" were inscribed upon them, and they were numbered so that no more could be put into circulation than represented the sum agreed to be expended on the undertaking. On the first instalment being due to the contractor, he was paid in these notes, which he again paid away to his workmen and others, who passed them to the shopkeepers; the landlords took them for rent, and the treasurer of the States and the constables received them in discharge of dues and taxes. At length the building was completed, when butchers took the stalls at an annual rent, and as that rent was received the meat-market notes were destroyed. In due course of time this rent wholly extinguished the notes; and the market remains, to this day, a permanent source of national revenue, applicable to other national improvements; and, strange as it may sound, no individual has been taxed one farthing for its construction! Here, then, is a practical illustration of the uses of a symbolic currency, and of the mode in which it may be made to work. Not an ounce of gold was employed; not a shilling of interest was paid. The States of Guernsey were their own guarantees for their own paper; they created the substance with the symbol, realising the allegory of Aladdin's lamp.

As bullion, the precious metals are mere commodities, and therefore possess no more intrinsic value than any other commodity, under the laws of supply and demand; as coin, they are still bits of bullion, and it is the act of ourselves, or of the legislature who represents us, that gives them the character and the power of a legal tender. And yet we have the folly to kneel down to this graven image, and measure individual happiness and national greatness by its presence or its departure. Foreign trade, however valuable, must ever be subsidiary to the home trade. This doctrine none will contest; being admitted, then it follows that the chief care of the government should be to provide a currency suited to the home trade, and leave to merchants the care of adjusting the foreign exchanges, which never, for any long period, can be adverse or favourable ; for what the ebb tide takes away the flood returns. It is an axiom in political economy that a favourable state of the exchanges acts as a *bounty on imports* and as a *duty on exports*, while the reverse takes place when the exchanges are unfavourable. The true *par* forms the centre of these oscillations, and though peculiar circumstances will rarely allow that *par* to be *exactly* hit, yet the tendency to approach it is constant, and the divergence from it is always evanescent. But the home trade is governed by very different influences; for, while we pay taxes on all we consume, the foreigner pays none on what he purchases from us, since he deals with us according to the measure of value, while we deal with each other according to price. Gold represents the *natural* price of commodities, not the taxed price. Therefore, we ought to have two sorts of currency ; let bullion serve for foreign trade, but let us have government paper, convertible into gold at the *market price*—not the *Mint price*—as the medium of internal exchanges. When gold is scarce, let it rise in value measured in the Bank or National note, and we need not fear a drain of bullion.

There can be no freedom nor safety, much less prosperity, for any people till they obtain just laws to regulate landed tenures, credit, and commercial interchange. With such laws there could not exist a bad government, nor would oppression in any form be possible. Without such laws there cannot be a good government, be its form, its administration, its institutes, or its franchises what they may. Land, and whatever else the Deity has made for man's use, must be expropriated, by commutation, on equitable terms for the general good. and never again be made private property. Credit must be accessible for every member of the community, on terms beneficial for the individual, and just and safe for the public. And all commerce must be gradually reduced to equitable exchange on the principle of equal values for equal values, measured by a labour or corn standard.

Under the systems of Landed Tenures, Currency, and Commerce which at present prevail in England and in France, it is no exaggeration to say, that those who live upon *rents, profits, usury, discounts, dividends, commissions, fees*, &c., absorb from 300 to 350 million pounds sterling worth of the people's produce in each country every year, over and above what they give the people any value whatever for, in money or service of any appreciable kind. In fact, for this enormous annual drain the useful classes of both countries receive no consideration whatever. It is sheer robbery, disguised under plausible names and forms. The Seven Propositions of the National Reform League present what would seem the only feasible means of ridding the country of this crushing incubus, consistent with acknowledging legal rights and vested interests. Unless some such compromise be agreed on between rich and poor, both in England and in France, a convulsion, sooner or later, that will engulf both, must be the inevitable consequence. No country could long sustain two such existing drains by the idle and baneful classes upon the laborious producers—drains equal to from 300 to 350

millions every year in each country—without at last collapsing
after protracted agonies to preserve national life. The system of
equitable Exchange substituted for the present nefarious one of profitmongering would save the *souls* as well as the *bodies* of both nations;
but *that* is absolutely impossible without such antecedent laws on
Land and Currency as we have pointed out.

It is the same with Currency. You may, for instance, by
repealing Peel's Currency Acts of 1819 and 1844, by making an
annual issue of Exchequer paper, equal to the taxation, our legal
tender, and by superadding to this the advantage of a free but sound
commercial currency, in the form of private and joint-stock paper
issues adequately secured,—you may by such a reform as this, and by
making gold a mere merchandise to rise and fall in the market like
all other merchantable commodities according to the law of supply
and demand,—you may by this means make money more plentiful
and come-at-able for trade purposes, and thus relieve society of a
large proportion of its distress,—you may do all this and so far effect
much good for society without any other accompanying reforms;
but the benefits of such a reform *per se* would, we contend, be only
temporary; they could not be permanent, for want of the other
reforms. For a time money would be plentiful, employment abundant, prices and wages high, and trade what is called prosperous;
but this very prosperity would soon work its own destruction ; it
would lead to increased speculation, increased production, increased
competition, increased rents for lands and houses, increase of expenditure and taxation, and to a terrific increase of what are called
vested interests ; it would soon overstock the markets, and glut
the warehouses with unsaleable goods. Then would come a crash—
a fearful, ruinous crash; mills would run short time or stop; the
factories and the workshops would dismiss their hands; multitudes
accustomed for some time to full employment and good living would
be cast suddenly adrift to beg, borrow, or steal ; the workhouses
would overflow as the mills and workshops became empty; the
shopkeepers would be ruined by forced sales and the lack of
legitimate custom. This would react on the manufacturers and
merchants, and, through them, on the artisans and labourers.
Meanwhile the increased pressure of inflamed rents, taxes, and
vested interests would be found intolerable by a people without
trade and without employment. Down would go prices and wages
again, in despite of the superabundance of money, which would have
found its way to and accumulated in the hands of usurers, fixed-
income men, and non-productive, overgrown capitalists. In short,
we should see a repetition on a larger scale than ever of one of those
periodic crises in the commercial world which, under the present
system, we invariably find to follow close upon the heels of every
great development of our manufacturing and trading prosperity.

It is with Land-reform as with Currency; it would be of comparatively little use to nationalise landed property with the view of
throwing open the land to labourers and small farmers, unless you
at the same time enabled them, by a sound system of Credit, to

procure implements and stock for their holdings, and to subsist themselves till after they gathered in the first year's crop. And even with competent allotments of Land and Credit to stock them, the occupants' condition would be still but a very indifferent one without the aid of an efficient Currency wherewith to effect easy and equitable exchanges of their surplus agricultural produce for money or for other produce, as their wants might require. In short, each element is imperfect in itself as the means of social reform. But all, from operating conjointly and harmoniously, go to make social reform perfect. And seeing that it is just as easy to legislate upon all forms conjointly as upon each separately, it appears to us a sad waste of time and labour to agitate for any one without including the rest at the same time, the more especially as the peculiar virtues of each are only brought into full play and development by being made to operate in unison with the other three.

There is not one warrior that ever fought for king, people, or commonwealth : they have all fought for landlords and profitmongers, to whom alone they could look for pay and promotion ; consequently, no good to the human race ever accrued from their conquests or victories. Nor will the millions ever gain by any war not waged by themselves on their own account, nor by any victories not won by themselves over their hereditary eternal foes, the landlords and profitmongers—over the latter especially, the more numerous, deadly, and irreclaimable of the two. Profitmongers are, indeed, perfectly irreclaimable enemies of the human race, because as such they can possess no one virtue, no one quality of head, heart, or conscience, by which they could be won over to God or humanity. In all the higher professional callings—in those associated with the arts and sciences—the pursuit of truth, and the culture of a taste for the Sublime, the Beautiful, the Chaste, the Sympathetic, form an essential part of their studies and the very foundation of success. Such is the case with engineers, architects, sculptors, painters, musicians, historians, mathematicians, physicians and surgeons, artists of every kind, orators, poets, professors of science, advocates, &c. The higher qualities of the human mind must be more or less cultivated by all those descriptions of persons, if they would excel ; and it is in the very nature of their studies to generate in them some appreciation of truth, taste, sympathy, or refinement. But the profitmongering devils of society neither need nor care for such ennobling pursuits. Indeed, the less they are tinctured with them, the more fitted they are for their nefarious callings. Genius, taste, culture, are not required for buying in the cheapest markets and selling in the dearest, for lying, deceiving, adulterating goods, giving short weight, or cheating our fellow-creatures out of their substance, either by underpaying them for their work or giving them less than the value for their money. Still less are the superior moral qualities required in profitmongering pursuits ; indeed, such qualities are only drawbacks and impediments in the way of success in business. Hence no clever profitmonger ever thinks of encumbering himself with them. True, mercantile men have a proverb which has become trite from use—"*Honesty is the best policy;*" but they use it, like other good things, only to improve their opportunities of cheating. A tacit understanding not to cheat one another is often necessary to their success in cheating the rest of mankind, which, after all, is the main business of their lives. As this iniquitous class can grow rich only by grinding and cheating their fellow-creatures, that is, by robbery and oppression, they are, by the very nature of their pursuits and practices, irreconcilable enemies of society. It is their interest that the working-classes should be always at variance amongst themselves—always a prey to ignorance—given to mutual jealousy and mistrust—and filled with prejudices and superstitions, by which they may at all times have their passions inflamed against those who would unite, enlighten, and emancipate them from bondage. It is the interest of this class, too, that the mass of the people should never own a house, nor even rent an acre of land, so that they may be forced to become wages-slaves to profitmongers, and pay to them every few years in rent more than the value of their wretched tenements. In short, profitmongers, as the main supports of all aristocracies and of all tyrannies in the world, are constrained by the very necessities of their positition and by the very nature of their pursuits, to ignore the Ten Commandments in practice, and to trample under foot the Gospel of the Saviour. There cannot, then, be even a semblance of real reform in society without beginning with clipping the claws and drawing the teeth of the profitmongers. The human race is, indeed, without hope of salvation either in this world or the next, until their present unlimited and irresponsible power of murder and robbery over the mass of mankind shall be wrenched from profitmongers and landlords.

CHAPTER XXII.

EVILS OF MONOPOLIES AND EXPLOITATIONS OF INDUSTRIES.

False Principle of Law-made Property—Absurdity of Funding System and Borrowing from Investors—Evil of Public Works in hands of Profit-mongers and Speculators—Rapacity of Predatory Classes—Efforts of Robespierre to abolish the nefarious System—his legal Assassination in consequence—All Evils of Society the work of Landlords and Profit-mongers.

ANOTHER false principle at the root of our system (mark it well! for it is a most diabolical one) is, that laws may legitimately *make* property for one set of people at the expense of another set, without the consent of the latter, and without giving them an equivalent. This principle lurks insidiously at the root of scores of different sorts of property, well known to exist in this country, and to be wholly and solely the offspring of class-legislation. The dividends payable on the National Debt are of this class of property; so are railway dividends; so are the dividends or revenues accruing from canals, docks, wharfs, fisheries, insurance offices, gas-companies, water-companies, mining-companies, and private companies of all sorts, which are chartered by private Acts of Parliament to do for the public what the public ought to be empowered to do for themselves. There is no subject upon which more gross and general ignorance prevails than upon this. Most people imagine that a man may as legitimately possess property of the kinds here alluded to, as he may possess a house, a horse, or a gross of Birmingham buttons. No delusion can be more ridiculous. Parliaments are chosen, and laws are designed, not to *make* property for people, but to *protect* it for those who have made it for themselves, or obtained it from those that *did*. If a man builds a house, or buys an ox, it is his rightful property irrespectively of Acts of Parliament. The law did not give him the house or the ox; neither has it a right to take it away, unless for a good and sufficient reason, and then only upon awarding adequate compensation. The same principle applies to every other legitimate description of property. All such legitimate descriptions of property are acquired or made by the owners themselves, and not by the law. The law only *protects* such property; it does not *create* or *make* it.

The State plan of borrowing money from its subjects on the perpetual-interest system is replete with folly and extravagance; unless it be admitted to be an artful scheme for robbing the wealth-producers, by taxing them with the payment of the interest of money which they never borrowed. An honest government would quickly set about paying this debt off, by offering life annuities to a certain number of stock-holders every year.   A real State power ought never to *borrow* money; it ought to *make* it when required to cancel its obligations, receiving the same money back in the form of taxes, so as to prevent depreciation.   The government practice of borrowing money on Exchequer bills is also absurdly wasteful; surely the credit of the State ought to be above that of any of its subjects!

What is true of funded property is equally applicable to the various other descriptions of property referred to.   Railroads should not be private property; neither should canals, docks, fisheries, mines, the supplying of gas, water, etc.   Works of this sort, designed for the use of the public, should be constructed or executed only at the public cost, and the public, and the public only, should have the advantage.   They should not be suffered to fall into the hands of private speculators, for whom they are only a legal disguise to enable them to rob the public.   A universal-suffrage parliament would never sanction such a system, unless it were stark mad.   Like the funding system, it only tends to breed idle schemers to prey upon the industrious classes.   All profits upon their outlay received by such private companies, while they preserve their capital intact, is in reality so much public plunder handed over to them by the law. Indeed, not unfrequently the profits for a single year are greater than the outlay itself, whilst the original shares are proportionately enhanced in value.   Thus, shares in the New River Company, originally worth £100, are now worth £16,000; in other words, the annual interest is equal to eight times the original capital.   It is superfluous to say such *property* is the sole creation of law, which, whenever it deviates from its original function of *protecting* property, to that of *creating* or *making* it, only robs one set of people to enrich another—a species of act which laws are intended to punish, and not to set the example of.

The mercantile middle-classes are everywhere organizing chartered companies to give themselves perpetual vested interests in the labour of the working-classes, and mortgage the latter to posterity, through public loans and State indebtedness.   Wars are now got up or waged every year merely to create fresh batches of "*stocks*" or "*public securities*" to be thrown, as marketable wares, upon the stock-exchanges of the world, in order that lazy, worthless, swindling villains, who have got rich by profitmongering, may be able to convert definite money-capitals into interminable annuities, or perennial streams of income wrung from the labouring classes in taxes, for which the said classes never receive a particle of consideration or value in any shape, while the "*investors*," as they are called, not only retain their money-capitals under the name of stock, but, as a general rule, can always sell that stock at a premium, or for more than the sum originally lent or invested; while, till they choose to sell out, they are privileged to live securely on the taxes.

All slavery in all countries called civilised is the work of landlords and profitmongers.   These two classes, which have no right to form an integral portion of society at all, have everywhere made them-

THE

IMMORTAL ·HISTORY

OF

SOUTH AFRICA.

(COMPLETE IN TWO VOLUMES.

THE ONLY TRUTHFUL, POLITICAL, COLONIAL, LOCAL,
DOMESTIC, AGRICULTURAL, THEOLOGICAL, NATIONAL,
LEGAL, FINANCIAL AND INTELLIGENT HISTORY OF
MEN, WOMEN, MANNERS AND FACTS OF THE
CAPE COLONY, NATAL, THE ORANGE FREE
STATE, TRANSVAAL, AND SOUTH AFRICA.

By MARTIN JAMES BOON,

AUTHOR OF

*How to Colonise South Africa, and by whom ; Jottings by
the Way in South Africa ; Home Colonisation ; How to
Construct and Nationalise Railways ; National Paper Money,
to enable all Nations to Construct Public Works without Bonds,
Mortgages, or Interest, &c., &c., &c.*

VOL. I.

LONDON :
WILLIAM REEVES, 185, FLEET STREET ;
MARTIN JAMES BOON, 170, FARRINGDON ROAD.

SOUTH AFRICA :
HAY BROS., WHOLESALE AGENTS, KING WILLIAM'S TOWN.

—

1885.

CONTENTS

OF VOLUME I.

------◦◦◦------

Reviews.

—:o:—

IMMORTAL SOUTH AFRICA.

By Martin James Boon.

" We have just had the pleasure of perusing the first volume of one of the most remarkable, instructive, and entertaining books ever presented to the public—*Immortal South Africa*— by Martin James Boon. Past, recent, and current events, all combine to enhance the interest and anxiety that we doubt not exist in the public mind with regard to all that pertains to the African Continent; and assuredly no Englishman, worthy of the name, can look with indifference upon the kaleidoscopic-like events now passing before his mental view in that veritable *terra incognita*. Egypt, the Soudan, the Transvaal, Basutoland, Zululand, Bechuanaland, &c., &c., are names now "Familiar as Household Words" in every English-speaking home, and naturally so; for where is the one to be found of the Anglo-Saxon race, from lisping infancy to the threshold of the grave, who has not read or heard, and on reading or hearing, of our African triumphs or disasters, felt the warm glow of patriotism and pride suffuse the brow, or sought refuge in tears from the agony of unavailing grief, and mentally resolved that the transient stain upon the national escutcheon must be removed? Under such influences and conditions as these, we feel not only that no apology is needed for inviting and commending to public attention *Immortal South Africa*; but that it makes its appearance at a singularly opportune and felicitous moment; and we confidently hope that it will obtain what it undoubtedly merits— the liberal patronage of the reading world. Although, as indicated by its title, the work is mainly devoted to South Africa, including the Orange River, Free State and Transvaal Republics, nothing has been left untouched where "British

Interests " are concerned—and where are they not? Few men have had better opportunities than Mr. Boon of acquiring the materials necessary to complete the Herculean task he has so successfully accomplished; and certainly no contemporary writer has brought to bear upon the subject greater natural ability and honesty of purpose, or more dauntless courage in maintaining the right and denouncing the wrong. As a resident in the country during a period of eleven years, Mr. Boon writes with all the authority of personal experience, and a sincerity as apparent as it is exceptional in the penultimate decade of the nineteenth century. "Fear, favour, or affection" on the one hand; "malice, hatred, or ill-will" on the other; appear to be *unknown quantities* to Martin James Boon. His descriptions of the natural features of the country are realistically beautiful. His defence of the poor Aborigines, plundered, cajoled, goaded, banished, and at times wantonly murdered, is a marvel of eloquent pleading, that appears unanswerable on the part of the oppressors. His denunciation of the Jews and their malpractices; of all shams, humbugs, and impostures, whether Governmental, official, or individual, are couched in language of crushing impetuosity, convincing and overwhelming. With unerring precision, and resistless force, he strikes at every abuse; tearing away with the mighty power of righteous indignation, the mask that has too long concealed them, and ruthlessly exposes them in all their nude hideousness, to the scorn and contempt of the world. Mr. Boon is far too much of an Englishman to have left untouched the German element—a by no means unimportant factor in the great South African problem; more especially now that Bismarck has shown the cloven hoof of acquisition in his Colonial Policy at Angra Pequena and New Guinea, &c.; combined with his ill-disguised hostility to us in Egypt —and with a master-hand, he has cleared away all the obscurity in which that portion of the question was enshrouded; and by virtue of his rare powers of perception and description, presented it to us in a form as intelligible, as the subject is interesting and important. Nothing worthy of notice appears to have been overlooked. Politics and agriculture in all their bearings; social, sanitary and domestic topics, the "Race" question, and a thousand and one other matters are dealt with in an able and comprehensive manner, revealing to the reader the *minutiæ* of the conditions of daily life in South Africa, as distinctly as though he looked upon the subject through the medium of some powerful mental microscope. Throughout the entire work

—for we will take the public into our confidence, and say at once, that we have enjoyed the pleasure of a peep into the second volume, which is in an advanced stage of the arrangements necessary to enable it to follow Vol. I. into the " Hearts and Homes," doubtless waiting to welcome its arrival, where we opine it will prove to be of " metal more attractive" even than its predecessor—the readers interest is never allowed to flag. The diversified contents of the book, and their mode of treatment by the Author render *Immortal South Africa* a mental *pabulum* upon which the appetite never palls. All English-speaking folk who value the principles and attributes of right and justice, truth and purity, will greet Mr. Boon's book with a hearty welcome; whilst to the agriculturist, the settler in South Africa, or the intending emigrant, it is of supreme importance that " one and all " should be possessed of it, as they undoubtedly will be, if they have any genuine regard for their own interests. Although Mr. Boon makes no pretensions to literary style or polish, he is a writer possessing singular power and originality of ideas, fascinating by reason of their very freshness, accompanied by a rich vein of humour and keen sense of the ridiculous, whereby he at times completely deprives us of all control over our risible faculties. On the other hand we are now and again moved to the tenderest of human emotions by his simple, pure and unaffected pathos. Neither can we pass over without notice his trenchant criticisms of evil-doers in high places, his scathing sarcasms when dealing with organised or individual hypocrisies, or his truly terrible power of invective when delivering an onslaught upon social, political or ecclesiastical malefactors. With his perfect freedom from all conventualism, Mr. Boon is a literary gem of the first water, a veritable rough diamond ; and it requires no great stretch of imagination to picture his pen as the magician's wand, whose vigorous strokes shall bring about the moral redemption of South Africa, and hand down to posterity the name of Martin James Boon, as the Nineteenth Century literary Bayard. *Sans peur et sans reproche."*

MONEY AND ITS USE.

In these days, when " hard times" is the universal, and un - happily but too well founded cry, certainly, any proposition, that appears feasible, for the amelioration of matters must be somewhat more than welcome. Whatever the cause, it is a fact, which cannot be gainsaid, for all of us are only too painfully aware of it, that our country in common with others, is in a state of commercial prostration, the like of which has rarely, if ever, been experienced; and thousands upon thousands of our "horny-handed sons of toil" are in a state of semi-starvation through want of employment. Of such gigantic proportions is the evil, that private effort, however well intended, is utterly helpless even to mitigate it to any appreciable extent, and our wilfully blind or mentally paralysed Government seems to be either unwilling or hopelessly incapable of grasping the difficulty, and dealing with it in an effectual and statesmanlike manner. Innumerable plans and suggestions—all of a more or less impracticable character—have been promulgated by the Press, and mouthed from the platform or in the Senate, but nothing—absolutely nothing has as yet been *done*. The latest scheme for improving our condition and exorcising from our midst, or stalling off that rapidly approaching dread gaunt goblin Famine aye, famine; surrounded by plenty, wealth, luxury and sumptuousness, appears to be the construction of subways in different parts of the Metropolis, thereby providing employment for a considerable number of our idle hands. Employment! Yes; just the thing English working men want, and "don't they wish they may get it?" Whilst our Municipal or Local Government pettifoggers are discussing the matter, and turning about in all directions to find the ways and means—the indispensable, the *sine qua non*, absolutely and indisputably of our very existence on this sublunary planet, it is simply but a repetition of the "old, old story" that *while the grass grows, the steed starves*. What then is to be done? Why simply this:—Let every statesman, every politician, every political economist, every philanthropist, the clergy and ministers of all denominations, in fact, every man who wishes himself and his country well, procure at once the little *brochure*, entitled "Money and Its Use," by MARTIN JAMES BOON, author of "The Immortal History of South Africa," "History of the Orange Free State," &c., &c., &c. Having purchased it, let them read and ponder carefully its contents. Having done so, we are persuaded that all then remaining to be done, will be for every one in his respective sphere and capacity to do all that lies within him to carry, or cause to be carried immediately into practice the great and indisputable truths, and plans sketched out by the author. Let what was done in Jersey be repeated to the extent necessary in England, and then we shall have achieved our emancipation for the greatest and grossest thraldom that ever disgraced, outraged, and held in bondage the world of manhood—that of the gold exploiters and monopolists. Then shall we have effected, noiselessly and peacefully, the greatest social revolution of this or any other age, and we make bold to prophesy that the name of Martin James Boon will be hailed with universal assent and acclamation as the talisman whereby this wondrous transformation was brought about.

THE RISE, PROGRESS, AND PHASES OF HUMAN SLAVERY: HOW IT CAME INTO THE WORLD, AND HOW IT SHALL BE MADE TO GO OUT. By JAMES BRONTERRE O'BRIEN, B.A. London: William Reeves, 185, Fleet Street, E.C.; G. Standing, 8 & 9, Finsbury Street; Martin James Boon, 170, Farringdon Road, W.C.

THIS little Work, by an eloquent denunciator of the manifold evils of Profitmongering and Landlordism, whose entire life was devoted to the advocacy of Social Rights, is now given to the world for the first time in complete form.

The Author, in his lifetime, was frustrated in his design of finishing his History, through the ceaseless machinations of working-class exploiters and landlords. This has been at length accomplished by the aid of his various writings preserved in print. The object steadily kept in view has been to give the *ipsissima verba* of the Author, so that no foreign pen may garble or mislead.

In order to provide room for so much additional matter as was essential to the elucidation of the great reforms needed in the subjects of Land Nationalisation, Credit, Currency, and Exchange, it has been found expedient to omit from this edition some disquisitions on subjects of ephemeral and passing interest, not closely connected with the scope of the Work. Ample compensation has, however, been given in the additions which have had to be made for the elucidation and enforcement of the saving truths therein contained.

> A man who lived for truth, and truth alone,
> Brave as the bravest—generous as brave ;
> A man whose heart was rent by every moan
> That burst from every trodden, tortured slave ;
> A man prepared to fight, prepared to die.
> To lighten, banish, human slavery.
> The mighty scorned him, villified, oppressed ;
> The bitter cup of poverty and pain
> Forced him to drink. He was misfortune's guest

Thro' weary, weary years : his anguished brain
Shed tears of pity—wrath—for mankind's woe ;
For his own sorrows tears could never flow.
He loved the people with a brother's love :
He hated tyrants with a tyrant's hate.
He turned from kings below, to God above—
The King of kings who smites the wicked great.
The shame, the scourge, the terror of their race,
Those demons in earth's holy dwelling place.
Thou noble soul ! Around thee gathered those
Who, poor and trampled patriots were like thee.
Thou art not dead ! Thy martyred spirit glows
In us, a band devoted of the free :
We best can celebrate thy natal day,
By virtues, valours, such as marked thy way.
WILLIAM MACCALL.

We have been privileged with a sight of the proof-sheets of
O'Brien's " Rise, Progress, and Phases of Human Slavery,'
and are sure that the thousands of Socialists throughout
the world will hail with delight its appearance, for the first
time in a complete form. It seems to us as the rising from
the dead, after a long sleep, of the mighty great who
electrified his audiences with his eloquence. With what
convincing arguments does the writer show the horrors of
slavery, tracing its progress from brutal chattel-slavery down
to its more refined and diabolic form of wage-slavery. He
does not, however, leave us here; but in fixing the evil, he
also, at the same time, gives the full and sufficient remedy.
It is like the voice of the Deity, speaking from the dead to
living. Let the people heed the voice, and their redemption
draweth nigh.

HISTORY OF THE ORANGE FREE STATE.

UNDER the above title, another aspirant for public favour will
shortly make its appearance in the book market. The work
will be complete in one handsomely bound volume, and is from
the able pen of MARTIN JAMES BOON, author of " The Immortal History of South Africa," a work we had occasion to
notice with unqualified eulogy, some short time back—
" Money and Its Use," and other works on social and political
economy. "Immortal South Africa," with all its encyclo-
pædic comprehensiveness, from the immense variety of subjects
it dealt with, could hardly do more than touch the fringe, as
it were, of that many-coloured geographical entity, the
Orange Free State. Those who have been fortunate enough,
or had the good sense, to read Mr. BOON's more general work,
cannot but have felt eager, when perusing the valuable and

interesting generalities, anent the Free State, therein contained, for more detailed information from the same authoritative source; and in the work under notice they will find it in abundance, variety and beauty. Mr. Boon has handled his subject, as only one in possession of absolutely personal knowledge and great natural gifts, could. In this book we positively feel as though we were onlookers or participators in the stirring events described. Public affairs generally—State, Local and Municipal—are treated with a copiousness that leaves nothing to be desired, and with a boldness of assertion, welcome and refreshing in these degenerate days of pandering to "authority," and cloaking its manifold transgressions and iniquities. Semitic and Teutonic rascality, appears to be rampant in the Free State, and the victims thereof seem, for the most part, to be Englishmen. So mean, contemptible, and dastardly; so utterly abhorrent to all the instincts of right and justice; in short, so fiendish, one might say, are the practices of these degenerate Cousins-German, and nefarious descendants of Abraham, that the Orange Republic must indeed be a sort of terrestial pandemonium. If Mr. Boon is correct—and he certainly fortifies his assertions, both by direct and collateral evidence—the malpractices referred to are openly encouraged, or secretly connived at, by the Free State officials of all grades. Whilst the experiences narrated, are engrossingly interesting, throwing a flood of light upon that mysterious, but ever existent inner circle of social and political life in the Free State; the warnings given should not only be read, but engraven upon the memory of every Englishman contemplating a residence in that unfortunate and really little-known Republic. Whether as a supplementary, or companion work to "The Immortal History of South Africa," or from its own inherent merits and attractions, "The Orange Free State" should find a welcome and a home in every public and private library.

"HOW TO NATIONALIZE OUR COMMONS, WASTE LANDS AND RAILWAYS."

Such is the title of a little work of very unpretending appearance, but whose contents are of paramount interest and importance to all classes, and especially to that unfortunate stalking-horse of political parties—the working man. Whilst the author, who has evidently studied the question carefully and earnestly, expresses his views with all the energy of an enthusiast who has unlimited confidence in the soundness of his conclusions; he is remarkably felicitous in his mode of illustration, which is characterised by such force and perspicuity, that not even the humblest capacity can fail to grasp his meaning. The author contends that the appropriation, with the public money, of our Commons and Waste lands is the only way to work out the great Land Question; and he urges that if this were done, and the whole brought into a proper state of cultivation, there would be no necessity for our agricultural labourers to emigrate, and that our own lands would yield sufficient sustenance for a population of "one hundred and twenty millions." The historical and legal bearings of the Commons Question are ably and copiously dealt with; and the statistics upon which the author bases his deductions, are collated from the most authoritative sources, including the report of the Enclosure Commissioners, from which he estimates the annual loss of revenue to the United Kingdom, through the present condition of our commons and waste lands, at the enormous sum of forty millions. Formidable as this amount appears, the author has something still more astounding in store. He says that if these lands were to be allotted to farm labourers for cultivation, they would in a few years yield, in the form of rent, an annual income to the State of "from sixty to eighty millions!" Such are a few only of the numerous items of interest contained in this truly valuable pamphlet, which not only points out existing evils, but—what is of infinitely greater importance— it shows the way out of them, in "short, sharp and decisive" fashion; and greater, better, and more wonderous still— "without a farthing's loss or cost to any one." Of the "Railway Question," the exigencies of space only permit us to say—without intending a joke — that it is dealt with exactly on the same lines. In conclusion, we cannot give better advice concerning this marvellous little work, than that contained in the words, "Go and buy it." The price places this little treasure within the reach of all, and it is written by that staunch, true friend of the working man, MARTIN JAMES BOON, author of the "Immortal History of South Africa," "History of the Orange Free State," "Money and Its Use," &c., &c., &c.

"JOTTING'S BY THE WAY, OR BOON'S MADNESS ON THE ROAD."—By MARTIN JAMES BOON.

LONDON: GEORGE STANDRING, 8 & 9, Finsbury Street.

" This is a very remarkable book by a very remarkable man. Mr. Boon is an ethusiast of the most indomitable type. He is irrepressible in his hopefulness. He presents us, in this volume, with a philosophical view of life—past, present and to come—in the Orange Free State, Natal, and Cape Colony. He has lived long and travelled much, and seen a great deal in these parts; and he believes that his thoughts, speculations, fancies, and facts will be of service to Englishmen—hence this work. Mr. Boon is a most pronounced Republican, and an ardent advocate of the nationalization of the land. He is a reformer, and is never happy, but as he is either destroying what he believes to be evil, or is uplifting and supporting what he believes to be good and true. His volume is interesting, instructive, and suggestive, and ought to be read by all reformers and those who take any interest in foreign policy. Mr. William Maccall, well known to advanced thinkers in this religion, introduces this book of colonial genius. We must not say, for the author is English born—but his ideas seem to have been strengthened, if not developed, by his colonial life and experience. In 1869 Mr. Maccall, at the Hall of Science, London, delivered four lectures on Pauperism. Among his hearers were the author of this book. The lecturer and his boon companions recognised a kinship of spirit, and this kinship has been strengthened by time. He is a merchant at Bloemfontein, Orange Free State. His "favourite ideas" do not let business muzzle his soul. *Maworm*, in the play of the Hypocrite, boasted that "he extorted [exhorted] all who came to the shop," and Martin Boon, who is a true man and no hypocrite, finds that his ideas being freely communicated and fearlessly maintained, do not hinder his progress in business. As Mr. Maccall's name is a sufficient voucher for the book we have only to add that it abounds with racy writing, which will amuse the cursory reader, and with thoughts that will interest the graver student of this mad world."—*Western Times.*

George Standring, 8 & 9, Finsbury Street, London, publishes "Jottings by the Way," and "How to Construct Free State Railways," by Martin James Boon. They are two thoughtful, earnest, and vigorous works. They are fresh, striking, drastic; brimful of all sorts of information and suggestions, and ought to be read by all reformers.—The Propagandist (Vail & Co., 170, Farringdon-road), is a twopenny monthly of the most advanced type, edited by Martin James Boon. It is a fearless, outspoken, daring periodical, advocating views of the most uncompromising kind. Martin Boon is far ahead of his age and country.—*Oldham Chronicle.*

"A SCHEME OF IMPERIAL COLONIZATION:
How to Coloninize South Africa, and by Whom."
By Martin J. Boon.

Many readers must recall with pleasure and esteem the name of Martin James Boon, who, twelve years ago, played a conspicuous part as a social and political reformer, and who was the first popular champion of what has recently attracted so much attention—land nationalisation. The more disinterested and devoted we are in the service of truth, the more we have to suffer; and brave, benevolent Boon was not an exception. His worldly affairs having fallen into confusion, he went, early in 1874, as a settler to South Africa. If in England he had been a hero, in Caffraria he was destined to be a martyr. For a considerable time he has resided as a merchant at Bloemfontein, Orange Free State. His tribulations have not diminished his enthusiasm, and he continues to write and speak with the valiant zeal which he displayed in England. His pamphlet, "How to Colonise South Africa," contains many ingenious suggestions.

At the risk of being called a Jingo, I think that England should have a great foreign policy and a great colonial policy, and that England should be for the modern world what Rome was for the ancient world. I was amused the other day, when reading a lecture by Mr. Conway, to find Benjamin Disraeli treated as an earnest man, with something of the old Hebrew prophetic fire. It seemed to me the height of comicality that the most detestable impostor of modern days should be regarded as a serious and honest personage. It is enough to make me hate Benjamin Disraeli that, by his contemptible trickeries, he brought a vigorous foreign and colonial policy into disrepute. To that policy we must return if England is to maintain or to extend its place among the nations. Whenever that policy is revived South Africa is sure to be sought as an admirable field for colonizing experiments. Boon's main idea includes the rapid extension of a peasant proprietary in connection with an immense issue of redeemable paper money. As all money is simply representative, I see no reason for deeming Boon's plan unworkable. But I cannot discuss the plan here, and must content myself with trying to excite the interest of the reader in Boon's pamphlet. My own currency has always been extremely limited; and I might be too much influenced by prejudices if I were to enter on the debate of currency questions. That these questions have been profoundly studied and are thoroughly understood by Boon, I am convinced; and his sincerity and generosity are beyond the reach of doubt.   William Maccall.

HOW TO CONSTRUCT FREE TRADE RAILWAYS, &c.

"THE manifold advantages of a thorough system of railway communication are so well known and appreciated in those countries fortunate enough to possess this universally recognised desideratum, that any recapitulation thereof is totally unnecessary. The chief ground for surprise in connection with the matter is, that any Nation or State, claiming to be considered civilised, should be without, or inadequately pro‧vided with railways ; and as we cannot for a moment imagine any people to be so blind to the interests of themselves and their country as not to be possessed of an earnest desire to have them, we are forced to the conclusion that the want of *means,* rather than the want of wit, is the real stumbling block in the way. We are led to these observations by the perusal of a pamphlet bearing the title at the head of this notice, written by that well known militant Apostle of Progress, Martin James Boon, author of the *Immortal History of South Africa, National Paper Money and Its Use, History of the Orange Free State,* &c., &c. The author having for a considerable time been an observant resident in the Free State is pre‧eminently entitled to speak upon the question, which he treats from the point of view that the railways should be constructed by and become the property of the State, the cost thereof being provided for by the issue of State paper-money in the form of Notes, marked to denote the purpose for which they were issued, and made legal tender for all purposes within the confines of the Free State. The security upon which the notes were issued would be the railway plant and works themselves. Upon the completion of the line five per cent. of the receipts after paying all expenses to be called in, and notes representing that amount cancelled annually, until the whole would be passed out of circulation and the property left as a source of income, either to carry out other works or to relieve the burdens of the taxpayers, and all effected, entirely free of cost. Such is a brief outline of the author's general idea, and it is worked out in detail with admirable reasoning, illustrated by convincing examples. Every member of that somewhat cosmopolitan community, The Orange Free State, should invest sixpence, and study the question for himself."

www.ingramcontent.com/pod-product-compliance
Lightning Source LLC
Chambersburg PA
CBHW030850270326
41928CB00008B/1303